Auditing and Accounting Cases

Investigating Issues of Fraud and Professional Ethics

Fourth Edition

Jay C. Thibodeau

Deborah Freier

McGraw-Hill Irwin

AUDITING AND ACCOUNTING CASES: INVESTIGATING ISSUES OF FRAUD
AND PROFESSIONAL ETHICS, FOURTH EDITION

1 2 3 4 5 6 7 8 9 0 DOC/DOC 1 0 9 8 7 6 5 4 3

ISBN 978-0-07-8025563
MHID 0-07-8025567

Senior Vice President, Products & Markets:
Kurt L. Strand
Vice President, Content Production &
Technology Services: Kimberly Meriwether David
Managing Director: Tim Vertovec
Brand Manager: Donna Dillon
Managing Development Editor: Gail Korosa
Marketing Manager: Dean Karampelas
Director, Content Production: Terri Schiesl

Project Manager: Judi David
Buyer: Nicole Baumgartner
Media Project Manager: Prashanthi Nadipalli
Cover Designer: Studio Montage, St. Louis, MO.
Cover Image: (c) 2007 Getty Images, Inc.
Typeface: 10/12 Palatino
Compositor: Laserwords Private Limited
Printer: R.R.Donnelley

Library of Congress Cataloging-in-Publication Data

Thibodeau, Jay C.
    [Auditing after Sarbanes-Oxley]
    Auditing and accounting cases : investigating issues of fraud and professional ethics /
Dr. Jay C. Thibodeau, Deborah Freier. — Fourth edition.
        pages cm
Revision of the authors' Auditing after Sarbanes-Oxley.
    ISBN 978-0-07-802556-3 (alk. paper)
    ISBN 0-07-802556-7 (alk. paper)
    1. Corporations—Accounting—Corrupt practices—United States--Case studies. 2. Corporations—
United States—Auditing—Case studies. 3. Corporations—Moral and ethical aspects—United States—
Case studies. 4. Professional ethics—United States—Case studies. 5. United States. Sarbanes-
Oxley Act of 2002. I. Freier, Deborah. II. Title.
    HF5686.C7T48 2014
    657'.450973—dc23
                                                                            2012049770

www.mhhe.com

This book is dedicated to Ellen, my extraordinary wife of 23 years, and my children, Jenny, Eric, and Jessica. You have all provided the inspiration for me to undertake and complete this project. I could not have accomplished it without your love. Thank you.

This book is also dedicated to the loving memory of my father, Jacques Thibodeau, who inspired me to reach for the stars. Thank you.

Jay C. Thibodeau

I dedicate this book in loving memory of my father, Martin Freier, who inspired me to work hard and to strive for excellence. He also inspired me and others with his strength, his integrity, his dedication to family and friends, his desire to help others, his deep abiding love for learning, his wide array of talents and interests, and his appreciation for life. He was a great man and will truly be missed.

This book is also dedicated to Matt, who always believed in me and was a constant source of support.

Deborah Freier

About the Authors

Jay C. Thibodeau, CPA

Dr. Thibodeau is a Professor at Bentley University. He received his BS degree from the University of Connecticut in December 1987 and his Ph.D. from the University of Connecticut in August 1996. He joined the faculty at Bentley in September of 1996 and has worked there ever since. At Bentley, he serves as the coordinator for all audit and assurance curriculum matters. In addition, he currently consults with the Audit Learning and Development group at KPMG and has consulted in the past with the Learning and Education group at PricewaterhouseCoopers.

Dr. Thibodeau's scholarship is focused on auditor judgment and decision making and audit education. In that spirit, he is a co-author of two books, Auditing and Accounting Cases: Investigating Issues of Fraud and Professional Ethics (Irwin/McGraw-Hill–4th Edition) and Auditing and Assurance Services (Irwin/McGraw-Hill – 5th Edition). In addition, he has published over forty articles and book chapters in a variety of academic and practitioner outlets, including *Contemporary Accounting Research, Auditing: A Journal of Practice & Theory, Accounting Horizons* and *Issues in Accounting Education.*

Dr. Thibodeau has received national recognition for his work three times. First, for his doctoral dissertation, winning the 1996 Outstanding Doctoral Dissertation Award presented by the American Accounting Association's ABO section. Second, for curriculum innovation, winning the 2001 Joint AICPA/AAA Collaboration Award. And third, also for curricular innovation, winning the 2003 Innovation in Assurance Education Award.

Deborah Freier

Deborah Freier is a recent graduate of the MBA program at the Wharton School at the University of Pennsylvania. Ms. Freier worked for several years as a research associate in the Strategy department at Harvard Business School. She collaborated with professors to create content for case studies, presentations, and articles that explored issues related to competitive advantage, intellectual property strategies, network effects and standards wars, and expansion into new geographic and strategic markets. She also developed teaching materials for an elective course about game theory and its application to business strategy. After Harvard Business School, Freier worked as a senior analyst in the Strategy and Product Development department at Tufts Health Plan, where she played a key role in developing and presenting financial and competitive analyses for senior management.

Freier graduated as the valedictorian of her undergraduate class at Bentley University. She was honored by the Financial Executives Institute as the Outstanding Graduating Student and received *The Wall Street Journal* Student Achievement Award. She was also inducted into Beta Gamma Sigma, Beta Alpha Psi, Omicron Delta Epsilon, and the Falcon Society. Freier placed in the semifinals of the Institute for Management Accountants 2000 National Student Case Competition and was the co-chair of Beta Alpha Psi's student leadership conference during her senior year.

Table of Contents

SECTION TWO
ETHICS AND PROFESSIONAL RESPONSIBILITY CASES   53

SECTION THREE
FRAUD AND INHERENT RISK ASSESSMENT CASES   83

Preface

Welcome to the fourth edition of our case book. For those of you who have already worked with our short cases, thank you very much for your support of our innovative approach to auditing and accounting education. For those of you who are trying out our short cases for the first time, welcome! We truly believe that you and your students will come to enjoy the use of our short cases in your classes.

The fourth edition of *Auditing and Accounting Cases: Investigating Issues of Fraud and Professional Ethics* continues in its quest to be known as the most current auditing and accounting case book on the market. In that spirit, all case questions in the fourth edition have been revised to incorporate the eight new standards adopted by the PCAOB (i.e., AS 8 – AS 15) that relate to the auditor's assessment of and response to risk in an audit and that include guidance related to audit planning, supervision, materiality, and evidence.

In this edition, we have added three new cases that provide important details about the historic fraud perpetrated by Bernie Madoff. The first new case, Case 1.8 - Bernard L. Madoff Investment and Securities: Broker-Dealer Fraud is designed to introduce students to some of the key details of the fraud, including the definition of a Ponzi scheme and a description of the "split-strike" strategy that was allegedly employed by Madoff. In addition, the case allows instructors an opportunity to introduce students to a number of the key provisions of the Dodd-Frank Wall Street Reform and Consumer Protection Act that relate to the regulation of broker-dealers like Bernie Madoff.

The second new case, Case 1.12 - Bernard L. Madoff Investment and Securities: The Role of the Securities & Exchange Commission (SEC) is designed to highlight the failure of the SEC in responding to the evidence submitted by Harry Markopolos that questioned the legitimacy of the returns on Madoff's hedge fund. The failure to respond by the SEC led to dramatic changes at the government agency in their enforcement division, which the case allows students to understand. Importantly, the case also provides an opportunity for instructors to highlight the new whistleblower provision of the Dodd-Frank Wall Street Reform and Consumer Protection Act.

The third new case, Case 3.6 - Bernard L. Madoff Investment and Securities: Understanding the Client's Business and Industry is designed to highlight the important relationship enjoyed by Bernie Madoff with the many "feeder funds" that were instrumental to attracting investors into the Madoff fund. The case provides students with an opportunity to learn that Madoff did not charge a fee on the money it managed. Rather, the Madoff fund allegedly only earned money by charging commissions on trades executed for the accounts of its feeder funds. This was a highly unusual practice that should have raised red flags about the Madoff fund. In addition, students are instructed that the feeder funds were not allowed to tell their investors that their money was actually being managed by Madoff. Overall, the case is quite helpful in helping students to understand the complex web of relationships that characterized the Madoff fraud.

Finally, the fourth Madoff case, Case 2.6 Bernard L. Madoff Investment and Securities: A Focus on Auditors' and Accountants' Legal Liability has been revised to reflect the latest developments related to Madoff's accountant, David Friehling. In addition, the case highlights the possible legal liability faced by auditors of the feeder funds. Despite the culpability of David Friehling, several courts have made decisions affirming that the auditors of the feeder funds could not be found guilty of fraud or malpractice. The decisions were appealed, but later upheld. Nevertheless, it is important for students to understand the legal exposure faced by accountants and auditors.

We also decided to add a new section to the book, Section Six, which features seven comprehensive company cases and eliminates the Appendix. This change reflects the fact that our comprehensive cases are being used quite effectively by professors throughout the world. As a result, we decided to include these cases in the primary part of the book, instead of relegating the cases to the Appendix. In addition, we decided to remove three of the short cases that feature the Fund of Funds fraud. These cases are still available on the book's website to those instructors that would like to continue to use them in the classroom.

Overall, we believe that our short cases provide a highly focused approach to help students better understand the framework of specific rules related to the auditing and accounting profession. Indeed, we believe it is critically important that students learn how to refer to the technical auditing standards and be able to apply them in specific auditing contexts. An important feature of this book is the extensive coverage of the Auditing Standards issued by the Public Company Accounting Oversight Board (PCAOB). As a result, this book provides students with extensive opportunities to apply technical knowledge to auditing contexts.

In the face of ever-changing regulations, auditing educators need to rise to the challenge of preparing future audit professionals. *Auditing and Accounting Cases: Investigating Issues of Fraud and Professional Ethics* provides instructors with 45 cases focusing on specific audit issues that were directly impacted by Sarbanes-Oxley and Dodd-Frank, using the actual companies— Enron, World-Com, Qwest—that have become synonymous with the capital markets' crisis in confidence. Importantly, these cases provide in-depth, up-to-date coverage of the Sarbanes-Oxley Act of 2002 (SARBOX), the technical audit guidance that has been issued by the PCAOB and the Dodd-Frank Wall Street Reform and Consumer Protection Act.

Our approach to this book emphasizes the substantial benefits of using real-life case examples in helping impart knowledge related to the practice of auditing. In the education psychology literature, this type of approach has long been acknowledged as a superior manner in which to teach. In addition, evidence from other disciplines shows that the use of cases as a mechanism to impart a range of critical auditing skills, including technical skills, interpersonal relations, and ethical analysis, will be quite effective. So by presenting the concepts of auditing using actual corporate contexts, we seek to provide readers with a real-life appreciation of these issues and clearly demonstrate the value of the Sarbanes-Oxley Act of 2002, the technical audit guidance issued by the PCAOB and the Dodd-Frank Wall Street Reform and Consumer Protection Act.

Overall, we set out to design a case book that could be easily adopted by instructors in their classes. The cases run only three to five pages in length, which dramatically reduces the time necessary for students to grasp key learning objectives. In addition, each case focuses on a specific topic to help ensure student mastery of that topic. Our approach can be contrasted with many traditional audit cases that range from 10 to 20 pages in length and introduce multiple learning objectives concurrently.

Once again, we have grouped our cases into the following categories: (1) fraud cases: violations of accounting principles; (2) ethics and professional responsibility; (3) fraud and inherent risk assessment; (4) internal control systems: entity-level controls; (5) internal control systems: control activities ; and (6) comprehensive company cases. The category structure is designed to make it easier for instructors to align the cases in the book with the needs of the class. We believe that the first section of the book can be effectively used in both financial accounting courses (to illustrate violations of accounting principles) and auditing courses (to illustrate examples of fraud). We believe that the remaining five sections of the book explore topics that are primarily covered in auditing or fraud courses.

In looking over the table of contents for this book, instructors who have used previous editions will note that each category has multiple cases that can be chosen for classroom coverage. This allows instructors to illustrate the critically important technical concepts with multiple real-life contexts if they so choose. And, it lets instructors assign the cases on a rotating basis. With 38 different short cases, instructors can assign 8 to 9 different cases for each of four different semesters. This will reduce the possibility of case solutions circulating around campus.

Importantly, we have also provided comprehensive company cases (in Section Six) to give instructors the option of presenting longer cases that focus concurrently on multiple learning objectives related to a particular company. We believe that the longer cases can be used quite effectively as an end of the semester project.

Technical Audit Guidance

To maximize a student's knowledge acquisition of this material, this book has been designed to be read in conjunction with the post–Sarbanes-Oxley technical audit guidance. All of the PCAOB Auditing Standards that are referenced in this book are available for free at http://pcaobus.org/STANDARDS/Pages/default.aspx. In addition, a summary of the provisions of the Sarbanes-Oxley Act of 2002 is available for free on the book's website at www.mhhe.com/thibodeau4e or at http://www.aicpa.org/Pages/Default.aspx.

Acknowledgments

We gratefully acknowledge the unwavering support of our families throughout this process. Without their support, creating this book would not have been possible. We also gratefully acknowledge the contributions and support of Donna Dillon, Gail Korosa, Dean Karampelas, Judi David, Art Levine, and Joy Golden at McGraw-Hill/Irwin. We also wish to acknowledge the contributions of Ellen Thibodeau, insights of JP Lenney at ALEKS Corporation and the inspiration of Larry Thibodeau, John Cizeski, James Corso, John Buccino, Steve Albert, Mark Mistretta, and Jim and Nicole Tobin.

We gratefully acknowledge the contributions of Mary Parlee, Michael Albert, Erin Burke, Scott Morency, and Xin Zheng. Their tireless efforts on the teaching materials are much appreciated. In addition, the contributions of Sheena Pass, Zeche Ionut, Katie Skrzypczak, and the members of Dr. Thibodeau's auditing classes at Bentley in the fall semester of 2004 and the spring semester of 2005 are gratefully acknowledged.

Finally, we want to express our sincere gratitude to James Bierstaker (Villanova University) and Christine Earley (Providence College) for their willingness to class-test several of the early cases. In addition, we express our gratitude to the following reviewers for their contributions: Pervaiz Alam, *Kent State University;* D'Arcy Becker, *University of Wisconsin Eau Claire;* Faye Borthick, *Georgia State University;* Robert Braun, *Southeastern Louisiana University.* Kimberly Burke, *Millsaps College;* Bryan Church, *Georgia Tech;* Sandra Clayton, *Regis University;* Jeff Cohen, *Boston College;* Mary Curtis, *University of North Texas;* Cynthia Daily, *University of Arkansas–Little Rock;* Laura DeLaune, *Louisiana State University;* Timothy Dimond, *Northern Illinois University;* Carla Feinson, *Bethune Cookman College;* Anita Feller, *University of Illinois at Urbana Champaign;* Parveen Gupta, *Lehigh University;* Janet Jamieson, *University of Dubuque;* Jordan Lowe, *Arizona State University;* Joseph Maffia, *Hunter College;* Marshall Pitman, *University of Texas–San Antonio;* Barbara Reider, *University of Montana–Missoula;* John Rigsby, *Mississippi State University;* Dan Royer, *Harrison College;* Christian Schaupp, *University of North Carolina–Wilmington;* Cindy Seipel, *New Mexico State University;* Kathleen Simons, *Bryant University;* Bernice Sutton, *Florida Southern College;* Susan Toohey, *Lehigh University;* Steve Wells, *Western Kentucky University;* Thomas Wetzel, *Oklahoma State University;* and other anonymous reviewers.

Fraud Cases: Violations of Accounting Principles

In July 2002 the Sarbanes-Oxley Act was passed by the U.S. Senate by a vote of 98 to 0. The bipartisan support for the legislation emanated directly from the investing public's lack of tolerance for financial statement fraud. Not surprisingly, when formulating its post-Sarbanes technical audit guidance, the Public Company Accounting Oversight Board (PCAOB) made it clear that detecting fraud must be the focus of the audit process. Consider that in the board's first internal control standard (Auditing Standard No. 2), *fraud* was mentioned 76 times.

The PCAOB has continued its focus on preventing and detecting fraud in each of its auditing standards, in particular its revised standard on Auditing Internal Control Over Financial Reporting (Auditing Standard No. 5) and its standards related to the Auditor's Assessment Of and Response to Risk (Auditing Standard No. 8–15). This book includes detailed coverage of each of these PCAOB Auditing Standards.

At its fundamental core, financial statement auditors must employ a process to determine whether the economic transaction activity that occurred has been accounted for by its audit client in accordance with Generally Accepted Accounting Principles (GAAP). This process must be completed in accordance with Generally Accepted Auditing Standards. In this spirit, the cases in this section are designed to illustrate different types of GAAP violations that have occurred in the recent past. In addition, the cases have been designed to illustrate how the proper application of the prevailing auditing standards by auditors may have been helpful in detecting the fraud.

The case readings have been developed solely as a basis for class discussion. The case readings are not intended to serve as a source of primary data or as an illustration of effective or ineffective auditing.

Case 1.1

Waste Management: The Expense Recognition Principle

Synopsis

In February 1998 Waste Management announced that it was restating the financial statements it had issued for the years 1993 through 1996. In its restatement, Waste Management said that it had materially overstated its reported pretax earnings by $1.43 billion. After the announcement, the company's stock dropped by more than 33 percent and shareholders lost over $6 billion.

The SEC brought charges against the company's founder, Dean Buntrock, and five other former top officers. The charges alleged that management had made repeated changes to depreciation-related estimates to reduce expenses and had employed several improper accounting practices related to capitalization policies, also designed to reduce expenses.[1] In its final judgment, the SEC permanently barred Buntrock and three other executives from acting as officers or directors of public companies and required payment from them of $30.8 million in penalties.[2]

Waste Management's Major Fixed Assets

The major fixed assets of Waste Management's North American (WMNA) business consisted of garbage trucks, containers, and equipment, which amounted to approximately $6 billion in assets. The second largest asset of the company (after vehicles, containers, and equipment) was land, in the form of the more than 100 fully operational landfills that the company both owned and operated. Under Generally Accepted Accounting Principles (GAAP), depreciation expense is determined by allocating the historical cost of tangible capital assets (less the salvage value) over the estimated useful life of the assets.

[1] SEC, Accounting and Auditing Enforcement Release No. 1532, March 26, 2002.
[2] SEC, Accounting and Auditing Enforcement Release No. 2298, August 29, 2005.

Unsupported Changes to the Estimated Useful Lives of Assets

From 1988 through 1996, management allegedly made numerous unsupported changes to the estimated useful lives and/or salvage values of one or more categories of vehicles, containers, and equipment.[3] Such changes reduced the amount of depreciation expense recorded in a particular period. In addition, such changes were recorded as top-side adjustments at the corporate level (detached from the operating unit level). Most often the entries were made during the fourth quarter, and then improperly applied cumulatively from the beginning of the year. Management did not appear to disclose the changes or their impact on profitability to the investors.

In a letter to the management team dated May 29, 1992, Arthur Andersen's team wrote, "[i]n each of the past five years the Company added a new consolidating entry in the fourth quarter to increase salvage value and/or useful life of its trucks, machinery, equipment, or containers." Andersen recommended that the company conduct a "comprehensive, one-time study to evaluate the proper level of WMNA's salvage value and useful lives," and then send these adjustments to the respective WMNA groups. However, top management allegedly continued the practice of making unsupported changes to WMNA's salvage value and useful lives at headquarters as a way to reduce depreciation expense and increase net income.

Carrying Impaired Land at Cost

Because of the nature of landfills, GAAP also requires that a company compare a landfill's cost to its anticipated salvage value, with the difference depreciated over the estimated useful life of the landfill.[4] Waste Management disclosed in the footnotes to the financial statements in its annual reports that "[d]isposal sites are carried at cost and to the extent this exceeds end use realizable value, such excess is amortized over the estimated life of the disposal site." However, in reality, the Securities and Exchange Commission (SEC) found evidence that Waste Management allegedly did not depreciate the assets and carried almost all of its landfills on the balance sheet at full historical cost.

In response to this treatment of landfills on the balance sheet, after its 1988 audit, Andersen issued a management letter to the board of directors recommending that the company conduct a "site by site analysis of its landfills to compare recorded land values with its anticipated net realizable value based on end use." Andersen further instructed that any excess needed to be amortized over the "active site life" of the landfill. Andersen made similar demands after

[3] SEC, Accounting and Auditing Enforcement Release No. 1532, March 26, 2002.
[4] SEC, Accounting and Auditing Enforcement Release No. 1532, March 26, 2002.

its audit in 1994. In reality, management never conducted such a study; they also failed to reduce the carrying values of overvalued land, despite their commitment to do so after Andersen's audit in 1994.

Case Questions

1. Consider the principles, assumptions, and constraints of Generally Accepted Accounting Principles (GAAP). Define the *expense recognition principle (sometimes referred to as the "matching" principle)* and explain why it is important to users of financial statements.

2. Based on the case information provided, describe specifically how Waste Management violated the expense recognition principle. In your description, please identify a journal entry that may have been used by Waste Management to commit the fraud.

3. Consult Paragraph 2 of PCAOB Auditing Standard No. 5. Do you believe that Waste Management had established an effective system of internal control over financial reporting related to the depreciation expense recorded in its financial statements? Why or why not?

4. Consult Paragraphs 5–6 of PCAOB Auditing Standard No. 15. As an auditor, what type of evidence would you want to examine to determine whether Waste Management's decision to change the useful life and salvage value of its assets was appropriate under GAAP?

5. Visit the PCOAB website (i.e., www.pcaobus.org), search for the "tip and referral center" and review the guidelines. Can you report a violation to the PCAOB anonymously? Next, consider the role of the Waste Management employee who was responsible for recording the proper amount of depreciation expense in the financial statements. Assuming that the employee knew that the consolidating entries in the fourth quarter recorded by upper management were fraudulent, do you believe that the employee had a responsibility to report the behavior to the audit committee? Why or why not?

Case 1.2

WorldCom: The Revenue Recognition Principle

Synopsis

On June 25, 2002, WorldCom announced that it would be restating its financial statements for 2001 and the first quarter of 2002. Less than one month later, on July 21, 2002, WorldCom announced it had filed for bankruptcy. It was later revealed that WorldCom had engaged in improper accounting that took two major forms: overstatement of revenue by at least $958 million and understatement of line costs, its largest category of expenses, by over $7 billion. Several executives pled guilty to charges of fraud and were sentenced to prison terms, including CFO Scott Sullivan (five years) and Controller David Myers (one year and one day). Convicted of fraud in 2005, CEO Bernie Ebbers was the first to receive his prison sentence: 25 years.

"Hit" the Numbers

Even as conditions in the telecommunications industry deteriorated in 2000 and 2001, WorldCom continued to post impressive revenue numbers. In April 2000 CEO Ebbers told analysts that he "remain[ed] comfortable with . . . 13.5 to 15.5 percent revenue growth in 2000." In February 2001 Ebbers again expressed confidence that WorldCom Group could repeat that performance: "On the WorldCom side of the business, we are sticking with our 12 percent to 15 percent revenue growth guidance for 2001. Let me restate that. On the WorldCom side of the business, we are sticking with our 12 percent to 15 percent revenue growth guidance for 2001."[1]

---

[1] Board of Directors' Special Investigative Committee Report, June 9, 2003, p. 133.

Monitoring of Revenue at WorldCom

According to several accounts, revenue growth was emphasized within World-Com; in fact, no single measure of performance received greater scrutiny. On a regular basis, the sales groups' performances were measured against the revenue plan. At meetings held every two to three months, each sales channel manager was required to present and defend his or her sales channel's performance against the budgeted performance.

Compensation and bonus packages for several members of senior management were also tied to double-digit revenue growth. In 2000 and 2001, for instance, three executives were eligible to receive an executive bonus only if the company achieved double-digit revenue growth over the first six months of each year.[2]

Monthly Revenue Report and the Corporate Unallocated Schedule

The principal tool by which revenue performance was measured and monitored at WorldCom was the monthly revenue report ("MonRev"), prepared and distributed by the revenue reporting and accounting group (hereafter referred to as the revenue accounting group). The MonRev included dozens of spreadsheets detailing revenue data from all of the company's channels and segments. However, the full MonRev also contained the Corporate Unallocated schedule, an attachment detailing adjustments made at the corporate level and generally not derived from the operating activities of WorldCom's sales channels. WorldCom's Chief Financial Officer and Treasurer Scott Sullivan had ultimate responsibility for the items booked on the Corporate Unallocated schedule.[3]

In addition to CEO Ebbers and CFO Sullivan, only a handful of employees outside the revenue accounting group regularly received the full MonRev. Most managers at WorldCom received only the portions of the MonRev that were deemed relevant to their positions. Sullivan routinely reviewed the distribution list for the full MonRev to make sure he approved of everyone on the list.[4]

The total amounts reported in the Corporate Unallocated schedule usually spiked during quarter-ending months, with the largest spikes occurring in those quarters when operational revenue lagged farthest behind quarterly revenue targets—the second and third quarters of 2000 and the second, third, and fourth quarters of 2001. Without the revenue that was recorded in the Corporate Unallocated account, WorldCom would have failed to achieve the double-digit growth it reported in 6 out of 12 quarters between 1999 and 2001.[5]

---

[2] Ibid., pp. 133–134.
[3] Ibid., pp. 135–139.
[4] Ibid., pp. 135–139.
[5] Ibid., pp. 140–141.

Process of Closing and Consolidating Revenues

WorldCom maintained a fairly automated process for closing and consolidating operational revenue numbers. By the 10th day after the end of the month, the revenue accounting group prepared a draft "preliminary" MonRev that was followed by a final MonRev, which took into account any adjustments that needed to be made. In non-quarter-ending months, the final MonRev was usually similar, if not identical, to the preliminary MonRev.[6]

In quarter-ending months, however, top-side adjusting journal entries, often very large, were allegedly made during the quarterly closing process in order to hit revenue growth targets. Investigators later found notes made by senior executives in 1999 and 2000 that calculated the difference between "act[ual]" or "MonRev" results and "target" or "need[ed]" numbers, and identified the entries that were necessary to make up that difference. CFO Scott Sullivan directed this process, which was allegedly implemented by Ron Lomenzo, the senior vice president of financial operations, and Lisa Taranto, an employee who reported to Lomenzo.[7]

Throughout much of 2001, WorldCom's revenue accounting group tracked the gap between projected and targeted revenue—an exercise labeled "close the gap"—and kept a running tally of accounting "opportunities" that could be exploited to help make up that difference.[8]

Many questionable revenue entries were later found within the Corporate Unallocated revenue account. On June 19, 2001, as the quarter of 2001 was coming to a close, CFO Sullivan left a voicemail message for CEO Ebbers that indicated his concern over the company's growing use of nonrecurring items to increase revenues reported:

> Hey Bernie, it's Scott. This MonRev just keeps getting worse and worse. The copy, um the latest copy that you and I have already has accounting fluff in it . . . all one time stuff or junk that's already in the numbers. With the numbers being, you know, off as far as they are, I didn't think that this stuff was already in there. . . . We are going to dig ourselves into a huge hole because year to date it's disguising what is going on the recurring, uh, service side of the business.[9]

A few weeks later, Ebbers sent a memorandum to WorldCom's COO Ron Beaumont that directed him to "see where we stand on those one time events that had to happen in order for us to have a chance to make our numbers." Yet Ebbers did not give any indication of the impact of nonrecurring items on revenues in his public comments to the market in that quarter or in other quarters. For that matter, the company did not address the impact of nonrecurring items on revenues in its earnings release or public filing for either that quarter or prior quarters.[10]

---

[6] Ibid., pp. 140–141.

[7] Ibid., p. 14.

[8] Ibid., p. 141.

[9] Ibid., p. 15.

[10] Ibid., p. 15.

Case Questions

1. Consider the principles, assumptions, and constraints of Generally Accepted Accounting Principles (GAAP). Define the *revenue recognition principle* and explain why it is important to users of financial statements.

2. Provide one specific example of how WorldCom violated the revenue recognition principle in this situation. In your description, please identify a journal entry that may have been used by WorldCom to commit the fraud.

3. Consult Paragraph A5 (in Appendix A) of PCAOB Auditing Standard No. 5 and Paragraph 68 of PCAOB Auditing Standard No. 12. Do you believe that WorldCom had established an effective system of internal control over financial reporting related to the revenue recorded in its financial statements?

4. Consult Paragraph 25 of PCAOB Auditing Standard No. 5. Define what is meant by *control environment*. Next explain why the control environment is so important to effective internal control over financial reporting at an audit client like WorldCom.

5. Consult Paragraphs 6–7 of PCAOB Auditing Standard No. 13. If you were auditing WorldCom, what type of documentary evidence would you require to evaluate the validity and propriety of a top-side journal entry made to the revenue account?

6. Consult Paragraphs 1–2 of Ethics Rule 102 (ET 102). Next, consider the roles of Ron Lomenzo and Lisa Taranto. Assuming that these employees knew that the entries being proposed by Scott Sullivan were fraudulent, do you believe that Lomenzo and Taranto should have recorded the journal entries as directed by Sullivan? Why or why not?

1.3

Qwest: The Full Disclosure Principle

Synopsis

When Joseph Nacchio became Qwest's CEO in January 1997, the company's existing strategy began to shift from just building a nationwide fiber-optic network to include increasing communications services. By the time it released earnings in 1998, Nacchio proclaimed Qwest's successful transition from a network construction company to a communications services provider. "We successfully transitioned Qwest . . . into a leading Internet protocol-based multimedia company focused on the convergence of data, video, and voice services." [1]

During 1999 and 2000, Qwest consistently met its aggressive revenue targets and became a darling to its investors. Yet, when the company announced its intention to restate revenues in August 2002, its stock price plunged to a low of $1.11 per share in August 2002, from a high of $55 per share in July 2000.[2] Civil and criminal charges related to fraudulent activity were brought against several Qwest executives, including CEO Joseph Nacchio. Nacchio was convicted on 19 counts of illegal insider trading, and was sentenced to six years in prison in July 2007. He was also ordered to pay a $19 million fine and forfeit $52 million that he gained in illegal stock sales.[3]

[1] *SEC v. Joseph P. Nacchio, Robert S. Woodruff, Robin R. Szeliga, Afshin Mohebbi, Gregory M. Casey, James J. Kozlowski, Frank T. Noyes,* Defendants, Civil Action No. 05-MK-480 (OES), 11–14.

[2] *SEC v. Qwest,* pp. 1–2.

[3] Dionne Searcey, "Qwest Ex-Chief Gets 6 Years in Prison for Insider Trading," *Wall Street Journal,* July 28, 2007 A3.

Background

To facilitate its growth in communications services revenue, Qwest unveiled an aggressive acquisition strategy in the late 1990s. Indeed, after a slew of other acquisitions, Qwest entered into a merger agreement with telecommunications company US West on July 18, 1999. The merger agreement gave US West the option to terminate the agreement if the average price of Qwest stock was below $22 per share or the closing price was below $22 per share for 20 consecutive trading days. Less than a month after the merger announcement, Qwest's stock price had dropped from $34 to $26 per share. So to prevent any further drops in its stock price, executives and managers were allegedly pressured by CEO Nacchio to meet earnings targets to ensure that the price per share did not fall below the level specified in the agreement. Although Qwest's stock price had dropped from $34 to $26 per share less than a month after the merger announcement, Qwest stock was trading above $50 per share by June 2000, less than a year after the acquisition. Qwest was, therefore, able to acquire US West by using Qwest's common stock.

Following the merger, Qwest's senior management set ambitious targets for revenue and earnings of the merged company.[4] These targets were especially ambitious in the face of difficult industry conditions. For example, in Qwest's earnings release for the second quarter of 2000, on July 19, 2000, Nacchio said that Qwest would "generate compound annual growth rates of 15–17 percent revenue . . . through 2005." At a January 2001 all-employee meeting, Nacchio stated his philosophy on the importance of meeting targeted revenues:

> [T]he most important thing we do is meet our numbers. It's more important than any individual product, it's more important than any individual philosophy, it's more important than any individual cultural change we're making. We stop everything else when we don't make the numbers.

Challenges

By 1999 Qwest encountered several obstacles that challenged its ability to meet its aggressive revenue and earnings targets. It faced increased competition from long distance providers, steep declines in the demand for Internet services, an overcapacity in the market resulting from the formation of other major fiber-optic networks, and a decline in the price at which Qwest could sell its excess fiber-optic capacity.[5]

Despite these significant industry challenges, Qwest's senior management publicly claimed that the company would continue its pattern of dramatic revenue increases because of a "flight to quality" that customers would enjoy when they left competitors to use Qwest's services. Within the company, Qwest senior

[4] *SEC v. Qwest,* pp. 6–7.
[5] *SEC v. Qwest,* pp. 7–8.

management exerted extraordinary pressure on subordinate managers and employees to meet or exceed the publicly announced revenue targets. In addition, it paid bonuses to management and employees only for periods when they achieved targeted revenue.[6]

Sale of Network Assets Initially Held for Use and Capital Equipment

To help meet revenue targets, senior management also began to sell portions of its own domestic fiber-optic network. Originally this network was to be held for Qwest's own use and had previously been identified as the "principal asset" of Qwest. Specifically, Qwest sold indefeasible rights of use (IRUs) for specific fiber capacity that it had constructed and used in its own communications services business. In addition, Qwest sold pieces of the network it had acquired from other third parties. Finally, Qwest sold used capital equipment to generate additional revenue.

Unlike recurring service revenue from its communication services business that produced a predictable amount of revenue in future quarters, revenue from IRUs and other equipment sales had no guarantee of recurrence in future quarters. In fact, both IRUs and equipment sales were referred to internally as "one hit wonders."[7]

In its earnings releases during 1999 through 2001, Qwest executives would often fail to disclose the impact of nonrecurring revenues. (See Table 1.3.1.) In its earnings releases and the management's discussion and analysis portion of its SEC filings, Qwest improperly characterized nonrecurring revenue as service revenue, often within the "data and internet service revenues" line item on the financial statements. Qwest's nonrecurring revenue was included primarily in the wholesale services segment and, to a lesser extent, the retail services segment.[8]

---

[6] *SEC v. Qwest,* p. 8.
[7] *SEC v. Qwest,* pp. 9–10.
[8] *SEC v. Qwest,* pp. 12–13.

TABLE 1.3.1 **Management's Failure to Disclose Impact of Nonrecurring Revenue**[9]

2Q 1999	Qwest failed to disclose that nonrecurring revenue made up 96 percent of data and Internet services revenue, 192 percent of the growth in data and internet services, and 19 percent of total revenue. Excluding nonrecurring revenue, data and Internet services revenue actually declined 92 percent from the same quarter of the previous year.
3Q 1999	Qwest failed to disclose that nonrecurring revenue made up 140 percent of Qwest's reported data and internet services revenue, and 32 percent of total revenue. Excluding nonrecurring revenue, total revenue actually declined 13 percent from the same quarter of the previous year.
4Q 1999	By the end of 1999, nonrecurring revenue comprised 33 percent of total revenue for the fourth quarter, and 26 percent of Qwest's total revenue for the year. Without inclusion of the nonrecurring revenue, Qwest's fourth quarter total revenue declined 9 percent from the same quarter of the previous year. Qwest's corporate accounting department drafted proposed disclosure language for the company's 1999 Form 10-K detailing the amount of revenue earned from sale of IRUs, but Qwest's CFO and CEO rejected the language and refused to disclose any material information about nonrecurring revenue in the 1999 Form 10-K filed on March 7, 2000.
1Q 2000	By the end of the quarter, nonrecurring revenue comprised 97 percent of data and internet services revenue, and 29 percent of total revenue. Without nonrecurring revenue, data and Internet services declined 92 percent from the same quarter of the prior year, and total revenue grew only 17 percent over the same quarter of the previous year. (This information was not disclosed.)
2Q 2000	Qwest did not disclose that nonrecurring revenue made up 86 percent of data and internet services revenue, and 29 percent of total revenue. Excluding nonrecurring revenue, total revenue grew by 23 percent.
3Q 2000	Even after acquiring US West, which resulted in a fivefold increase in revenue, nonrecurring revenue made up 35 percent of data and internet service revenue, and 8 percent of total revenue. The company continued not to disclose this information to the public.
1Q 2001	Contrary to Qwest's statements, during the first quarter 2001, nonrecurring revenue was 36 percent of data and internet services revenue, 11 percent of total revenue, and 35 percent of Qwest's total revenue growth. Excluding nonrecurring revenue, Qwest's total revenue grew only 8 percent over the same period of the previous year.
2Q 2001	Qwest did not disclose that nonrecurring revenue had grown to 13 percent of total revenue, and 39 percent of data and internet services revenue. Without including the nonrecurring revenue, Qwest's total revenue grew only 6 percent over the same period of the previous year.

[9] *SEC v. Qwest*, pp. 13–18. Data for 4Q 2000 unavailable.

Case Questions

1. Consider the principles, assumptions, and constraints of Generally Accepted Accounting Principles (GAAP). Define the *full disclosure principle* and explain why it is important to users of financial statements.

2. Explain specifically why Qwest's failure to disclose the extent of nonrecurring revenue violated the full disclosure principle in this situation.

3. Consult Paragraph 67 of PCAOB Auditing Standard No. 12. Do you believe that Qwest had established an effective system of internal control over financial reporting related to the presentation and disclosure of its nonrecurring revenue? Why or why not?

4. Consult Paragraph A4 (in Appendix A) of PCAOB Auditing Standard No. 5. What is the auditor's responsibility related to information disclosed by management at the time of an earnings release, if any? What is the auditor's responsibility related to the information disclosed by management in the management's discussion and analysis section, if any? Do you agree with these responsibilities? Why or why not?

5. Do you believe it is ethical for a CEO to establish a company's earnings expectation at an unreasonably high number and then require the company's employees to meet or exceed that expectation to keep their jobs? Why or why not?

1.4

Sunbeam: The Revenue Recognition Principle

Synopsis

In April 1996 Sunbeam named Albert J. Dunlap as its CEO and Chairman. Formerly with Scott Paper Co., Dunlap was known as a turnaround specialist and was even nicknamed "Chainsaw Al" because of the cost-cutting measures he typically employed. Almost immediately, Dunlap began replacing nearly all of the upper management team and led the company into an aggressive corporate restructuring that included the elimination of half of its 12,000 employees and the elimination of 87 percent of Sunbeam's products.

Unfortunately, in May 1998 Sunbeam disappointed investors with its announcement that it had earned a worse-than-expected loss of $44.6 million in the first quarter of 1998.[1] Dunlap was fired in June 1998. In October 1998 Sunbeam announced that it would need to restate its financial statements for 1996, 1997, and 1998.[2]

Sunbeam's Customer Discounts and Other Incentives and Sales to Distributors

Under GAAP, sales revenue can be recognized and earned only if the buyer assumes the risks and rewards of ownership of merchandise—for example, the risk of damage or physical loss. But what happens if the customer returns the merchandise with an expectation of a full refund? In such a situation, a sale with a right of return can be recognized as revenue only if the seller takes a reserve against possible future returns. The size of this reserve must be based on the company's history with returns; the sales revenue may not be recorded if no such history exists.

[1] Robert Frank and Joann S. Lublin. "Dunlap's Ax Falls—6,000 Times—at Sunbeam." *The Wall Street Journal,* November 13, 1996, p. B1.
[2] GAO-03-138, Appendix XVII, "Sunbeam Corporation," p. 201.

Beginning with the first quarter of 1997, Sunbeam began offering its customers discounts and other incentives if they placed their orders in the current period rather than holding off until the next period. Sunbeam did not disclose its practice of accelerating expected sales from later periods in its financial statements, however. In the other quarters of 1997, Sunbeam also allegedly relied on additional price discounting and other incentives in an attempt to accelerate recognition of revenue from future periods.[3]

One example of a special arrangement with a customer took place at the end of March 1997, just before the first quarter closed. Sunbeam recognized $1.5 million in revenue and contributed $400,000 toward net income from the sale of barbecue grills to a wholesaler. The contract with the wholesaler provided that the wholesaler could return all of the merchandise, with Sunbeam paying all costs of shipment and storage, if it was unable to sell it. In fact, the wholesaler wound up returning all of the grills to Sunbeam during the third quarter of 1997, and the wholesaler incurred no expenses in the transaction.[4]

Sales to Distributors

In December 1997 Sunbeam devised a "distributor program" that would help improve the company's sales. The program was designed to help Sunbeam accelerate the recognition of sales revenue for merchandise it placed with distributors in advance of actual retail demand. Sunbeam allegedly used favorable payment terms, discounts, guaranteed markups, and, consistently, the right to return unsold product as incentives for distributors to participate in the program.

The sales under the distributor program represented a new distribution channel for the company. Therefore Sunbeam was unable to set an appropriate level of reserves for any returns.[5]

Bill and Hold Sales

In the second quarter of 1997 Sunbeam recognized $14 million in sales revenue from bill and hold sales. By the fourth quarter Sunbeam had recognized $29 million in revenues and contributed an additional $4.5 million toward net income in bill and hold sales after it began promoting its bill and hold program. In all, bill and hold sales contributed to 10 percent of the fourth quarter's revenue.[6]

At year-end 1997, Sunbeam disclosed in its annual filing to the SEC that "the amount of [the] bill and hold sales at December 29, 1997, was approximately 3 percent of consolidated revenues." It did not disclose the extent to which the bill and hold sales had been booked in the final quarter.[7]

[3] SEC Accounting and Auditing Enforcement Release No. 1393, May 15, 2001.
[4] SEC Accounting and Auditing Enforcement Release No. 1393, May 15, 2001.
[5] SEC Accounting and Auditing Enforcement Release No. 1706, January 27, 2003.
[6] SEC Accounting and Auditing Enforcement Release No. 1394, May 15, 2001.
[7] SEC Accounting and Auditing Enforcement Release No. 1394, May 15, 2001.

Revenue Recognition Criteria for Bill and Hold Sales

The SEC had stipulated that the following criteria must be met for revenue to be recognized in bill and hold transactions:[8]

- The risks of ownership must have passed to the buyer.
- The buyer must have made a fixed commitment to purchase the goods.
- The buyer must request that the transaction be on a bill and hold basis and must have a substantial business purpose for this request.
- There must be a fixed schedule for delivery of the goods.
- The seller must not have retained any specific performance obligations such that the earning process is not complete.
- The ordered goods must be segregated from the seller's inventory.
- The goods must be complete and ready for shipment.

Characteristics of Sunbeam's Bill and Hold Sales

The SEC found that Sunbeam's bill and hold sales were not requested by Sunbeam's customers and served no business purpose other than to accelerate revenue recognition by Sunbeam. Sunbeam's bill and hold sales were typically accompanied by financial incentives being offered to customers, such as discounted pricing, to encourage the sale to occur long before the customer actually needed the goods. Sunbeam would then typically hold the product until delivery was requested by the customer. Sunbeam also paid the costs of storage, shipment, and insurance related to the products. In addition, Sunbeam's customers had the right to return the unsold product.[9]

Restatement of Revenues

In 1998 Sunbeam restated its revenues for 1997 from $1.168 to $1.073 billion. In an amended filing of its 10-K to the SEC, management wrote, "Upon examination, it was determined that certain revenue was improperly recognized (principally 'bill and hold' and guaranteed sales transactions)."[10] The company had reversed all bill and hold sales, which amounted to $29 million in 1997, and about $36 million in guaranteed or consignment sales, whose liberal return policies made the recognition of their revenue improper.[11]

---

[8] Staff Accounting Bulletin No. 101.

[9] SEC Accounting and Auditing Enforcement Release No. 1393, May 15, 2001.

[10] Amended 1997 10K filing to SEC.

[11] Martha Brannigan, "Sunbeam Slashes Its 1997 Earnings in Restatement," *The Wall Street Journal,* October 21, 1998.

Case Questions

1. Consider the principles, assumptions, and constraints of Generally Accepted Accounting Principles (GAAP). Define the *revenue recognition principle* and explain why it is important to users of financial statements.

2. Provide one specific example of how Sunbeam violated the revenue recognition principle in this situation. In your description, please identify a journal entry that may have been used by Sunbeam to commit the fraudulent act.

3. Consult Paragraph 2 of PCAOB Auditing Standard No. 5. Do you believe that Sunbeam had established an effective system of internal control over financial reporting related to revenue recorded in its financial statements? Why or why not?

4. Consult Paragraphs 7–9 of PCAOB Auditing Standard No. 15. As an auditor, what type of evidence would you want to examine to determine whether Sunbeam was inappropriately recording revenue from special discount sales?

5. Consult Paragraph 68 of PCAOB Auditing Standard No. 12. Next, consider a customer that receives extraordinary discounts and terms to purchase merchandise at the end of the year (e.g., the wholesaler that purchased grills from Sunbeam). Do you believe that an auditor has an obligation to investigate these type of situations during revenue testing? Why or why not?

Case 1.5

Waste Management: The Definition of an Asset

Synopsis

In February 1998 Waste Management announced that it was restating the financial statements it had issued for the years 1993 through 1996. In its restatement, Waste Management said that it had materially overstated its reported pretax earnings by $1.43 billion. After the announcement, the company's stock dropped by more than 33 percent, and shareholders lost over $6 billion.

The SEC brought charges against the company's founder, Dean Buntrock, and five other former top officers. The charges alleged that management had made repeated changes to depreciation-related estimates to reduce expenses and had employed several improper accounting practices related to capitalization policies, also designed to reduce expenses.[1] In its final judgment, the SEC permanently barred Buntrock and three other executives from acting as officers or directors of public companies and required payment from them of $30.8 million in penalties.[2]

Capitalization of Landfill Costs and Other Expenses

Under Generally Accepted Accounting Principles (GAAP), a cost can be capitalized if it provides economic benefits to be used or consumed in future operations. A company is required to write off, as a current period expense, any deferred costs at the time the company learns that the underlying assets have been either impaired or abandoned. Any costs to repair or return property to its original condition are required to be expensed when incurred. Finally, interest

[1] SEC, Accounting and Auditing Enforcement Release No. 1532, March 26, 2002.
[2] SEC, Accounting and Auditing Enforcement Release No. 2298, August 29, 2005.

can be capitalized as part of the cost of acquiring assets for the period of time that it takes to put the asset in the condition required for its intended use. However, GAAP requires that the capitalization of interest must cease once the asset is substantially ready for its intended use.

Capitalization of Landfill Permitting Costs[3]

Waste Management capitalized the costs related to obtaining the required permits to develop and expand its many landfills. It also capitalized interest on landfill construction costs, as well as costs related to systems development at its landfills.

As part of its normal business operations, Waste Management allocated substantial resources toward the development of new landfills and the expansion of existing landfills. A significant part of the landfill development and expansion costs related to the process of obtaining required permits from government authorities. Over the years, the company faced increasing difficulty in obtaining the required landfill permits, and had already invested significantly in many projects that had to be abandoned or were materially impaired when the required permits could not be obtained.

The company routinely capitalized the costs related to obtaining the required permits, so it could defer recording expenses related to those landfills until they were put into productive use. However, instead of writing off the costs related to impaired and/or abandoned landfill projects and disclosing the impact of such write-offs, management disclosed in its Form 10-K filed with the SEC only the *risk* of future write-offs related to such projects.

The management team of Waste Management also allegedly transferred the costs of unsuccessful efforts to obtain permits to other sites that had received permits or sites for which the company was still seeking permits. In effect, it was commingling impaired or abandoned landfill project costs with the costs of a permitted site (a practice known as "basketing," which did not comply with GAAP). In addition to basketing, the company also allegedly transferred unamortized costs from landfill facilities that had closed earlier than expected to other facilities that were still in operation (a practice known as "bundling," which also did not comply with GAAP). Management never disclosed the use of bundling or basketing in its Form 10-Ks.

In 1994, after its auditor Arthur Andersen discovered these practices, management allegedly agreed to write off $40 million related to dead projects over a span of 10 years, and also promised to write off future impairments and abandonments in a prompt manner. However, during 1994, 1995, 1996, and 1997, management effectively buried the write-offs related to abandoned and impaired projects by netting them against other gains, as opposed to identifying the costs separately as it had promised Andersen.

---

[3] Ibid.

Capitalization of Interest on Landfill Construction Costs[4]

In accordance with GAAP, Waste Management was able to capitalize interest related to landfill development because of the relatively long time required to obtain permits, construct landfills, and prepare them to receive waste. However, Waste Management utilized the "net book value (NBV) method," which essentially enabled it to avoid GAAP's requirement that interest capitalization cease once the asset became substantially ready for its intended use. Waste Management's auditor, Arthur Andersen, advised the company from its first use of the NBV method (in 1989) that this method did not conform to GAAP.

Corporate Controller Thomas Hau admitted that the method was "technically inconsistent with FAS Statement No. 34 [the controlling GAAP pronouncement] because it included interest [capitalization] related to cells of landfills that were receiving waste." Yet the company wrote in the footnotes to its financial statements that "[i]nterest has been capitalized on significant landfills, trash-to-energy plants and other projects under development in accordance with FAS No. 34."

Ultimately the company agreed to utilize a new method that conformed to GAAP, beginning on January 1, 1994. Corporate Controller Thomas Hau and CFO James Koenig allegedly determined that the new GAAP method would result in an increased annual interest expense of about $25 million; therefore they chose to phase in the new method over three years, beginning in 1995. However, the company continued to utilize the NBV method for interest capitalization through 1997.

Capitalization of Other Costs[5]

The company also chose to capitalize other costs, such as systems development costs, rather than record them as expenses in the periods in which they were incurred. In fact, it used excessive amortization periods (10- and 20-year periods for the two largest systems) that did not recognize the impact of technological obsolescence on the useful lives of the underlying systems.

The SEC found evidence that the company's auditor, Arthur Andersen, proposed several adjusting journal entries to write off the improperly deferred systems development costs. Andersen also repeatedly advised management to shorten the amortization periods. In 1994 management finally agreed to shorten the amortization periods and to write off financial statement misstatements resulting from improperly capitalized systems costs over a period of five years. During 1995 the company changed the amortization periods and wrote off improperly capitalized systems costs by netting them against other gains.

[4] Ibid.

[5] Ibid.

Case Questions

1. Consider the principles, assumptions, and constraints of Generally Accepted Accounting Principles (GAAP). What is the specific definition of an *asset?*

2. Consider the practices of basketing and bundling. Briefly explain why each practice is not appropriate under GAAP.

3. Consult Paragraphs 6–7 of PCAOB Auditing Standard No. 13. Next, describe why netting write-offs against other gains would be effective for Waste Management's management team in trying to cover up their fraudulent behavior.

4. Consult Paragraph 10 of PCAOB Auditing Standard No. 15. As an auditor, what type of evidence would allow you to detect whether your client was engaging in behaviors that are designed to mask fraudulent behavior (such as basketing, bundling, or netting)?

5. Consider the decision by CFO James Koenig and Corporate Controller Thomas Hau to phase in the new GAAP method to capitalize interest expense over three years. Do you believe that this decision was in the best interests of the shareholders in the long run? Why or why not?

Case 1.6

Enron: The Revenue Recognition Principle

Synopsis

In its 2000 annual report, Enron prided itself on having "metamorphosed from an asset-based pipeline and power generating company to a marketing and logistics company whose biggest assets are its well-established business approach and its innovative people."[1] Enron's strategy seemed to pay off; in 2000 it was the seventh largest company on the Fortune 500, with assets of $65 billion and sales revenues of $100 billion.[2] From 1996 to 2000, its revenues had increased by more than 750 percent, which was unprecedented in any industry.[3] Yet just a year later, in December 2001, Enron filed for bankruptcy, and billions of shareholder and retirement savings dollars were lost.

Background

Enron was created in 1985 by the merger of two gas pipeline companies: Houston Natural Gas and InterNorth. Enron's mission was to become the leading natural gas pipeline company in North America. As it adapted to changes in the natural gas industry, Enron changed its mission, expanding into natural gas trading and financing and into other markets, such as electricity and other commodity markets.

In the process, Enron made significant changes to several of its accounting procedures. For example, Enron began using mark-to-market (MTM) accounting for its trading business. Firms in the financial services industry typically used MTM

[1] Enron 2000 annual report, p. 7.

[2] Joseph F. Berardino, Remarks to U.S. House of Representatives Committee on Financial Services, December 12, 2001.

[3] Bala G. Dharan and William R. Bufkins, "Red Flags in Enron's Reporting of Revenues and Key Financial Measures," March 2003, prepublication draft (www.ruf.rice.edu/~bala/files/dharan-bufkins_enron_red_flags_041003.pdf), p. 4.

to value their trading portfolios. That is, every day they adjusted the values of their portfolios according to their current values in the market.[4] Enron was the first company outside the financial services industry to use MTM accounting.[5]

Enron's Use of Mark-to-Market Accounting

In 1992 the SEC's chief accountant, Walter Scheutz, granted Enron permission to use MTM during the first quarter of its fiscal year ended December 31, 1992. However, he also indicated that MTM could be used *only* in Enron's natural gas trading business.[6] Enron's CFO, Jack Tompkins, wrote back to Scheutz informing him that "Enron has changed its method of accounting for its energy-related price risk management activities effective January 1, 1991 . . . the cumulative effect of initial adoption of mark-to-market accounting, as well as the impact upon 1991 earnings is not material."[7]

For some time, there has been debate about whether MTM should be used for assets that are actively traded. For certain assets, like stock portfolios, an active trading market exists and the determination of value is straightforward. However, the value of natural gas contracts is harder to assess because they often require complex valuation formulas with multiple assumptions for the formulas' variables, such as interest rates, customers, costs, and prices. These assumptions have a major impact on value and are related to very long time periods—in some cases as long as 20 years.

Early Application of MTM Accounting: Sithe Energies Agreement

One of the earliest contracts for which Enron employed MTM accounting was an agreement for Enron to supply Sithe Energies with 195 million cubic feet of gas per day for 20 years for a plant that Sithe was going to build in New York. The estimated value of the gas to be supplied was $3.5 to $4 billion. Interestingly, by using MTM, Enron was able to book profits from the contract even before the plant started operating.[8]

---

[4] Bethany McLean and Peter Elkind, *The Smartest Guys in the Room: The Amazing Rise and Scandalous Fall of Enron* (New York: Penguin Group, 2003), p. 40.

[5] Bala G. Dharan and William R. Bufkins, "Red Flags in Enron's Reporting of Revenues and Key Financial Measures," March 2003, prepublication draft (www.ruf.rice.edu/~bala/files/dharan-bufkins_enron_red_flags_041003.pdf), pp. 7–11.

[6] Robert Bryce, *Pipe Dreams: Greed, Ego, and the Death of Enron* (New York: Perseus Book Group, 2002), p. 67.

[7] Robert Bryce, *Pipe Dreams: Greed, Ego, and the Death of Enron* (New York: Perseus Book Group, 2002), p. 67.

[8] Bethany McLean and Peter Elkind, *The Smartest Guys in the Room: The Amazing Rise and Scandalous Fall of Enron* (New York: Penguin Group, 2003), pp. 60–61.

Prior to the use of MTM, Enron would have recognized the *actual* costs of supplying the gas and the *actual* revenues received from selling the gas in each time period. Using MTM, at the moment a long-term contract was signed, the *present value* of the stream of future inflows under the contract was recognized as revenues, and the *present value* of the expected costs of fulfilling the contract was expensed.[9] Changes in value were recognized as additional income or loss (with a corresponding change to the relevant balance sheet account) in subsequent periods.[10]

Enron's Expanded Use of MTM Accounting

Although the SEC had initially given approval for Enron to use MTM in the accounting of natural gas futures contracts, Enron quietly began using MTM for electric power contracts and trades as well.[11] In one example, Enron signed a 15-year, $1.3 billion contract to supply electricity to Eli Lilly in the state of Indiana. Enron calculated the present value of the contract as more than half a billion dollars and recognized this amount as revenue. It also reported estimates for the costs associated with servicing the contract. Interestingly, at the time of this contract, the state of Indiana had not yet deregulated electricity. Thus Enron needed to predict when Indiana would deregulate, as well as the impact of the deregulation on the contract valuation.[12]

Enron also extended MTM accounting to other business lines. In another example, Enron signed a 20-year agreement with Blockbuster Video in July 2000 to introduce entertainment on demand. Enron set up pilot projects in Portland, Seattle, and Salt Lake City to store the entertainment and then distribute it over its broadband network. Based on these pilot projects, Enron recognized estimated profits of more than $110 million for the Blockbuster deal, although the technical viability and market demand were difficult to predict in these initial pilot stages.[13] Canceled in March 2001, the Blockbuster deal never went past the initial pilot stages.

---

[9] Bala G. Dharan and William R. Bufkins, "Red Flags in Enron's Reporting of Revenues and Key Financial Measures," March 2003, prepublication draft (http://www.ruf.rice.edu/~bala/files/dharan-bufkins_enron_red_flags_041003.pdf), pp. 7–11.

[10] Bethany McLean and Peter Elkind, *The Smartest Guys in the Room: The Amazing Rise and Scandalous Fall of Enron* (New York: Penguin Group, 2003), p. 39.

[11] Bethany McLean and Peter Elkind, *The Smartest Guys in the Room: The Amazing Rise and Scandalous Fall of Enron* (New York: Penguin Group, 2003), p. 127.

[12] Paul M. Healy and Krishna Palepu, "The Fall of Enron," *Journal of Economic Perspectives* 17, no. 2 (Spring 2003), p. 10.

[13] Paul M. Healy and Krishna Palepu, "The Fall of Enron," *Journal of Economic Perspectives* 17, no. 2 (Spring 2003), p. 10.

Case Questions

1. Consider the principles, assumptions, and constraints of Generally Accepted Accounting Principles (GAAP). Define the *revenue recognition principle* and explain why it is important to users of financial statements.

2. Consider the Sithe Energies contract described in the case. Does the accounting for this contract provide an example of how Enron violated the revenue recognition principle? Why or why not? Please be specific.

3. Consult Paragraph 14 of PCAOB Auditing Standard No. 5 and Paragraph 68 of PCAOB Auditing Standard No. 12. Based on the case information, do you believe that Enron had established an effective system of internal control over financial reporting related to the contract revenue recorded in its financial statements? Why or why not?

4. Consult Paragraphs 4–8 of PCAOB Auditing Standard No. 15. As an auditor, what type of evidence would you want to examine to determine whether Enron was inappropriately recording revenue from the Sithe Energies contract?

5. Consult Paragraphs 1–2 of Ethics Rule 102 (ET 102). Next, consider the role of the Enron employee who was responsible for applying MTM accounting rules to electric power contracts, like the Eli Lilly contract. Assuming the employee was a CPA and knew that the use of MTM accounting was beyond the scope of the SEC approval parameters, do you believe that the employee had a responsibility to report the behavior to the audit committee? Why or why not?

Case 1.7

WorldCom: The Expense Recognition Principle

Synopsis

On June 25, 2002, WorldCom announced that it would be restating its financial statements for 2001 and the first quarter of 2002. Less than one month later, on July 21, 2002, WorldCom announced that it had filed for bankruptcy. It was later revealed that WorldCom had likely engaged in improper accounting that took two major forms: the overstatement of revenue by at least $958 million and the understatement of line costs, its largest category of expenses, by over $7 billion. Several executives pled guilty to charges of fraud and were sentenced to prison terms, including CFO Scott Sullivan (five years) and Controller David Myers (one year and one day). Convicted of fraud in 2005, CEO Bernie Ebbers was the first to receive his prison sentence: 25 years.

Line Cost Expenses

WorldCom generally maintained its own lines for local service in heavily populated urban areas. However, it relied on non-WorldCom networks to complete most residential and commercial calls outside of these urban areas and paid the owners of these networks to use their services. For example, a call from a WorldCom customer in Boston to Rome might start on a local (Boston) phone company's line, flow to WorldCom's own network, and then get passed to an Italian phone company to be completed. In this example, WorldCom would have to pay both the local Boston phone company and the Italian provider for the use of their services.[1] The costs associated with carrying a voice call or data transmission from its starting point to its ending point were called *line cost expenses*.

---

[1] Board of Directors' Special Investigative Committee Report, June 9, 2003, p. 58.

Line cost expenses were WorldCom's largest single expense. They accounted for approximately half of the company's total expenses from 1999 to 2001. World-Com regularly discussed its line cost expenses in public disclosures, emphasizing, in particular, its *line cost E/R ratio*—the ratio of line cost expense to revenue.[2]

GAAP for Line Costs

Under Generally Accepted Accounting Principles (GAAP), WorldCom was required to estimate its line costs each month and to expense the estimated cost immediately, even though many of these costs would be paid later. To reflect an estimate of amounts that had not yet been paid, WorldCom would set up a liability account, known as an *accrual,* on its balance sheet. As the bills arrived from its outside parties, sometimes many months later, WorldCom would pay them and reduce the previously established accruals accordingly.[3]

Because accruals are estimates, a company is required under GAAP to reevaluate them periodically to see if they have been stated at appropriate levels. If charges from service providers were lower than estimated, an accrual is "released." The amount of the release is set off against the reported line cost expenses in the period when the release occurred. For example, if an accrual of $500 million was established in the first quarter and $25 million of that amount was deemed excess or unnecessary in the second quarter, then $25 million should be released in that second quarter, thus reducing reported line cost expenses by $25 million.[4]

WorldCom's Line Cost Releases

Beginning in the second quarter of 1999, management allegedly started ordering several releases of line cost accruals, often without any underlying analysis to support the releases. When requests were met with resistance, management allegedly made the adjustments themselves. For example, in the second quarter of 2000, David Myers, a CPA who served as senior vice president and controller of World-Com, requested that UUNET (a largely autonomous WorldCom subsidiary at the time) release $50 million in line cost accruals. UUNET's acting CFO David Schneeman asked that Myers explain the reasoning for the requested release, but Myers insisted that Schneeman book the entry without an explanation. When Schneeman refused, Myers wrote to him in an e-mail, "I guess the only way I am going to get this booked is to fly to DC and book it myself. Book it right now, I can't wait another minute." After Schneeman refused again, Betty Vinson in general accounting allegedly completed Myers's request by making a "top-side" corporate-level adjusting journal entry releasing $50 million in UUNET accruals.[5]

[2] Ibid., pp. 58–59.
[3] Ibid., pp. 62–63.
[4] Ibid., pp. 63–64.
[5] Ibid., p. 83.

In 2000, senior members of WorldCom's corporate finance organization allegedly directed a number of similar releases from accruals established for other reasons to offset domestic line cost expenses. For example, in the second quarter of 2000, Senior Vice President and Controller David Myers asked Charles Wasserott, director of Domestic Telco Accounting, to release $255 million in domestic line cost accruals to reduce domestic line cost expenses. Wasserott refused to release such a large amount. It later emerged that the entire $255 million used to reduce line cost expenses came instead from a release of a Mass Markets accrual related to WorldCom's Selling General & Administrative expenses.[6]

The largest release of accruals from other areas to reduce line cost expenses occurred after the close of the third quarter of 2000. During this time, a number of entries were made to release various accruals that reduced domestic line cost expenses by $828 million.[7]

In addition to allegations that WorldCom's management released line cost accruals without proper support for doing so and released accruals that had been established for other purposes, there were also allegations that management often did not release certain line costs in the period in which they were identified. Rather, certain line cost accruals were kept as "rainy-day" funds that could be released when management needed to improve reported results.[8]

[6] Ibid., pp. 87–88.
[7] Ibid., pp. 88–89.
[8] Ibid., p. 10.

Case Questions

1. Consider the principles, assumptions, and constraints of Generally Accepted Accounting Principles (GAAP). Define the *matching principle* and explain why it is important to users of financial statements.

2. Based on the case information provided, describe specifically how WorldCom violated the matching principle. In your description, please identify a journal entry that may have been used by WorldCom to commit the fraud.

3. Consult Paragraph A5 (in Appendix A) of PCAOB Auditing Standard No. 5. Do you believe that WorldCom had established an effective system of internal control over financial reporting related to the line cost expense recorded in its financial statements? Why or why not?

4. Consult Paragraphs 13–21 of PCAOB Auditing Standard No. 15. As an auditor at WorldCom, what type of evidence would you want to examine to determine whether the company was inappropriately releasing line costs? Please be specific.

5. Consult Paragraphs 1–2 of Ethics Rule 102 (ET 102). Next, consider the actions of David Schneeman and Charles Wasserott. Assuming that they were CPAs, do you believe that these employees should have recorded the journal entries as directed by Senior Vice President and Controller David Myers? Why or why not?

Case 1.8

Bernard L. Madoff Investment and Securities: Broker-Dealer Fraud

Synopsis

During 2008, Bernie Madoff became famous for a Ponzi scheme that defrauded investors out of as much as $65 billion. To satisfy his clients' expectations of earning returns greater than the market average, Madoff falsely asserted that he used an innovative "split-strike conversion strategy," which provided the appearance that he was achieving extraordinary results.[1] In reality, he was a fraudster. Madoff was arrested on December 11, 2008, and convicted in 2009 on 11 counts of fraud, perjury, and money laundering. As a result, Madoff was sentenced to 150 years in prison.

The Beginning

Bernard Madoff created Madoff Investment Securities in the 1960s with $5,000 that he had earned from installing refrigeration systems and working as a lifeguard. His brother Peter, who joined the firm in 1965, was the head of trading and the chief compliance officer for the firm's investment advisory and the broker-dealer businesses. Madoff's nephew, Charles Wiener, joined the firm in 1978 and became the firm's director of administration. Madoff's sons, Mark and Andrew, joined the business in the 1980s (becoming directors), and in the 1990s, Madoff's niece (Peter's daughter) Shana came on board as in-house legal counsel.

---

[1] "Plea Allocution of Bernard L. Madoff," March 12, 2009 (http://news.findlaw.com/hdocs/docs/madoff/bernard-guilty-plea31209statement.html).

A Ponzi Scheme

A Ponzi scheme is any fraudulent investment plan that pays its returns to an investor from either that investor's own principal or principal paid by future investors, not from legitimate investment returns. To carry out his plan, Bernie Madoff represented to clients and potential clients that he would invest their money in "shares of common stock, options and other securities of well-known corporations, and upon request, would return to them their profits and principal."[2] In fact, Madoff never invested the funds in the securities that had been promised. Rather, the funds were deposited into a bank account at Chase Manhattan Bank, based in New York City. If clients requested to receive "profits earned" or redeem their investment principal, Madoff merely used the money in the bank account at Chase Manhattan Bank that had belonged to either that client or other clients to pay off the requested sum.[3]

The Split-Strike Conversion Strategy

In the early 1990s, Madoff began to receive investment commitments from key institutional investors. While he did not promise specific rates of return to clients, Madoff knew that the investors expected that their investment would perform at a level higher than the market average. To meet their expectations, Madoff claimed to have mastered a "split-strike conversion strategy."[4]

Under his split-strike conversion strategy, Madoff promised clients and prospective clients that their funds would be invested in a "basket of stocks that would closely mimic the price movements of the Standard & Poor's 100 Index." He further promised to "opportunistically time these purchases and would be out of the market intermittently, investing client funds during these periods in United States Government-issued securities such as United States Treasury bills." Madoff also promised to hedge the investments in common stocks "by using client funds to buy and sell option contracts related to those stocks, thereby limiting potential client losses caused by unpredictable changes in stock prices." Madoff promised that his strategy would lead to consistent returns for his investors. And, the strategy appeared to be working. Harry Markopolos, the whistleblower that informed the SEC about Madoff, commented that "in 1993 when the S&P 500 returned 1.33%, Bernie returned 14.55%; in 1999 the S&P returned 21.04%, and there was Bernie at 16.69%. His returns were always good, but rarely spectacular. For limited periods of time, other funds returned as much, or even more, than Madoff's. So it wasn't his returns that bothered me so much – his returns each month were possible – it was that he always returned a profit. There was no existing mathematical model that could explain the consistency."[5] Madoff, in reality, never made the investments that he promised to clients.[6]

[2] Ibid.
[3] Ibid.
[4] Ibid.
[5] Harry Markopolos, *No One Would Listen* (Hoboken NJ: John Wiley & Sons, 2010), 33.
[6] Ibid.

Concealment Techniques

"For many years up until my arrest on December 11, 2008, I operated a Ponzi scheme through the investment advisory side of my business, Bernard L. Madoff Securities LLC," admitted Madoff on March 12, 2009. He continued:

> To conceal my fraud, I misrepresented to clients, employees and others, that I purchased securities for clients in overseas markets. Indeed, when the United States Securities and Exchange Commission asked me to testify as part of an investigation they were conducting about my investment advisory business, I knowingly gave false testimony under oath to the staff of the SEC on May 19, 2006, that I executed trades of common stock on behalf of my investment advisory clients and that I purchased and sold the equities that were part of my investment strategy in European markets. In that session with the SEC . . . I also knowingly gave false testimony under oath that I had executed options contracts on behalf of my investment advisory clients and that my firm had custody of the assets managed on behalf of my investment advisory clients . . . Another way that I concealed my fraud was through the filing of false and misleading certified audit reports and financial statements with the SEC."

In addition, Madoff created "false trading confirmations and client account statements that reflected the bogus transactions and positions" and then sent them to investment clients. According to Madoff, "The clients receiving trade confirmations and account statements had no way of knowing by reviewing these documents that I had never engaged in the transactions represented on the statements and confirmations."[7]

Interestingly, auditors of nonpublic broker-dealers were not subject to oversight by the Public Company Accounting Oversight Board(PCAOB) at this time. However, the Dodd-Frank Wall Street Reform and Consumer Protection Act of 2010 provided the PCAOB with new authority over the audits of brokers and dealers that are registered with the SEC. As a result of the act, the financial statements of such brokers and dealers must now be audited by a public accounting firm that is registered with the PCAOB. In addition, the Act gave the PCAOB the authority to inspect the audit workpapers for broker-dealer audits. Title IX of the Act focuses in part on the role of the Securities and Exchange Commission (SEC) in protecting investors. The Act established a whistleblower program to help produce tips about securities fraud. The program features a generous reward structure for suppliers of original information (10–30 percent of the recovered capital, when more than $1 million is recovered). In addition, the Act expands the oversight of the SEC to be completed by the Government Accountability Office (GAO) and calls for changes that are designed to improve the management of the SEC.

---

[7] Ibid.

Case Questions

1. Define a Ponzi scheme. Next, describe why the Madoff fraud is considered a Ponzi scheme. Please be specific in your explanation.
2. Describe what is meant by a "split-strike" strategy. Do you believe that this strategy is viable? Why or why not?
3. Consider the Dodd-Frank Wall Street Reform and Consumer Protection Act of 2010. According to the Act, the PCAOB now has authority to inspect the work of audit firms auditing broker-dealer firms. Do you believe that this provision is going to make a difference? Why or why not?
4. Title IX of the Dodd-Frank Wall Street Reform and Consumer Protection Act of 2010 appears to be driven in part by the Madoff Ponzi scheme. Indeed, after the SEC's investigations failed to detect the Madoff fraud (see Case 1.12), many sections of Title IX sought to improve the performance of the Securities and Exchange Commission (SEC). How?

Case 1.9

Qwest: The Revenue Recognition Principle

Synopsis

When Joseph Nacchio became Qwest's CEO in January 1997, the company's existing strategy began to shift from just building a nationwide fiber-optic network to include increasing communications services. By the time it released earnings in 1998, Nacchio proclaimed Qwest's successful transition from a network construction company to a communications services provider. "We successfully transitioned Qwest into a leading Internet protocol-based multimedia company focused on the convergence of data, video, and voice services."[1]

During 1999 and 2000, Qwest consistently met its aggressive revenue targets and became a darling to its investors. Yet, when the company announced its intention to restate revenues in August 2002, its stock price plunged to a low of $1.11 per share in August 2002, from a high of $55 per share in July 2000.[2] Civil and criminal charges related to fraudulent activitity were brought against several Qwest executives, including CEO Joseph Nacchio. Nacchio was convicted on 19 counts of illegal insider trading, and was sentenced to six years in prison in July 2007. He was also ordered to pay a $19 million fine and forfeit $52 million that he gained in illegal stock sales.[3]

[1] *SEC v. Joseph P. Nacchio, Robert S. Woodruff, Robin R. Szeliga, Afshin Mohebbi, Gregory M. Casey, James J. Kozlowski, Frank T. Noyes, Defendants*, Civil Action No. 05-MK-480 (OES), 11–14.

[2] *SEC v. Qwest*, 1–2.

[3] Dionne Searcey, "Qwest Ex-Chief Gets 6 Years in Prison for Insider Trading," *Wall Street Journal*, July 28, 2007 A3.

Background[4]

Qwest executives allegedly made false and misleading disclosures concerning revenues from its directory services unit, Qwest Dex Inc. (Dex). In addition, executives were charged with having manipulated revenue from Dex for 2000 and 2001 by secretly altering directory publication dates and the lives of directories.

Dex's Changes to Publication Dates and Lives of Directories

Dex published telephone directories year-round in approximately 300 markets in 14 states. It earned revenue by selling advertising space in its directories. Each of its directories typically had a life of 12 months, and Qwest traditionally recognized directory revenue over the life of the directory. However, in late 1999 Dex adopted a "point of publication" method of accounting and began to recognize all advertising revenue for a directory as soon as Dex began deliveries of that directory to the public.

In August 2000 Dex executives allegedly informed Qwest senior management that Dex would be unable to achieve the aggressive 2000 earnings' targets that management had set for it. As one option for making up for the shortfall, Dex suggested that it could publish Dex's Colorado Springs directory in December 2000 rather than January 2001 as scheduled, thereby allowing Qwest to recognize revenue from the directory in 2000 rather than 2001. One Dex executive expressed opposition, citing his concern that such a schedule change would merely reduce 2001 revenue and earnings. He also expressed his view that Qwest probably would be required to disclose the change in the regulatory filings with the SEC. Despite this executive's opposition, Qwest senior management allegedly instructed Dex to move forward with the proposed change.

By recognizing revenue from the Colorado Springs directory in 2000, Qwest generated $28 million in additional revenue and $18 million in additional earnings before interest and tax, depreciation, and amortization (EBITDA) for the year. The additional revenue generated in 2000 accounted for about 30 percent of Dex's 2000 year-over-year revenue increase. It further allowed Dex to show 6.6 percent year-over-year revenue growth versus 4.6 percent if the schedule change had not been made.

In Qwest's 2000 Form 10-K, Qwest informed investors that Dex's revenue for 2000 increased by almost $100 million. It wrote that the increase was due in part to "an increase in the number of directories published." At the same time, it failed to inform investors that Dex generated nearly one-third of that amount by publishing the Colorado Springs directory twice in 2000. It also did not inform investors that the schedule change would produce a corresponding decline in Dex revenue for the first quarter of 2001.

---

[4] Much of the information in this case is based on *SEC v. Qwest*, pp. 40–42.

For 2001 Qwest senior management established revenue and EBITDA targets for Dex that were higher than what Dex management believed was possible to achieve. In fact, the EBITDA target was allegedly $80–100 million greater than the amount Dex management believed was achievable. The SEC found that Dex management complained to Qwest's senior management about the unrealistic targets. Yet Qwest's senior management not only allegedly refused to change the targets but also did not allow Dex a reduction in the targets to compensate for the revenue from the Colorado Springs directory that was recognized in 2000.

In March 2001 Dex management met with some of Qwest's senior management to discuss "gap-closing" ideas for the first two quarters of 2001 in an attempt to achieve its 2001 financial targets. One idea was to advance the publication dates of several directories, thus allowing Dex to recognize revenue in earlier quarters; another idea was to lengthen the lives of other directories from 12 to 13 months, thereby allowing Dex to bill each advertiser for one additional month of advertising fees in 2001. Senior managers at Qwest allegedly instructed the Dex managers to implement the changes, as well as other changes to allow it to meet its third- and fourth-quarter financial targets.

During 2001 Dex advanced the publication dates or extended the lives of 34 directories. Those schedule changes produced $42 million in additional revenue and $41 million in additional EBITDA. Qwest's Form 10-Qs for the first three quarters of 2001 stated that period-over-period improvements in Dex's revenue were due in part to changes in the "mix" and/or the "lengths" of directories published. Like the 2000 Form 10-K, these reports did not include any information about the directory schedule changes or the reasons for those changes.

Case Questions

1. Consider the principles, assumptions, and constraints of Generally Accepted Accounting Principles (GAAP). Define the *revenue recognition principle* and explain why it is important to users of financial statements.

2. Describe specifically why the revenue recognition practices of Dex were not appropriate under GAAP.

3. Consult Paragraph A5 (in Appendix A) of PCAOB Auditing Standard No. 5 and Paragraph 68 of PCAOB Auditing Standard No. 12. Do you believe that Qwest had established an effective system of internal control over financial reporting related to the revenue recorded by Dex in its financial statements? Why or why not?

4. Consult Paragraph 25 of PCAOB Auditing Standard No. 5. Next consider the impact of the pressure exerted by Qwest's senior management team to meet aggressive revenue and earnings targets. Comment about why such a "tone at the top" would have a pervasive effect on the reliability of financial reporting at a company like Qwest.

5. Consider the role of an upper manager at Dex. Do you believe that a "point of publication" method of accounting is allowable under Generally Accepted Accounting Principles? Whether you do or not, please make an argument that supports the recognition of revenue related to the Colorado Springs directory in December 2000, as opposed to 2001. Consult Paragraphs 1–2 of Ethics Rule 102 (ET 102). Assuming that they were CPAs, do you believe that the actions of the upper managers at Dex were ethical? Why or why not?

1.10

The Baptist Foundation of Arizona: The Conservatism Constraint

Synopsis

The Baptist Foundation of Arizona (BFA) was organized as an Arizona non-profit organization primarily to help provide financial support for various Southern Baptist causes. Under William Crotts's leadership, the foundation engaged in a major strategic shift in its operations. BFA began to invest heavily in the Arizona real estate market and also accelerated its efforts to sell investment agreements and mortgage-backed securities to church members.

Two of BFA's most significant affiliates were ALO and New Church Ventures. It was later revealed that BFA had set up these affiliates to facilitate the "sale" of its real estate investments at prices significantly above fair market value. In so doing, BFA's management perpetrated a fraudulent scheme that cost at least 13,000 investors more than $590 million. In fact, Arizona Attorney General Janet Napolitano called the BFA collapse the largest bankruptcy of a religious nonprofit in the history of the United States.[1]

Background

Under William Crotts's leadership, BFA began to invest heavily in the Arizona real estate market, and also accelerated its efforts to sell investments to church members. Although Arizona real estate prices skyrocketed in the early 1980s, the upward trend did not continue, and property values declined substantially in 1989. Soon after this decline, management decided to establish a number

[1] Terry Greene Sterling, "Arthur Andersen and the Baptists," *Salon.com Technology,* February 7, 2002.

of related affiliates. These affiliates were controlled by individuals with close ties to BFA, such as former board members. For example, one former BFA director incorporated both ALO and New Church Ventures. The entities had no employees of their own, and both organizations paid BFA substantial management fees to provide accounting, marketing, and administrative services. As a result, both ALO and New Church Ventures owed BFA significant amounts by the end of 1995. On an overall basis, BFA, New Church Ventures, and ALO had a combined negative net worth of $83.2 million at year-end 1995, $102.3 million at year-end 1996, and $124.0 million at year-end 1997.[2] From 1984 to 1997, BFA's independent auditor, Arthur Andersen, issued unqualified audit opinions on BFA's combined financial statements.

Year-End Transactions

In December of each year, BFA engaged in significant year-end transactions with its related parties, ALO and New Church Ventures. These related party transactions primarily included real estate sales, gifts, pledges, and charitable contributions. Without these year-end transactions, BFA, on a stand-alone basis, would have been forced to report a significant decrease in net assets in each year from 1991 to 1994. Yet BFA did not disclose any information about these material related party transactions in its financial statements for the years 1991 to 1994.[3]

As an example, the significant real estate transactions that occurred in December 1995 with Harold Friend, Dwain Hoover, and subsidiaries of ALO enabled BFA to report an increase in net assets of $1.6 million for the year ended December 31, 1995, as opposed to a decrease in net assets that would have been reported. Importantly, for BFA to recognize a gain on these transactions in accordance with GAAP, the down payment for the buyer's initial investment could not be "funds that have been or will be loaned, refunded, or directly or indirectly provided to the buyer by the seller, or loans guaranteed or collateralized by the seller for the buyer."[4] However, in reality, the cash for the initial down payments on many of these real estate sales could be traced back to BFA via transactions with affiliates of ALO and New Church Ventures.

Foundation Investments, Inc.'s Sale of Santa Fe Trails Ranch II, Inc., Stock

Santa Fe Trails Ranch II, Inc., was a subsidiary of Select Trading Group, Inc., which was a subsidiary of ALO. The only significant asset owned by Santa Fe Trails Ranch II was 1,357 acres of undeveloped land in San Miguel County, New Mexico.

[2] Notice of Public Hearing and Complaint No. 98.230-ACY, Before the Arizona State Board of Accountancy, pp. 3–4.

[3] Ibid., pp. 19–20.

[4] Notice of Public Hearing and Complaint No. 98.230-ACY, Before the Arizona State Board of Accountancy, p. 25.

On December 26, 1995, 100 percent of the issued and outstanding common stock of Santa Fe Trails Ranch II was transferred from Select Trading Group to ALO. ALO then sold the stock to New Church Ventures in exchange for a $1.6 million reduction in ALO's credit line that was already owed to New Church Ventures. On the same day, New Church Ventures sold the Santa Fe Trails Ranch II stock to Foundation Investments, Inc., a BFA subsidiary, in exchange for a $1.6 million reduction in the New Church Ventures's credit line that was already owed to Foundation Investments. Also on the same day, Foundation Investments sold the Santa Fe Trails Ranch II stock to Harold Friend for $3.2 million, resulting in Foundation Investments recognizing a gain of $1.6 million in its financial statements.

The terms of the sale of the Santa Fe Trails Ranch II stock by Foundation Investments to Friend for $3.2 million was a 25 percent cash down payment ($800,000) with the balance of $2.4 million in a carryback note receivable to Foundation Investments. To audit the transaction, Arthur Andersen's senior auditor John Bauerle vouched the payment received from Friend via wire transfer back to the December 31, 1995, bank statement. However, he did not complete any additional work to determine the source of the cash down payment.

To assess the true nature and purpose of this series of transactions, Arthur Andersen reviewed a feasibility study and a 1993 cash flow analysis for the proposed development of Cedar Hills. An independent appraisal was not obtained. Arthur Andersen prepared a net present value calculation using the 1993 cash flow analysis to support the $3.2 million value that Friend paid to Foundation Investments on December 26, 1995. Arthur Andersen accepted the $3.2 million value without questioning why that same property was valued at only $1.6 million when New Church Ventures sold it to Foundation Investments on the same day.

TFCI's Sale to Hoover[5]

In December 1995 The Foundation Companies, Inc., a for-profit BFA subsidiary, sold certain joint venture interests in real estate developments to Dwain Hoover and recognized a gain on the transaction of approximately $4.4 million. In this particular transaction, the cash down payment from Hoover to The Foundation Companies of approximately $2.9 million was funded by a loan to Hoover from FMC Holdings, Inc., a subsidiary of ALO. Importantly, FMC received its own funding from BFA and New Church Ventures.

The details of this transaction were documented in Arthur Andersen's workpapers, primarily through a memorandum prepared by Arthur Andersen senior auditor John Bauerle on April 13, 1996. According to his memo, Bauerle concluded that the transaction did meet the criteria for gain recognition pursuant to SFAS No. 66. However, Bauerle's memorandum did not include

[5] Notice of Public Hearing and Complaint No. 98.230-ACY, Before the Arizona State Board of Accountancy, pp. 27–28.

any documentation to support how Arthur Andersen tested the source of the cash down payment to help ensure that the down payment was not directly or indirectly provided by BFA.

In early 1996 Arthur Andersen was auditing The Foundation Companies and prepared their annual management representation letter to be signed by the Foundation Companies' Chief Financial Officer, Ron Estes. However, because of the previously described Hoover transaction, Estes refused to sign the management representation letter. CFO Estes protested against the Hoover transaction and ultimately resigned in June 1996. Arthur Andersen's audit workpapers related to the Foundation Companies 1995 audit did not address the absence of Estes's signature on the final management representation letter or indicate whether it asked Estes why he refused to sign the letter.

Case Questions

1. Consider the principles, assumptions, and constraints of Generally Accepted Accounting Principles (GAAP). Define the *conservatism constraint* and explain why it is important to users of financial statements.
2. Consider the significant year-end transactions consummated by BFA. Do you believe that the accounting for these transactions violated the conservatism constraint? Why or why not? Please be specific when answering the question.
3. Consult Paragraph 14 of PCAOB Auditing Standard No. 5. Do you believe that BFA had established an effective system of internal control over financial reporting related to its significant year-end transactions? Why or why not?
4. Consult Paragraphs 12–15 of PCAOB Auditing Standard No. 13. Consider the sale of the Santa Fe Trails Ranch II stock by Foundation Investments to Friend. Do you believe that the auditor should have completed any additional testing beyond vouching the payment received from Friend? Provide the rationale for your decision.
5. Consider the role of president at BFA. Next, assume that as president, you are representing the upper management team at the Foundation's annual meeting. During the question-and-answer session, an investor asks you to justify the creation of ALO and whether the real estate transactions between BFA and ALO were legitimate. Develop a response that could potentially satisfy the investor's curiosity.

Case 1.11

WorldCom: The Definition of an Asset

Synopsis

On June 25, 2002, WorldCom announced that it would be restating its financial statements for 2001 and the first quarter of 2002. Less than one month later, on July 21, 2002, WorldCom announced it had filed for bankruptcy. It was later revealed that WorldCom had engaged in improper accounting that took two major forms: the overstatement of revenue by at least $958 million and the understatement of line costs, its largest category of expenses, by over $7 billion. Several executives pled guilty to charges of fraud and were sentenced to prison terms, including CFO Scott Sullivan (five years) and Controller David Meyers (one year and one day). Convicted of fraud in 2005, CEO Bernie Ebbers was the first to receive his prison sentence: 25 years.

Line Cost Expenses

WorldCom generally maintained its own lines for local service in heavily populated urban areas. However, it relied on non-WorldCom networks to complete most residential and commercial calls outside of these urban areas and paid the owners of the networks to use their services. For example, a call from a WorldCom customer in Boston to Rome might start on a local (Boston) phone company's line, flow to WorldCom's own network, and then get passed to an Italian phone company to be completed. In this example, WorldCom would have to pay both the local Boston phone company and the Italian provider for the use of their services.[1] The costs associated with carrying a voice call or data transmission from its starting point to its ending point are called line cost expenses.

---

[1] Board of Directors' Special Investigative Committee Report, June 9, 2003, p. 58.

Through the end of 2000, WorldCom incurred substantial line cost expenses when it made large capital investments to increase the size of its Internet backbone and expand its local and data networks. To do so, it entered into long-term, fixed-rate leases for network capacity to take advantage of a perceived boom in the technology sector. However, customer traffic did not grow as rapidly as anticipated. In addition, the telecommunications market became extremely competitive, forcing WorldCom to reduce the fees it charged to customers. As a result, in late 2000 and early 2001, WorldCom's ratio of line cost expense to revenue (line cost E/R ratio) was trending upward.[2]

Construction in Progress

In its first-quarter 2001 earnings announcement, WorldCom reported a line cost E/R ratio of 42 percent, which was in line with previously reported E/R ratios. WorldCom achieved this result in large part by capitalizing $544.2 million in line costs (rather than expensing the costs), despite the fact that the company had never previously capitalized these costs. In fact, WorldCom's internal accounting policy prohibited the capitalization of these operating line cost expenses. Importantly, the company did not disclose this change in accounting policy in its public filings.[3]

Once again, in the second quarter of 2001, WorldCom capitalized $560 million of operating line costs. The capitalized line costs in both the first and second quarters of 2001 were booked in asset accounts labeled "Construction in Progress." Employees in the Property Accounting group, which oversaw the company's assets, later transferred the capitalized line cost amounts from Construction in Progress to in-service asset accounts. Interestingly, the transfer of capitalized line cost amounts happened at about the same time that WorldCom's outside auditors expressed an interest in reviewing certain Construction in Progress accounts (as part of their normal substantive testing procedures).[4]

Due to the line cost capitalization entries in the first two quarters of 2001, line cost expenses were significantly below the amount budgeted for operating line cost expenses. In September of 2001, the company's Budget group was directed to retroactively reduce the line cost budget for 2001 by $2.7 billion. WorldCom also capitalized $743 million of operating line costs for the third quarter. By the fourth quarter of 2001, employees in Property Accounting and Capital Reporting began refusing to make such entries without proper documentation.[5]

---

[2] Board of Directors' Special Investigative Committee Report, June 29, 2003, pp. 109–151.

[3] Ibid.

[4] Ibid.

[5] Ibid.

The Audit Committee

In May 2002, the Internal Audit department began investigating the capitalization of line costs. In June 2002 the Internal Audit team informed Max Bobbitt, the chair of the audit committee of the board of directors, of entries that amounted to a total of $2.5 billion in capitalized line costs. Between June 21 and June 24, the board of directors engaged several attorneys and other professionals to review the issue in detail.[6]

WorldCom CFO Scott Sullivan explained his rationale for the line cost capitalizations in a document submitted to the board of directors. He supported his conclusion that the lease costs should not be expensed until WorldCom had recognized matching revenue. Sullivan reasoned that "the cost deferrals for the unutilized portion" of line leases were "an appropriate inventory of this capacity" which would be amortized before the expiration of the contractual commitment. The audit committee and the full board of directors rejected Sullivan's reasoning. They determined that WorldCom should restate its financial statements for 2001 and the first quarter of 2002. They also decided to terminate Sullivan without severance.[7]

[6] Board of Directors' Special Investigative Committee Report, June 29, 2003, pp. 24–46.
[7] Ibid.

Case Questions

1. Consider the principles, assumptions, and constraints of Generally Accepted Accounting Principles (GAAP). What is the definition of an *asset*? Please be specific in describing the requirements for recording an asset in the financial statements.
2. Based on the case information provided, do you believe that operating line cost expenses meet the requirement for recording an asset in the financial statements? Why or why not?
3. Consult Paragraph A5 (in Appendix A) of PCAOB Auditing Standard No. 5. Do you believe that WorldCom had established an effective system of internal control over financial reporting related to the line cost expense recorded in its financial statements? Why or why not?
4. Consult Paragraphs 4–6 of PCAOB Auditing Standard No. 15. As an auditor at WorldCom, what type of evidence could you have examined to determine whether the company was inappropriately capitalizing operating line cost expenses? Please be specific.
5. Consult Paragraphs 1–2 of Ethics Rule 102 (ET 102). Next, consider the role of the employees in the Property Accounting group at WorldCom. If the employees were CPAs and suspected that the entries being proposed by management were fraudulent, do you believe that the accountants had a responsibility to report the behavior to the audit committee? Why or why not?

1.12

Bernard L. Madoff Investment and Securities: The Role of the Securities & Exchange Commission (SEC)

Synopsis

During 2008, Bernie Madoff became famous for a Ponzi scheme that defrauded investors out of as much as $65 billion. To satisfy his clients' expectations of earning returns greater than the market average, Madoff falsely asserted that he used an innovative "split-strike conversion strategy," which provided the appearance that he was achieving extraordinary results. In reality, he was a fraudster. Madoff was arrested on December 11, 2008, and convicted in 2009 on 11 counts of fraud, perjury, and money laundering. As a result, Madoff was sentenced to 150 years in prison.

Background

Between June 1992 and December 2008, the SEC received several complaints regarding Madoff's hedge fund, including those from Harry Markopolos, a portfolio manager at Rampart Investment Management in Boston; yet, ultimately the SEC was unable to uncover Madoff's Ponzi scheme.

Markopolos' Complaints Submitted in 2000, 2001, and 2005

In May 2000, Markopolos submitted evidence to the SEC that questioned the legitimacy of the returns on Madoff's hedge fund. In his submission, Markopolos wrote that Madoff's reported performance, which when charted, rose roughly at a 45-degree angle, did not exist in finance. He wrote, "In 25 minutes or less, I will prove one of three scenarios regarding Madoff's hedge fund operation: (1) They are incredibly talented and/or lucky and I'm an idiot for wasting your time; (2) the returns are real, but they are coming from some process other than the one being advertised, in which case an investigation is in order; or (3) the entire case is nothing more than a Ponzi scheme."[1]

Markopolos e-mailed a second submission (less than a year later) to the SEC on March 1, 2001, in which he presented additional analysis of Madoff's returns. Markopolos wrote that Madoff reportedly earned over 15.5% a year for over seven years with an extremely low standard deviation of 4.3%. This was in contrast to the S&P 500 which earned over 19.5% but with an annual standard deviation of 12.9%. In addition, Madoff's fund had only three down months in contrast to the market being down 26 months during the same period. "For example, in 1993 when the S&P returned 1.33%, Bernie returned 14.55%; in 1999 the S&P returned 21.04%, and there was Bernie at 16.69%. His returns were always good, but rarely spectacular. For limited periods of time, other funds returned as much, or even more, than Madoff's. So it wasn't his returns that bothered me so much—his returns each month were possible—it was that he always returned a profit. There was no mathematical model that could explain the consistency."[2] "This program earned 80% of the market's return with only one third of the risk. Think about it! Is this really possible, or is it too good to be true?" wrote Markopolos.[3]

In October 2005 Markopolos made his third submission titled "The World's Largest Hedge Fund Is A Fraud," to the SEC. Markopolos' submission included 30 red flags that indicated that it was "highly likely" that Madoff was operating a Ponzi scheme. Each red flag fell into one of three categories: 1) Madoff's obsessive secrecy; 2) the impossibility of Madoff's returns, particularly the consistency of those returns; and 3) the unrealistic volume of options Madoff was supposedly trading.[4]

Reasons that the SEC Discounted Markopolos' Submissions

In an investigation conducted on why the SEC failed to uncover the Madoff Ponzi scheme, one of the SEC's examiners testified that the credibility of Markopolos' submissions were discounted because he was not an employee or an

---

[1] Harry Markopolos, *No One Would Listen* (Hoboken NJ: John Wiley & Sons, 2010), 59.

[2] Ibid, p. 33

[3] http://www.sec.gov/news/studies/2009/oig-509.pdf

[4] Ibid.

investor. The examiner testified that it's challenging to develop evidence in Ponzi scheme cases "until the thing actually falls apart."[5]

Another SEC examiner testified that part of the problem was that Markopolos could not technically be considered a "whistleblower" because he did not have "inside" or nonpublic information. In addition, the examiners testified they were skeptical of Markopolos' motives. One examiner testified she "had concerns that he was a competitor of Madoff's who had been criticized for not being able to meet Madoff's returns, and that he was looking for a bounty." The investigation at the SEC found that the examiners were also skeptical of Markopolos' claims because Madoff "didn't fit the profile of a Ponzi scheme operator;" the chief examiner acknowledged that there is an "inherent bias towards [the] sort of people who are seen as reputable members of society."[6]

SEC's Investigation

The SEC's Enforcement staff began investigating Madoff in 2005. Although the complaints from Markopolos suggested that Madoff was operating a Ponzi scheme, the SEC's investigation primarily focused on relatively insignificant registration and disclosure matters. During the investigation, the SEC Enforcement staff was comparing documents that Madoff had provided to the examination staff to documents that Madoff had sent his investors – both sets of documents had been fabricated by Madoff. In December 2005, during the investigation, the SEC Enforcement staff reviewed documents that Madoff had sent to his largest hedge fund investor. There was a discrepancy in the information, revealing that Madoff had lied in his previous representations to the SEC. "He seems to have failed to disclose to the examiners several billion dollars worth of options accounts," wrote one examiner to another in an e-mail exchange. On December 29, 2005 the SEC's Enforcement staff faxed a voluntary request to Madoff for certain documents related to three of his hedge fund clients—Fairfield, Kingate, and Tremont. Specifically, the SEC requested account opening documents, trading authorizations, account statements, trade confirmations, trade tickets, agreements (including options agreements), correspondence, audio records of telephone conversations, and documents sufficient to identify all persons who had custody of the assets in the accounts identified. After receiving Madoff's documentation, one examiner wrote in an e-mail to another examiner: "What's annoying is that he clearly created special write-ups in response to our request, instead of producing existing documents. The write-ups are helpful, but he should also be producing everything that existed."[7]

In January 2006, an examiner summarized the investigation to that point as follows:

> The staff received a complaint alleging that Bernard L. Madoff Investment Securities LLC, a registered broker-dealer in New York ("BLM"), operates an undisclosed multi-billion dollar investment advisory business, and that BLM operates

[5] Ibid.
[6] Ibid.
[7] Ibid.

this business as a Ponzi scheme. The complaint did not contain specific facts about the alleged Ponzi scheme, and the complainant was neither a BLM insider nor an aggrieved investor. Nevertheless, because of the substantial amounts at issue, the staff, in the abundance of caution, requested voluntary production of certain documents from BLM and two of its hedge fund customers . . . The staff found, first, that neither BLM nor [the hedge funds] disclose to investors that the investment decisions for [the hedge funds] are made by BLM . . . and that, in substance, BLM acts as an undisclosed investment adviser to [the hedge funds].[8]

Second, the staff found that, during an SEC examination of BLM that was conducted earlier this year, BLM—and more specifically, its principal Bernard L. Madoff, – mislead [sic] the examination staff about the nature of the strategy implemented . . . and also withheld from the examination staff information about certain of these customers' accounts at BLM . . . The staff is now seeking additional evidence, in the form of documents and witness testimony from BLM and its hedge fund customers, on the issues of BLM's role in those hedge funds' investment activities and the adequacy of related disclosures. Additionally, the staff is trying to ascertain whether the complainant's allegation that BLM is operating a Ponzi scheme has any factual basis.[9]

In February 2006 the SEC sent a second voluntary request to Madoff, and in May 2006 Madoff testified before the SEC. Eventually, however, the SEC's investigation stalled. When interviewed about why the investigation stalled, one of the examiners attributed it to the SEC's lack of resources: "I think given the resources that we had available to us and given what else we all had to do at the time, this was the best we could do."[10]

[8] Ibid.
[9] Ibid.
[10] Ibid.

Case Questions

1. Consider the Securities Act of 1933 and the Securities Exchange Act of 1934. What is the role of the SEC in regards to protecting individual investors?
2. Consider the information brought to the SEC by Harry Markopolos. Please explain the primary reasons why Mr. Markopolos believed that Madoff's fund was nothing more than a "Ponzi" scheme.
3. After the Madoff case, the SEC instituted a number of reforms to its operations. Please visit the SEC's website (www.sec.gov) and search for Post-Madoff reforms. Next, please identify the two reforms that you believe will have the best chance of catching a criminal like Madoff. Make sure to provide justification for your choices.
4. Consider the Dodd-Frank Wall Street Reform and Consumer Protection Act. Please explain the whistleblower provision that was mandated by the act and elaborate about the role of the SEC.

Ethics and Professional Responsibility Cases

It can be argued that the most dramatic change ushered in by the Sarbanes-Oxley Act of 2002 (SARBOX) is that the public company auditing profession is now regulated. The Public Company Accounting Oversight Board (PCAOB) is solely responsible for setting all auditing standards pertaining to audits of public companies. The PCAOB is also now required to perform detailed inspections of audit work completed and the quality control processes employed by audit firms. These changes have had a dramatic impact on audit quality and the auditing profession. The following cases are designed to illustrate the ethical and professional responsibility of auditors in the post-Sarbanes auditing environment.

The case readings have been developed solely as a basis for class discussion. The case readings are not intended to serve as a source of primary data or as an illustration of effective or ineffective auditing.

Case 2.1

Enron: Independence

Synopsis

In its 2000 annual report, Enron prided itself on having "metamorphosed from an asset-based pipeline and power generating company to a marketing and logistics company whose biggest assets are its well-established business approach and its innovative people."[1] Enron's strategy seemed to pay off. In 2000 it was the seventh largest company on the Fortune 500, with assets of $65 billion and sales revenues of over $100 billion.[2] From 1996 to 2000 Enron's revenues had increased by more than 750 percent, which was unprecedented in any industry.[3] Yet just a year later, in December 2001, Enron filed for bankruptcy, and billions of shareholder and retirement savings dollars were lost.

Arthur Andersen

Enron paid Arthur Andersen $46.8 million in fees for auditing, business consulting, and tax work for the fiscal year ended August 31, 1999; $58 million in 2000; and more than $50 million in 2001.[4] Andersen was collecting a million dollars a week from Enron in the year before its crash. Enron was one of Andersen's largest clients.

More than half of that amount was for fees that were charged for nonaudit services.[5] In 2000, for example, Enron paid Andersen $25 million for audit

---

[1] Enron 2000 annual report, p. 7.

[2] Joseph F. Berardino, remarks to U.S. House of Representatives Committee on Financial Services, December 12, 2001.

[3] Bala G. Dharan and William R. Bufkins, "Red Flags in Enron's Reporting of Revenues and Key Financial Measures," March 2003, prepublication draft (www.ruf.rice.edu/~bala/files/dharan-bufkins_enron_red_flags_041003.pdf), p. 4.

[4] Anita Raghavan, "Accountable: How a Bright Star at Andersen Fell Along with Enron," *The Wall Street Journal*, May 15, 2002. Accessed from Factiva (February 25, 2005).

[5] Jane Mayer, "The Accountants' War," *New Yorker*, April 22, 2002. Accessed from LexisNexis Academic (February 25, 2005).

services and $27 million for consulting and other services, such as internal audit services.[6]

In fact, Andersen had performed Enron's internal audit function since 1993. That year Andersen had hired 40 Enron personnel, including the vice president of internal audit, to be part of Andersen's team providing internal audit services.[7] In 2000, as SEC Chair Arthur Levitt was trying to reform the industry practice of an audit firm also offering consulting services to their audit clients, Enron Chair and CEO Ken Lay sent a letter to Levitt (the letter was secretly coauthored by Andersen partner David Duncan), in which he wrote,

> While the agreement Enron has with its independent auditors displaces a significant portion of the activities previously performed by internal resources, it is structured to ensure that Enron management maintains appropriate audit plan design, results assessment and overall monitoring and oversight responsibilities. . . . Enron has found its "integrated audit" arrangement to be more efficient and cost-effective than the more traditional roles of separate internal and external auditing functions.[8]

Interestingly, at Andersen, an audit partner's compensation depended in large part on his or her ability to sell other services (in addition to auditing) to clients.[9] Therefore, the nonaudit services provided to Enron had a big impact on the salary of the lead Andersen partner on the Enron engagement, David Duncan, who was earning around $1 million a year.[10]

Close Ties between Enron and Andersen

After graduating from Texas A&M University, Duncan joined Andersen in 1981, was made partner in 1995, and was named the lead partner for Enron two years later. Duncan developed a close personal relationship with Enron's Chief Accounting Officer Richard Causey, who himself had worked at Arthur Andersen for almost nine years. Duncan and Causey often went to lunch together, and their families had even taken vacations together.[11]

[6] Nanette Byrnes, "Accounting in Crisis," *BusinessWeek,* January 28, 2002. Accessed from LexisNexis Academic (February 25, 2005).

[7] Thaddeus Herrick and Alexei Barrionuevo, "Were Auditor and Client Too Close-Knit?" *The Wall Street Journal,* January 21, 2002. Accessed from ProQuest Research Library (February 26, 2005).

[8] "Letter from Kenneth Lay," Bigger Than Enron transcript, *Frontline,* aired on Public Broadcasting Service on June 20, 2002 (www.pbs.org/wgbh/pages/frontline/shows/regulation/congress/lay.html).

[9] Jane Mayer, "The Accountants' War," *New Yorker,* April 22, 2002. Accessed from LexisNexis Academic (February 25, 2005).

[10] Bethany McLean and Peter Elkind, *The Smartest Guys in the Room: The Amazing Rise and Scandalous Fall of Enron* (New York: Penguin Group, 2003), pp. 146–147.

[11] Susan E. Squires, Cynthia J. Smith, Lorna McDougal, and William R. Yeack, *Inside Arthur Andersen* (Upper Saddle River, NJ: Prentice Hall, 2003), p. 2.

Causey, who came to Enron in 1991, was appointed chief accounting officer in 1997 (the same year that Duncan was named lead audit partner for Enron). Causey was responsible for recruiting many Andersen alumni to work at Enron. Over the years, Enron hired at least 86 Andersen accountants.[12] Several were in senior executive positions, including Jeffrey McMahon, who had served as Enron's treasurer and president, and Vice President Sherron Watkins.

Although Andersen had separate offices in downtown Houston, Duncan and up to a hundred Andersen managers had a whole floor available to them within Enron's headquarters in Houston.[13] Duncan once remarked that he liked having the office space there because it "enhanced our ability to serve" and to "generate additional work."[14] Andersen boasted about the closeness of their relationship in a promotional video. "We basically do the same types of things. . . . We're trying to kinda cross lines and trying to, you know, become more of just a business person here at Enron," said one accountant. Another spoke about the advantage of being located in Enron's building: "Being here full-time, year-round, day-to-day gives us a chance to chase the deals with them and participate in the deal making process."[15]

In fact, Andersen and Enron employees went on ski trips and took annual golf vacations together. They played fantasy football against each other on their office computers and took turns buying each other margaritas at a local Mexican restaurant chain. One former senior audit manager at Andersen said that it was "like these very bright geeks at Andersen suddenly got invited to this really cool, macho frat party."[16]

[12] Bethany McLean and Peter Elkind, *The Smartest Guys in the Room: The Amazing Rise and Scandalous Fall of Enron* (New York: Penguin Group, 2003), p. 145.

[13] Susan E. Squires, Cynthia J. Smith, Lorna McDougal, and William R. Yeack, *Inside Arthur Andersen* (Upper Saddle River, NJ: Prentice Hall, 2003), p. 126.

[14] Rebecca Smith and John R. Emshwiller, *24 Days: How Two Wall Street Journal Reporters Uncovered the Lies That Destroyed Faith in Corporate America* (New York: HarperBusiness, 2003), p. 289.

[15] Bethany McLean and Peter Elkind, *The Smartest Guys in the Room: The Amazing Rise and Scandalous Fall of Enron* (Penguin Group, 2003), p. 146.

[16] Flynn McRoberts, "Ties to Enron Blinded Andersen," *Chicago Tribune,* September 3, 2002. Accessed from Factiva (February 3, 2004).

Case Questions

1. Consult PCAOB Ethics and Independence Rule 3520. What is *auditor independence,* and what is its significance to the audit profession? What is the difference between independence in appearance and independence in fact?

2. Refer to Section 201 of SARBOX. Identify the services provided by Arthur Andersen that are no longer allowed to be performed. Do you believe that Section 201 was needed? Why or why not?

3. Refer to Sections 203 and 206 of SARBOX. How would these sections of the law have impacted the Enron audit? Do you believe that these sections were needed? Why or why not?

4. Refer to Section 301 of SARBOX. Do you believe that Section 301 is important to maintaining independence between the auditor and the client? Why or why not?

Case # 2.2

Waste Management: Due Care

Synopsis

In February 1998 Waste Management announced that it was restating its financial statements issued for the years 1993 through 1996. In its restatement, Waste Management said that it had materially overstated its reported pretax earnings by $1.43 billion. After the announcement, the company's stock dropped by more than 33 percent, and shareholders lost over $6 billion.

The SEC brought charges against the company's founder, Dean Buntrock, and other former top officers. The charges alleged that management had made repeated changes to depreciation-related estimates to reduce expenses and had employed several improper accounting practices related to capitalization policies, also designed to reduce expenses.[1] In its final judgment, the SEC permanently barred Buntrock and three other executives from acting as officers or directors of public companies and required payment from them of $30.8 million in penalties.[2]

Background

Because the financial statements for the years 1993 through 1996 were not presented in conformity with Generally Accepted Accounting Principles (GAAP), Waste Management's independent auditor, Arthur Andersen, came under scrutiny for issuing unqualified opinions on the financial statements for these years. The SEC filed suit against Andersen on charges that it knowingly or recklessly issued materially false and misleading audit reports for the period 1993 through 1996. Andersen ultimately settled with the SEC for $7 million, the largest ever civil penalty at the time, without admitting or denying any allegations or

[1] SEC, Accounting and Auditing Enforcement Release No. 1532, March 26, 2002.
[2] SEC, Accounting and Auditing Enforcement Release No. 2298, August 29, 2005.

findings.[3] Three Andersen partners who worked on the Waste Management audit during this period also received sanctions from the SEC.

Waste Management's Relationship with Arthur Andersen

Even before Waste Management became a public company in 1971, Arthur Andersen served as the company's auditor. In 1991 Waste Management capped Andersen's corporate audit fees at the prior year's level, although it did allow the firm to earn additional fees for "special work." Between 1991 and 1997, Andersen billed Waste Management approximately $7.5 million in financial statement audit fees.[4] During this seven-year period, Andersen also billed Waste Management $11.8 million in fees related to other professional services.[5]

During the 1990s, at least 14 former Andersen employees worked for Waste Management.[6] While at Andersen, most of these individuals had worked in the group that was responsible for auditing Waste Management's financial statements prior to 1991.[7]

In fact, until 1997 every chief financial officer (CFO) and chief accounting officer (CAO) at Waste Management since it became public had previously worked as an auditor at Andersen. Waste Management's CAO and corporate controller from September 1990 to October 1997, Thomas Hau, was a former Andersen audit engagement partner for the Waste Management account. When Hau left Andersen, he was the head of the division within Andersen responsible for conducting Waste Management's annual audit, but he was not the engagement partner at that time.[8]

Andersen's Partners on the Waste Management Audit

In 1991 Andersen assigned Robert Allgyer, a partner at Andersen since 1976, to become the audit engagement partner for the Waste Management audit. Allgyer held the title of partner-in-charge of client service, and he also served as the marketing director for Andersen's Chicago office. Among the reasons for Allgyer's selection as engagement partner were his "extensive experience in Europe," his "devotion to client service," and his "personal style that . . . fit well with the Waste Management officers."[9] In setting Allgyer's compensation,

[3] SEC, "Arthur Andersen LLP Agrees to Settlement Resulting in First Antifraud Injunction in More Than 20 Years and Largest-Ever Civil Penalty ($7 million) in SEC Enforcement Action against a Big Five Accounting Firm," Press Release 2001–62.

[4] SEC Auditing and Enforcement Release No. 1410, June 19, 2001.

[5] Ibid.

[6] Ibid.

[7] Ibid.

[8] Ibid.

[9] Ibid.

Andersen considered fees earned on the Waste Management account for audit and nonaudit services.[10] Walter Cercavschi, who was a senior manager when he started working on the Waste Management engagement team in the late 1980s, also remained on the engagement after becoming a partner in 1994.

In 1993 Edward Maier became the concurring partner on the engagement. As concurring partner, Maier's duties included reading the financial statements; discussing significant accounting, auditing, or reporting issues with the engagement partner; reviewing certain key workpapers (such as the audit risk analysis, final engagement memoranda, and summaries of proposed adjusting entries); and inquiring about matters that could have a material effect on the financial statements or the auditor's report. Maier also served as the risk management partner for the Chicago office in charge of supervising the client acceptance and retention processes for the entire office.[11]

Andersen's Proposed Adjusting Journal Entries

In early 1994 the Andersen engagement team quantified several current and prior period misstatements and prepared proposed adjusting journal entries (PAJEs) in the amount of $128 million for Waste Management to record in 1993. If recorded, this amount would have reduced net income before special items by 12 percent. The engagement team also identified other accounting practices that gave rise to other (known and likely) misstatements primarily resulting in the understatement of operating expenses.[12]

Allgyer and Maier consulted with Robert Kutsenda, the practice director responsible for Andersen's Chicago, Kansas City, Indianapolis, and Omaha offices, about this issue. Kutsenda and the audit division head, who was also consulted, determined that the misstatements were not material and that Andersen could therefore issue an unqualified audit report on the 1993 financial statements. Nevertheless, the team did instruct Allgyer to inform management that Andersen expected the company to change its accounting practices and to reduce the cumulative amount of the PAJEs in the future.[13] After consulting with the managing partner of the firm, Allgyer proposed a "summary of action steps" to reduce the cumulative amount of the PAJEs, going forward, and to change the accounting practices that gave rise to the PAJEs, as well as to the other known and likely misstatements.[14]

Although Waste Management agreed to the summary of action steps, the company continued to engage in the accounting practices that gave rise to the PAJEs and the other misstatements. Despite Waste Management's failure to make progress on the PAJEs, Andersen's engagement team continued to issue unqualified audit reports on Waste Management's financial statements.

[10] Ibid.

[11] Ibid.

[12] Ibid.

[13] Ibid.

[14] Ibid.

Case Questions

1. What is *auditor independence,* and what is its significance to the audit profession? In what ways, if any, was Arthur Andersen's independence potentially impacted on the Waste Management audit?

2. Consult Paragraphs 3–6 of Quality Control Standard No. 20 (QC 20). Considering the example in the Waste Management case, explain why a review by the practice director and the audit division head is important in the operations of a CPA firm. In your opinion, was this review effective at Waste Management? Why or why not?

3. Consult Paragraph 7 of PCAOB Auditing Standard No. 13. Do you believe that Andersen's final decision regarding the PAJEs was appropriate under the circumstances? Would your opinion change if you knew that all of the adjustments were based on subjective differences (such as a difference in the estimate of the allowance for doubtful accounts) as compared to objective differences (such as a difference in the accounts receivable balance of the biggest customer)?

4. Refer to Sections 203 and 206 of SARBOX. How would these sections of the law have impacted the Waste Management audit? Do you believe that these sections were needed? Why or why not?

Case 2.3

WorldCom: Professional Responsibility

Synopsis

On June 25, 2002, WorldCom announced that it would be restating its financial statements for 2001 and the first quarter of 2002. Less than one month later, on July 21, 2002, WorldCom announced that it had filed for bankruptcy. It was later alleged that WorldCom had engaged in improper accounting that took two major forms: overstatement of revenue by at least $958 million and understatement of line costs, its largest category of expenses, by over $7 billion. Several executives pled guilty to charges of fraud and were sentenced to prison terms, including CFO Scott Sullivan (five years) and Controller David Myers (one year and one day). Convicted of fraud in 2005, CEO Bernie Ebbers was the first to receive his prison sentence: 25 years.

Andersen's Relationship with WorldCom

Andersen served as WorldCom's auditor from at least as far back as 1990 through April 2002. In a presentation to the audit committee on May 20, 1999, Andersen stated that the firm viewed its relationship with WorldCom as a "long-term partnership," in which Andersen would help WorldCom improve its business operations and grow in the future. In its Year 2000 audit proposal, Andersen told the audit committee that it considered itself "a committed member of [WorldCom's] team" and that WorldCom was "a flagship client and a 'crown jewel'" of its firm.[1]

In terms of the total fees charged to clients, WorldCom was one of Andersen's top 20 engagements in 2000 and was the largest client of its Jackson, Mississippi, office. From 1999 through 2001 WorldCom paid Andersen $7.8 million in fees

[1] Board of Directors' Special Investigative Committee Report, June 9, 2003, p. 225.

to audit the financial statements of WorldCom, Inc.; $6.6 million for other audits required by law in other countries; and about $50 million for consulting, litigation support, and tax services.[2]

Andersen's Restricted Access to Information

WorldCom allegedly severely restricted Andersen's access to information; several of Andersen's requests for detailed information and opportunities to speak with certain employees were denied. In fact, Andersen was denied access to WorldCom's computerized general ledger and had to rely on the printed ledgers. According to the person in charge of security for WorldCom's computerized consolidation and financial reporting system, WorldCom's treasurer in 1998 instructed him not to give Andersen access to this computerized reporting system.[3]

In addition, senior management of WorldCom allegedly berated employees who disclosed unauthorized information to Andersen. For example, in October 2000 Steven Brabbs, the director of international finance and control for EMEA (Europe, Middle East, and Africa), told Andersen's U.K. office that line cost expenses for EMEA were understated by $33.6 million because senior management had reduced its line cost accruals and that EMEA did not have any support for this entry. WorldCom's senior vice president and controller David Myers reprimanded Brabbs and directed him never to do it again. In early 2002, after learning about another conversation between Brabbs and Andersen about a planned restructuring charge, Myers specifically instructed U.K. employees that "NO communication with auditors is allowed without speaking with Stephanie Scott [vice president of financial reporting] and myself. This goes for anything that might imply a change in accounting, charges, or anything else that you would think is important." When Myers found out that the accountant had continued to speak with Andersen U.K. about the issue, he wrote the following message to the accountant:[4]

> Do not have any more meetings with Andersen for any reason. I spoke to Andersen this morning and hear that you are still talking about asset impairments and facilities. I do not want to hear an excuse just stop. Mark Wilson has already told you this once. Don't make me ask you again.

Although Andersen was aware that it was receiving less than full cooperation, it did not notify WorldCom's audit committee about this matter.[5] Indeed, the special investigative committee of the board of directors at WorldCom (the special committee) found no evidence that its independent auditor, Arthur Andersen, had determined that WorldCom's revenues or line costs were improperly reported. However, it did find that Andersen's failure to detect these improprieties likely stemmed, in part, from a failure to demand supporting

---

[2] Board of Directors' Special Investigative Committee Report, June 9, 2003, p. 225.

[3] Board of Directors' Special Investigative Committee Report, June 9, 2003, pp. 246–248.

[4] Board of Directors' Special Investigative Committee Report, June 9, 2003, pp. 250–251.

[5] Board of Directors' Special Investigative Committee Report, June 9, 2003, pp. 25–26.

evidence for certain recorded transactions and some other missed audit opportunities that might have resulted in the detection of these improprieties.[6]

Audit Approach

Apparently the auditors from Arthur Andersen understood the elevated risk associated with the WorldCom audit. Based on a review of the workpapers by the special investigative committee, it was discovered that Andersen rated WorldCom a "maximum risk" client. Because of the maximum risk classification, Andersen's internal policies required the engagement team to consult with Andersen's practice director, advisory partner, audit division head, and professional standards group (where appropriate) regarding all significant audit issues. In addition, the lead engagement partner was required to hold an annual expanded risk discussion with the concurring partner, the practice director, and the audit division head to consider the areas that caused greatest audit risk. Surprisingly Andersen did not disclose that WorldCom was considered a maximum risk client to the audit committee of WorldCom.[7]

The outcome of the expanded risk discussion after the 1999 and 2000 year-end audits was that Andersen did not find evidence of aggressive accounting or fraud at WorldCom.[8] However, during the discussion held in December 2001, concerns were voiced over WorldCom's use of numerous "top-side" journal entries. Such entries are typically recorded at the corporate level, detached from the economic activity that is occurring at each of the business units or divisions within WorldCom. A handwritten note in Andersen's workpapers read, "Manual Journal Entries How deep are we going? Surprise w[ith] look [at] journal entries." Yet there was no indication of further testing on these entries.[9] In all, the special investigative committee found hundreds of large, round-dollar journal entries that were made by WorldCom's general accounting group staff without any support other than Post-it® Notes or written instructions directing that the entries be made.

The special committee found that Andersen relied heavily on substantive analytical procedures and conducted only a limited amount of substantive tests of details. In addition, the element of surprise was lost because Andersen often provided WorldCom's senior management team with a list of the auditing procedures that it anticipated performing in the areas of revenues, line costs, accounts receivable, capital expenditures, and data integrity. Furthermore, Andersen's testing of capital expenditures, line costs, and revenues did not change materially from 1999 through 2001.[10]

---

[6] Ibid, p.25

[7] Board of Directors' Special Investigative Committee Report, June 9, 2003, p. 27.

[8] Board of Directors' Special Investigative Committee Report, June 9, 2003, pp. 232–233.

[9] Board of Directors' Special Investigative Committee Report, June 9, 2003, p. 236.

[10] Board of Directors' Special Investigative Committee Report, June 9, 2003, p. 228.

Case Questions

1. Consult PCAOB Ethics and Independence Rule 3520. What is *auditor independence,* and what is its significance to the audit profession? Based on the case information, do you believe that Andersen violated this rule? Why or why not?

2. Consult Paragraphs 5–7 of PCAOB Auditing Standard No. 13. Given the reluctance of WorldCom's management team to communicate with Andersen, do you believe that Andersen exercised due care and professional skepticism in completing the audit? Why or why not?

3. Consult Paragraphs 13–21 of PCAOB Auditing Standard No. 15. In terms of audit effectiveness and efficiency, briefly explain the difference between substantive analytical procedures and substantive tests of details. Do you believe it was appropriate for Andersen to rely primarily on substantive analytical procedures? Why or why not?

4. Consult Paragraphs 14 and A8 (in Appendix A) of PCAOB Auditing Standard No. 5. Provide an example of both a preventive control and a detective control that could address the risk that a fraudulent top-side adjusting journal entry could be made by a member of management.

Case 2.4

Enron: Quality Assurance

Synopsis

In its 2000 annual report, Enron prided itself on having "metamorphosed from an asset-based pipeline and power generating company to a marketing and logistics company whose biggest assets are its well-established business approach and its innovative people."[1] Enron's strategy seemed to pay off. In 2000 it was the seventh largest company on the Fortune 500, with assets of $65 billion and sales revenues of over $100 billion.[2] From 1996 to 2000 Enron's revenues had increased by more than 750 percent, which was unprecedented in any industry.[3] Yet just a year later, in December 2001, Enron filed for bankruptcy, and billions of shareholder and retirement savings dollars were lost.

Andersen's Professional Standard Group

Within Andersen there was a group of expert accountants tasked with reviewing and passing judgment on difficult accounting, auditing, and tax issues; this group was called the professional standards group (PSG). The PSG had objected strongly to several accounting issues related to the Enron audit. However, based on memos that were later uncovered, the PSG's objections had been overruled by the lead Andersen partner on the Enron audit, David Duncan. In addition, Duncan allegedly helped carry out Enron's request to have one of the PSG partners barred from advising on any issues related to the Enron audit.[4]

---

[1] Enron 2000 annual report, p. 7.

[2] Joseph F. Berardino, remarks to U.S. House of Representatives Committee on Financial Services, December 12, 2001.

[3] Bala G. Dharan and William R. Bufkins, "Red Flags in Enron's Reporting of Revenues and Key Financial Measures," March 2003, prepublication draft (www.ruf.rice.edu/~bala/files/dharan-bufkins_enron_red_flags_041003.pdf), p. 4.

[4] Mike McNamee, "Out of Control at Andersen," *BusinessWeek Online,* March 29, 2002. Accessed from Business Source Premier database (December 31, 2004).

The PSG's Disapproval of Special Purpose Entities and the Audit Team's Response

In 1999 Enron's chief financial officer, Andrew Fastow, spoke to David Duncan about Enron's plan to set up a special purpose entity (later called LJM), a financing vehicle used to access capital or increase leverage without adding debt to a firm's balance sheet. After the discussion with Fastow, Duncan asked for the advice of the PSG.

A member of the PSG, Benjamin Neuhausen, represented the group's disapproval in an e-mail message written to Duncan on May 28, 1999: "Setting aside the accounting, (the) idea of a venture equity managed by CFO is terrible from a business point of view. . . . Conflicts of interest galore. Why would any director in his or her right mind ever approve such a scheme?" he wrote.[5]

In addition, the PSG was firmly against the idea of Enron's recording gains on the sales of assets (or immediate gains on any transactions) to the Fastow-controlled special purpose entity. In response to the recording of gains, Duncan wrote in a June e-mail message, "I'm not saying I'm in love with this either . . . But I'll need all the ammo I can get to take that issue on . . . on your point 1, (i.e. the whole thing is a bad idea), I really couldn't agree more." Yet Duncan later told Fastow that Andersen would sign off on the transaction under a few conditions, one of which was that Fastow obtain the approval of Enron's chief executive and its board of directors.[6]

Shortly after, Carl Bass, a member of the PSG since December 1999, raised concerns over the sale of some equity options within the LJM special purpose entity. Bass wrote to his boss John Stewart via e-mail, "This is a big item and the team apparently does not want to go back to the client on this. I think at a minimum the Practice Director needs to be made aware of this history and our opposition to the accounting."[7] However, the memo Duncan's team prepared to document the deal indicated that Bass "concurred with our conclusions."[8]

Bass continued to object to the LJM transaction, writing in an e-mail message to Stewart (his boss) in February 2000, "This whole deal looks like there is no substance. The only money at risk here is $1.8 million in a bankrupt proof special purpose entity (SPE). All of the money here appears to be provided by Enron."[9] Duncan's team did not address Bass's concerns and, in fact, continued to misrepresent his views to the client.

---

[5] Anita Raghavan, "Accountable: How a Bright Star at Andersen Fell Along with Enron," *The Wall Street Journal*, May 15, 2002. Accessed from Factiva (February 25, 2005).

[6] Anita Raghavan, "Accountable: How a Bright Star at Andersen Fell Along with Enron," *The Wall Street Journal*, May 15, 2002. Accessed from Factiva (February 25, 2005).

[7] Carl E. Bass, Internal E-Mail to John E. Stewart, "Subject: Enron Option," December 18, 1999.

[8] Mike McNamee, "Out of Control at Andersen," *BusinessWeek Online*, March 29, 2002. Accessed from Business Source Premier database (December 31, 2004).

[9] Carl E. Bass, internal e-mail to John E. Stewart, "Subject: Enron Transaction," February 1, 2000.

In late 2000 Duncan asked Bass for more advice on how best to account for four Enron SPEs known as Raptors. Enron wanted to lump together the financial results for all the entities so that the more profitable ones could offset losses being garnered by others. Bass opposed the idea. Nevertheless, Duncan later decided that Andersen would "accept the client's position," with some modifications.[10]

In February 2001 Andersen held a routine annual risk assessment meeting to determine whether to keep Enron as a client. Some partners raised concerns related to how much debt Enron was *not* putting on its balance sheet, Fastow's conflict of interest, and the lack of disclosure in the company's financial footnotes.[11] Duncan reassured his fellow partners.

Carl Bass was removed from the Enron account in March 2001. Bass wrote to Stewart (his boss) in an e-mail message, "Apparently, part of the process issue stems from the client (Enron) knowing all that goes on within our walls on our discussions with respect to their issues. . . . We should not be communicating with the client that so and so said this and I could not get this past so and so in the PSG. . . . I have first hand experience on this because at a recent EITF meeting some lower level Enron employee who was with some else [sic] from Enron introduced herself to me by saying she had heard my name a lot—'so you are the one that will not let us do something. . . . ' I have also noted a trend on this engagement that the question is usually couched along the lines 'will the PSG support this?' When a call starts out that way, it is my experience that the partner is struggling with the question and what the client wants to do."[12] Stewart complained to a senior partner about Bass's removal. Duncan allegedly called Stewart and explained that two Enron executives, Richard Causey and John Echols, had pushed for Bass's removal.[13]

In October 2001 Enron announced that it had a loss of $600 million and a reduction of shareholder equity of $1.2 billion in its third quarter of that year; and that the SEC was conducting an investigation into an issue related to one of its partnerships. At that time, Bass discovered the memos written by the audit team that claimed he agreed with Enron's accounting. Bass asked that some of the memos be changed to reflect his true judgments.[14] In November, Enron announced that it would need to restate its financial statements for the previous five years to account for $586 million in losses.[15]

---

[10] Anita Raghavan, "Accountable: How a Bright Star at Andersen Fell Along with Enron," *The Wall Street Journal,* May 15, 2002. Accessed from Factiva (February 25, 2005).

[11] Mimi Swartz, *Power Failure: The Inside Story of the Collapse of Enron* (New York: Doubleday, 2003), pp. 235–236.

[12] Carl E. Bass, internal e-mail to John E. Stewart, "Subject: Enron," March 4, 2001.

[13] Anita Raghavan, "Accountable: How a Bright Star at Andersen Fell Along with Enron," *The Wall Street Journal,* May 15, 2002. Accessed from Factiva (February 25, 2005).

[14] Anita Raghavan, "Accountable: How a Bright Star at Andersen Fell Along with Enron," *The Wall Street Journal,* May 15, 2002.

[15] This was also foreshadowed by Enron's announcement in October 2001 that it had a loss of $600 million and a reduction of shareholder equity of $1.2 billion in its third quarter of that year; and that the SEC was conducting an investigation into an issue related to one of its partnerships.

Case Questions

1. Consult Paragraphs 3–6 of Quality Control Standard No. 20 (QC 20). Explain why an accounting and auditing research function (like Andersen's PSG) is important in the operations of a CPA firm. What role does the function play in completing the audit?
2. Consult Section 103 of SARBOX. Do you believe that the engagement leader of an audit (like David Duncan on the Enron audit) should have the authority to overrule the opinions and recommendations of the accounting and auditing research function (like the PSG)? Why or why not?
3. After Carl Bass was removed from the Enron account, he indicated to his boss that he did not believe Enron should have known about internal discussions regarding accounting and auditing issues. Do you agree with Bass's position? Why or why not?
4. Consult Section 203 of SARBOX. Do you believe that this provision of the law goes far enough? That is, do you believe the audit firm itself (and not just the partner) should have to rotate off an audit engagement every five years? Why or why not?

Case 2.5

Sunbeam: Due Care

Synopsis

In April 1996 Sunbeam named Albert J. Dunlap as its CEO and chair. Former-ly with Scott Paper Co., Dunlap was known as a turnaround specialist and was even nicknamed "Chainsaw Al" because of the cost-cutting measures he typically employed. Almost immediately, Dunlap began replacing nearly all of the upper management team and led the company into an aggressive corporate restructuring that included the elimination of half of its 12,000 employees and 87 percent of Sunbeam's products.

Unfortunately, in May 1998 Sunbeam disappointed investors with its an-nouncement that it had earned a worse-than-expected loss of $44.6 million in the first quarter of 1998.[1] CEO and Chair Dunlap was fired in June 1998. In October 1998 Sunbeam announced that it would need to restate its financial statements for 1996, 1997, and 1998.[2]

Arthur Andersen

Sunbeam's auditor, Arthur Andersen, came under fire for having issued an unqualified opinion on the company's financial statements for both 1996 and 1997. In January 1999 a class action lawsuit alleging violation of the federal securities laws was filed in the U.S. District Court for the Southern District of Florida against Sunbeam, Arthur Andersen, and Sunbeam executives. The suit reached the settlement stage in 2001. As part of the settlement, Andersen agreed to pay $110 million.[3]

---

[1] Robert Frank and Joann S. Lublin. "Dunlap's Ax Falls—6,000 Times—at Sunbeam," *The Wall Street Journal,* November 13, 1996, p. B1.

[2] GAO-03-138, Appendix XVII "Sunbeam Corporation," p. 201.

[3] Nicole Harris, "Andersen to Pay $110 Million to Settle Sunbeam Accounting-Fraud Lawsuit," *The Wall Street Journal,* May 2, 2001, p. B11.

Not surprisingly, Phillip Harlow, the engagement partner in charge of the Sunbeam audit during this period, also found himself under fire on an individual basis for his work on the audits. The Securities and Exchange Commission (SEC) barred Harlow from serving as a public accountant for three years after it found that Harlow failed to exercise due professional care in auditing Sunbeam's financial statements.[4]

The 1996 Audit

Through the 1996 audit, Andersen partner Phillip Harlow allegedly became aware of several accounting practices that failed to comply with GAAP. In particular, he allegedly knew about Sunbeam's improper restructuring costs, excessive litigation reserves, and an excessive cooperative advertising figure. Each of these items reduced net income for 1996.

Improper Restructuring Costs

During the 1996 audit, Harlow allegedly identified $18.7 million in items within Sunbeam's restructuring reserve that were improperly classified as restructuring costs because they benefited Sunbeam's future operations. Harlow proposed that the company reverse the improper accounting entries, but management rejected his proposed adjustments for these entries. Harlow relented on his demand after concluding that the items were immaterial for the 1996 financials.[5]

Excessive Litigation Reserves

Sunbeam also failed to comply with GAAP on a $12 million reserve recorded for a lawsuit that alleged Sunbeam's potential obligation to cover a portion of the cleanup costs for a hazardous waste site. Management did not take appropriate steps to determine whether the amount reflected a probable and reasonable estimate of the loss, as required by GAAP. Had it done so, the reserve would not have passed either of the criteria and would have been far lower than the amount recorded. The SEC determined that Harlow relied on statements from Sunbeam's general counsel and did not take additional steps to determine whether the litigation reserve level was in accordance with GAAP.[6]

The 1997 Audit

The SEC also found that Harlow discovered several items that were not compliant with GAAP during the 1997 audit. These items related to revenue, the restructuring reserves, and inventory, in particular. In several cases he

---

[4] Cassell Bryan-Low, "Deals & Deal Makers," *The Wall Street Journal,* January 28, 2003, p. C5.

[5] SEC Accounting and Auditing Enforcement Release No. 1393, May 15, 2001.

[6] SEC Accounting and Auditing Enforcement Release No. 1706, January 27, 2003.

proposed adjustments that management refused to make. In response to management's refusal, Harlow acquiesced, however. By the end of 1997, it appears Harlow knew that approximately 16 percent of Sunbeam's reported 1997 income came from items he found to be not in accordance with GAAP.[7] In fact, at least $62 million of Sunbeam's reported $189 million of income before tax failed to comply with GAAP.[8] The following examples illustrate two of the different techniques used by Sunbeam to overstate revenue earned in 1997.

Bill and Hold Sales

The SEC wrote in its findings that Harlow "knew or recklessly disregarded facts, indicating that the fourth-quarter bill and hold transactions did not satisfy required revenue recognition criteria."[9] Among other things, Sunbeam's revenues earned through bill and hold sales should not have been recognized because these sales were not requested by Sunbeam's customers, and they served no business purpose other than to accelerate revenue recognition by Sunbeam. Sunbeam offered its customers the right to return any unsold product. Further, several of Sunbeam's bill and hold transactions were also characterized by Sunbeam as offering its customers financial incentives, such as discounted pricing, to write purchase orders before they actually needed the goods.[10]

Sale of Inventory

Sunbeam's fourth-quarter revenue in 1997 included $11 million from a sale of its spare parts inventory to EPI Printers, which, prior to this transaction, had satisfied spare parts and warranty requests for Sunbeam's customers on an as-needed basis. As part of the transaction, Sunbeam agreed to pay certain fees and guaranteed a 5 percent profit for EPI Printers on the resale of the inventory. The contract with EPI Printers also stipulated that it would terminate in January 1998 if the parties did not agree on the value of the inventory underlying the contract.

Harlow allegedly knew that revenue recognition on this transaction did not comply with GAAP due to the profit guarantee and the indeterminate value of the contract. Thus Harlow proposed an adjustment to reverse the accounting entries that reflected the revenue and income recognition for this transaction. Yet Harlow acquiesced in management's refusal to reverse the sale.[11]

---

[7] SEC Accounting and Auditing Enforcement Release No. 1706, January 27, 2003.

[8] SEC Accounting and Auditing Enforcement Release No. 1393, May 15, 2001.

[9] SEC Accounting and Auditing Enforcement Release No. 1706, January 27, 2003.

[10] SEC Accounting and Auditing Enforcement Release No. 1393, May 15, 2001.

[11] SEC Accounting and Auditing Enforcement Release No. 1706, January 27, 2003.

Case Questions

1. Consult Paragraphs 4–8 of PCAOB Auditing Standard No. 15. Next, consider the alleged accounting improprieties related to increased expenses from the 1996 audit. If you were auditing Sunbeam, what type of evidence would you like to review to determine whether Sunbeam had recorded the litigation reserve amount and the cooperative advertising amount in accordance with GAAP?

2. For the excessive litigation reserves and excessive cooperative advertising amount, identify the journal entry that is likely to have been proposed by Andersen to correct each of these accounting improprieties. Why would Sunbeam be interested in recording journal entries that essentially reduced its income before tax in 1996?

3. Consult Paragraphs 17–23 of PCAOB Auditing Standard No. 14. As discussed in the case, during both the 1996 and 1997 audits, Phillip Harlow allegedly discovered a number of different accounting entries made by Sunbeam that were not compliant with Generally Accepted Accounting Principles (GAAP). Speculate about how Harlow might have explained his decision not to require Sunbeam to correct these alleged misstatements in the audit workpapers.

4. Consult Sections 204 and 301 of SARBOX. In the post-Sarbanes audit environment, which of the issues that arose in 1996 and 1997 would have to be reported to the audit committee at Sunbeam? Do you believe that communication to the audit committee would have made a difference in Harlow's decision not to record the adjusting journal entries? Why or why not?

2.6

Bernard L. Madoff Investment and Securities: A Focus on Auditors' and Accountants' Legal Liability

Synopsis

During 2008, Bernie Madoff became famous for a Ponzi scheme that defrauded investors out of as much as $65 billion. To satisfy his clients' expectations of earning returns greater than the market average, Madoff falsely asserted that he used an innovative "split-strike conversion strategy," which provided the appearance that he was achieving extraordinary results. In reality, he was a fraudster. Madoff was arrested on December 11, 2008, and convicted in 2009 on 11 counts of fraud, perjury, and money laundering. As a result, Madoff was sentenced to 150 years in prison.

Follow the Money

The Securities Investor Protection Corporation (SIPC), which provides aid to customers of failed brokerage firms when assets are missing from customer accounts, gave Madoff's victims $800 million and appointed Irving Picard as the trustee responsible for liquidating Madoff's firm in December 2008.

Picard filed claims totaling $100 billion in lawsuits against Madoff's feeder funds, banks that Picard believed to have aided Madoff in perpetrating his fraud, clients who took out more than they put in ("net winners"), and the

Madoff family.[1] In addition to the feeder funds coming under fire, the firms auditing these funds also became litigation targets.

Firms Auditing Feeder Funds

The first lawsuit against a feeder fund's auditor was brought in December 2008. The lawsuit, brought by New York Law School and the limited partners of feeder fund Ascot Partners, was against the Ascot Partners' auditor BDO Seidman (and J. Ezra Merkin, the feeder fund's general partner).

The lawsuit alleged that BDO Seidman was grossly negligent and failed to do the following:

- Use due professional care;
- Properly plan the audits;
- Maintain an appropriate degree of skepticism, and;
- Obtain sufficient competent evidential matter to support the conclusions of the audit reports.

The lawsuit alleged that Ascot Partners had made materially false and misleading statements to investors, implying that it would use "numerous third-party managers with varying execution strategies, thereby avoiding the risk of concentrating capital in too few investments or managers."[2] Virtually all of Ascot's $1.8 billion was invested with Madoff.

A spokesman for BDO Seidman released the following statement:

> It is understandable that investors affected by the massive fraud at Bernard L. Madoff Investment Securities are frustrated and angry . . . BDO Seidman is not and has never been the auditor of Madoff Securities. BDO Seidman's audits of Ascot Partners conformed to all professional standards and we will vigorously defend ourselves against these unfounded allegations.[3]

Madoff's Auditor

From 1991 through 2008, Bernard L. Madoff Investment and Securities' (BLMIS) financial statements were audited by the accounting firm Friehling & Horowitz. In March 2009, David Friehling, who was a CPA licensed by the state of New York, was arrested and charged with securities fraud, aiding Madoff

---

[1] Lisa Sandler, "Recovery Comes Slowly for Madoff Victims," Bloomberg Businessweek, May 3, 2012.

[2] New York Law School v. Ascot Partners, L.P., J. Ezra Merkin, and BDO Seidman, http://online.wsj.com/public/resources/documents/madoffmerkin.pdf.

[3] http://www.accountingtoday.com/news/30233-1.html

with investment advisor fraud, and filing false audit reports with the SEC. The charges brought against Mr. Friehling include that he failed to do the following[4]:

- Conduct independent verification of BLMIS revenues, assets, liabilities related to BLMIS client accounts, and the purchase and custody of securities by BLMIS;
- Test internal controls over areas such as the payment of invoices for corporate expenses or the purchase of securities by BLMIS on behalf of its clients;
- Examine a bank account through which BLMIS client funds flowed.

The SEC also filed a civil case against Mr. Friehling and his firm Friehling & Horowitz. The AICPA and the New York State Society of CPAs have since expelled Friehling from membership. Under the AICPA's peer review program, auditors are monitored through mandatory peer review every three years. Mr. Friehling's work was not peer-reviewed because, since 1993, he had informed the AICPA that he did not perform audits, and therefore, would not need a peer review.[5] Importantly, beginning January 1, 2012, New York firms with three or more accounting professionals must be peer-reviewed once every three years.[6]

On November 3, 2009, Mr. Friehling changed his plea from not guilty to guilty for the crimes involving the filing of falsely certified audits and financial statements with the SEC. "First and foremost, it is critical for Your Honor to be aware that at no time was I ever aware that Bernard Madoff was engaged in a Ponzi scheme," said Friehling to the presiding judge in his case. Friehling made a point to mention that he and many members of his family had lost their retirement savings on account of having invested with Madoff.[7]

Although Friehling was initially supposed to be sentenced in 2010, the sentencing had been repeatedly postponed due to his cooperation with the government; as of June 2012, he had not been sentenced. However, Friehling lost his CPA license in July 2010.

Several additional courts have also made decisions affirming that the auditors of the feeder funds could not be found guilty of fraud or malpractice. The decisions were appealed, but later upheld. Representative of the other major decisions in these cases, the appellate court upholding the dismissal of charges against KPMG and Ernst & Young (auditors for funds by Tremont Group

---

[4] United States Attorney, Southern District of New York, "Accountant for Bernard L. Madoff," Investment Securities, LLC Charged With Fraud Stemming From Accounting Violations," March 18, 2009.

[5] AccountingWeb, "Madoff's accountant: When is an auditor not an auditor?" http://www.accountingweb.com/item/107303, March 30, 2009.

[6] Alyssa Abkowitz, "Madoff's auditor . . . doesn't audit?," *Fortune*, December 19, 2008 (available via: http://money.cnn.com/2008/12/17/news/companies/madoff.auditor.fortune)

[7] Diana B. Henriques, The Wizard of Lies, 2012, p. 309.

Holdings Inc., which lost more than $3 billion in client money in Madoff's firm) agreed with the initial ruling and in its judgment asserted the following:

> Auditors were responsible for auditing the Tremont funds, not [Bernard L. Madoff Investment Securities] . . . many of the purported 'red flags' that plaintiffs contend should have put the auditors on notice of the Madoff fraud, such as the lack of an independent third-party custodian, and BLMIS's dual role as both investment manager and administrator, were risks inherent to BLMIS, not the Tremont entities.[8]

[8] Ross Todd, "Circuit Again Rejects Suit Against Auditors by Investors Caught in Madoff Scheme," *New York Law Journal*, July 12, 2012.

Case Questions

1. Refer to the fundamental principles governing an audit. Under the responsibilities principle, auditors are required to exercise due care and maintain professional skepticism throughout the audit. Based on the case information, discuss the ways in which the BLMIS auditor, David Friehling, disregarded his responsibility to uphold the fundamental principles governing an audit.

2. Consider the charges brought against the BLMIS auditor, David Friehling, regarding his failure to complete certain audit steps. If you were auditing BLMIS, what type of evidence would you like to review to determine whether BLMIS had (1) purchased, (2) sold, and (3) maintained proper custody of investment securities?

3. Consider an auditor's common law liability to third parties. Describe the difference among the three levels of failure to exercise due care: ordinary negligence, gross negligence, and fraud. Based on the case information, comment on the possible level of failure that was seemingly exhibited by BDO Seidman in their audit of Ascot Partners. Are there any factors that you believe could be used in defense of the auditing firm?

4. Consider Section 24 of the Securities Act of 1933 and Section 32 of the Securities Exchange Act of 1934. Based on the case information, do you believe that the BLMIS auditor, Friehling, should be facing criminal charges? Why or why not? Next, do you believe that the Ascot Partners auditor, BDO Seidman, should be facing criminal charges? Why or why not?

Case 2.7

Enron: Audit Documentation

Synopsis

In its 2000 annual report, Enron prided itself on having "metamorphosed from an asset-based pipeline and power generating company to a marketing and logistics company whose biggest assets are its well-established business approach and its innovative people."[1] Enron's strategy seemed to pay off. In 2000, it was the seventh largest company on the Fortune 500, with assets of $65 billion and sales revenues of over $100 billion.[2] From 1996 to 2000, Enron's revenues had increased by more than 750 percent, which was unprecedented in any industry.[3] Yet, just a year later, in December 2001, Enron filed for bankruptcy, and billions of shareholder dollars and retirement savings were lost.

Andersen's Document Retention Policy

On October 12, 2001, after reading through some of Andersen's internal memos related to the Enron audits, one of Andersen's lawyers, Nancy Temple, advised Andersen's practice director in Houston, Michael Odom, in an e-mail as follows: "It might be useful to consider reminding the engagement team of our documentation and retention policy. It will be helpful to make sure that we have complied with the policy."[4]

---

[1] Enron 2000 annual report, p. 7.

[2] Joseph F. Berardino, remarks to U.S. House of Representatives Committee on Financial Services, December 12, 2001.

[3] Bala G. Dharan and William R. Bufkins, "Red Flags in Enron's Reporting of Revenues and Key Financial Measures," March 2003, prepublication draft (www.ruf.rice.edu/~bala/files/dharan-bufkins_enron_red_flags_041003.pdf), p. 4.

[4] Bethany McLean and Peter Elkind. *The Smartest Guys in the Room: The Amazing Rise and Scandalous Fall of Enron* (New York: Penguin Group, 2003), p. 382.

Two days earlier, Odom had given a videotaped presentation on the firm's document-retention policy, in which he said that any documents that were not essential to the audit file (drafts, notes, internal memos, and e-mails) should be discarded, unless a lawsuit had been filed. "If it's destroyed in the course of normal policy and litigation is filed the next day, that's great, you know, because we've followed our own policy, and whatever there was that might have been of interest to somebody is gone and irretrievable."[5]

Andersen's In-House Lawyers

On October 16, Enron announced its third-quarter results, which included a loss of $638 million and a reduction of shareholder equity of $1.2 billion. Its stock price fell almost 40 percent in the following week alone. That same day, Temple e-mailed David Duncan, the lead engagement partner for the Enron audit, with suggestions on how he should edit his memo that documented auditing-related events surrounding Enron's third-quarter earnings release.

One of her suggestions was to delete his "reference to consultation with the legal group" as well as deleting her name from the memo. "Reference to the legal group consultation arguably is a waiver of attorney-client privilege and if my name is mentioned it increases the chances that I might be a witness, which I prefer to avoid," she wrote. Temple continued to edit internal memos. At one point, she even suggested deleting senior Andersen partners from the distribution list for Enron-related e-mails to decrease their likelihood of being called as witnesses in any subsequent litigation.[6]

Document Shredding

Seven days later, on October 23, the SEC announced its investigation into the Enron matter. That afternoon, Duncan gathered the members of his audit team and reminded them that they needed to make sure they complied with the firm's document-retention policy. Shortly after, Andersen's Houston office started shredding documents from the Enron audit files. Andersen's auditors wound up sending files it maintained onsite at Enron to its main downtown office.

The amount it sent to be shredded was more than the entire Houston office typically shredded in an entire year. Andersen eventually hired a shredding truck from a local disposal company called Shred-It. In addition, its offices in London, Portland, and Chicago began helping to shred documents. Andersen also destroyed almost all of the computer files and e-mail messages that related to Enron's audits.[7]

[5] Ibid.

[6] Ibid.

[7] Bethany McLean and Peter Elkind, *The Smartest Guys in the Room: The Amazing Rise and Scandalous Fall of Enron* (New York: Penguin Group, 2003), pp. 382–383.

On November 9, Andersen stopped shredding documents related to the Enron audits after it received a subpoena from the SEC the day before.[8] Duncan's assistant sent the following e-mail: "Per Dave: no more shredding. If you are asked, tell them Dave said we can't. We've been officially served by the attorneys for our documents."[9]

In January 2002, Andersen fired Duncan for his lead role in the shredding of documents. After Duncan pled guilty to the crime of obstruction of justice, the U.S. Justice Department filed a criminal indictment against Andersen in March 2002. The entire firm was indicted because of the several offices that had worked on the Enron account and that had been involved with shredding documents.[10] The indictment signaled the beginning of the end for Enron's auditor Arthur Andersen LLP, one of the five largest international public accounting firms.

In May 2002, Andersen was convicted on one charge of obstruction of justice in connection with the shredding of documents related to the Enron audit. And although this conviction was overturned in May 2005 by the United States Supreme Court, Andersen's decision to destroy evidence cast suspicion on whether Andersen was trying to cover up any guilt related to a failure to perform its professional responsibilities.

[8] Susan E. Squires, Cynthia J. Smith, Lorna McDougal, and William R. Yeack, *Inside Arthur Andersen* (Upper Saddle River, NJ: Prentice Hall, 2003), p. 4.

[9] Bethany McLean and Peter Elkind, *The Smartest Guys in the Room: The Amazing Rise and Scandalous Fall of Enron* (New York: Penguin Group, 2003), p. 383.

[10] Susan E. Squires, Cynthia J. Smith, Lorna McDougal, and William R. Yeack, *Inside Arthur Andersen* (Upper Saddle River, NJ: Prentice Hall, 2003), pp. 127–128.

Case Questions

1. Consult Paragraph 2 of PCAOB Auditing Standard No. 3. Define *audit documentation*. Explain why it is important for an auditor to retain audit documentation for a specific period of time?

2. Refer to Section 103 of SARBOX. Do you believe that this provision of the law goes far enough; that is, do you believe that the law is adequate related to audit documentation requirements? Why or why not?

3. Consult Paragraphs 4–6 of PCAOB Auditing Standard No. 3. In your own words, describe what is expected to be documented in the audit workpapers for each relevant financial statement assertion.

4. Consult Paragraphs 14–15 PCAOB Auditing Standard No. 3. Do you believe that the shredding of documents acquired during the audit process still occurs? Why or why not?

5. Consider the actions of Andersen lawyer Nancy Temple and practice director Michael Odom. Do you believe that their actions were appropriate under the circumstances? Why or why not?

Fraud and Inherent Risk Assessment Cases

Section

3

To identify areas of elevated risk in audits, auditors must take great care to get to know their clients' management and to understand their clients' businesses, industries, and ultimately their strategies to achieve competitive advantage. Because it can often be difficult for an auditor to make the connection between a client's strategic direction and the identification of significant audit risks, the cases in this section help illustrate the explicit linkage between a client's strategic direction and the identification of significant fraud and inherent risks.

The case readings have been developed solely as a basis for class discussion. The case readings are not intended to serve as a source of primary data or as an illustration of effective or ineffective auditing.

Case 3.1

Enron: Understanding the Client's Business and Industry

Synopsis

In its 2000 annual report, Enron prided itself on having "metamorphosed from an asset-based pipeline and power generating company to a marketing and logistics company whose biggest assets are its well-established business approach and its innovative people."[1] Enron's strategy seemed to pay off. In 2000 it was the seventh largest company on the Fortune 500, with assets of $65 billion and sales revenues of over $100 billion.[2] From 1996 to 2000 Enron's revenues had increased by more than 750 percent, which was unprecedented in any industry.[3] Yet just a year later, in December 2001, Enron filed for bankruptcy, and billions of shareholder and retirement savings dollars were lost.

Origins of Enron

Enron was created in 1985 by the merger of two gas pipeline companies: Houston Natural Gas and InterNorth. Enron's mission was to become the leading natural gas pipeline company in North America. As several changes occurred in the natural gas industry in the mid-1980s, Enron adapted and changed its mission, expanding into natural gas trading and financing, as well as into other markets, such as electricity and other commodity markets.

---

[1] Enron 2000 annual report, p. 7.

[2] Joseph F. Bernardino, remarks to U.S. House of Representatives Committee on Financial Services, December 12, 2001.

[3] Bala G. Dharan and William R. Bufkins, "Red Flags in Enron's Reporting of Revenues and Key Financial Measures," March 2003, prepublication draft (www.ruf.rice.edu/~bala/files/dharan-bufkins_enron_red_flags_041003.pdf), p. 4.

Enron's First Few Years

In 1985 Enron had assets along the three major stages of the supply chain of natural gas: production, transmission, and distribution. Natural gas was produced from deposits found underground. The natural gas was transmitted via pipelines, or networks of underground pipes, and either sold directly to industrial customers or sold to regional gas utilities, which then distributed it to smaller businesses and customers. Some companies in the industry had assets related to specific activities within the supply chain. For example, some companies owned pipelines but did not produce their own gas. These companies often entered into long-term "take or pay" contracts, whereby they paid for minimum volumes in the future at prearranged prices to protect against supply shortages.

In early 1986 Enron reported a loss of $14 million for its first year. As a result, the company employed a series of cost-cutting measures, including layoffs and pay freezes for top executives. Enron also started selling off assets to reduce its debt. Nevertheless, Enron's financial situation was still bleak in 1987. In that year Moody's downgraded its credit rating to junk bond status.[4]

Impact of Significant Industry Change on Enron

Enron faced significant change in its industry environment due to the government's decision in the mid-1980s to deregulate the once highly regulated industry. The government, which had dictated the prices pipeline companies paid for gas and the prices they could charge their customers, decided to allow the market forces of supply and demand to dictate prices and volumes sold. As part of this process, the government required that pipeline companies provide "open access" to their pipelines to other companies wanting to transport natural gas, so that pipeline companies would not have an unfair competitive advantage.[5]

Enron's Natural Gas Pipeline Business

Enron adapted by providing "open access" to its pipelines—that is, charging other firms for the right to use them. Enron also took advantage of the ability to gain such access to pipelines owned by other companies. For example, in 1988 Enron signed a 15-year contract with Brooklyn Union to supply gas to a plant being built in New York. Because Brooklyn Union was not connected to Enron's pipeline system, Enron needed to contract with another pipeline company to transport the gas to Brooklyn Union. Enron was, therefore, assuming added risks related to the transportation of the gas. The long-term nature of the

---

[4] Bethany McLean and Peter Elkind, *The Smartest Guys in the Room: The Amazing Rise and Scandalous Fall of Enron* (New York: Penguin Group, 2003), p. 14.

[5] Paul M. Healy and Krishna Palepu, "Governance and Intermediation Problems in Capital Markets: Evidence from the Fall of Enron," Harvard NOM Research Paper No. 02–27, August 2002, p. 7.

contract was also risky because prices could rise to a level that would make the contract unprofitable.[6]

Enron Expands into Natural Gas Trading and Financing

Enron capitalized on the introduction of market forces into the industry by becoming involved in natural gas trading and financing. Enron served as an intermediary between producers who contracted to sell their gas to Enron and gas customers who contracted to purchase gas from Enron. Enron collected as profits the difference between the prices at which it purchased and sold the gas. Enron's physical market presence (that is, owning the pipelines and charging a price for distribution that was proportional to the spot price of gas it might purchase) helped mitigate the risk of a price increase of the gas it was purchasing.[7]

In response to the problem of getting producers to sign long-term contracts to supply gas, Enron started giving such producers cash up-front instead of payment over the life of the contract. Enron then allowed the natural gas contracts it devised—which were quite complex and variable, depending on different pricing, capacity, and transportation parameters—to be traded.

Enron Expands beyond Natural Gas

Enron decided to apply its gas trading model to other markets, branching out into electricity and other commodity markets, such as paper and chemicals. To accomplish its expansion strategy, it sought to pursue an "asset-light" strategy. Enron's goal was to achieve the advantages of having a presence in the physical market without the disadvantages of huge fixed capital expenditures. For example, in natural gas, Enron divested its assets related to pumping gas at the wellhead or selling gas to customers, and then set out to acquire assets related to midstream activities such as transportation, storage, and distribution.[8] By late 2000 Enron owned 5,000 fewer miles of natural gas pipeline than at its founding in 1985; in fact, Enron's gas transactions represented 20 times its existing pipeline capacity.[9]

In addition, Enron undertook international projects involving construction and management of energy facilities outside the United States—in the United Kingdom, Eastern Europe, Africa, the Middle East, India, China, and Central

---

[6] Bethany McLean and Peter Elkind, *The Smartest Guys in the Room: The Amazing Rise and Scandalous Fall of Enron* (New York: Penguin Group, 2003), p. 34.

[7] Christopher L. Culp and Steve H. Hanke, "Empire of the Sun: An Economic Interpretation of Enron's Energy Business," *Policy Analysis* 470, February 20, 2003, p. 6.

[8] Christopher L. Culp and Steve H. Hanke, "Empire of the Sun: An Economic Interpretation of Enron's Energy Business," *Policy Analysis* 470, February 20, 2003, p. 7.

[9] Paul M. Healy and Krishna Palepu, "Governance and Intermediation Problems in Capital Markets: Evidence from the Fall of Enron," Harvard NOM Research Paper No. 02–27, August 2002, pp. 9–10.

and South America. Established in 1993, the Enron International Division did not adhere to the asset-light strategy pursued by other divisions. Enron also expanded aggressively into broadband—the use of fiber optics to transmit audio and video. Among its goals in that business were to deploy the largest open global broadband network in the world.[10]

[10] Christopher L. Culp and Steve H. Hanke, "Empire of the Sun: An Economic Interpretation of Enron's Energy Business," *Policy Analysis* 470, February 20, 2003, p. 4.

Case Questions

1. Consult Paragraphs 7–10 of PCAOB Auditing Standard No. 12. Based on your understanding of risk assessment and the case information, identify three specific factors about Enron's business model in the late 1990s that might cause you to elevate the risk of material misstatement at Enron.

2. Consult Paragraphs 5–7 of PCAOB Auditing Standard No. 13. Comment about how your understanding of the inherent risks identified at Enron (in Question 1) would influence the nature, timing, and extent of your audit work at Enron.

3. Consult Paragraphs 28–30 of PCAOB Auditing Standard No. 5. Next, consider how the change in industry regulation and Enron's resulting strategy shift would impact your risk assessment for the relevant assertions about revenue. Finally, identify the most relevant assertion for revenue before and after Enron's resulting strategy shift and briefly explain why.

4. Consult Paragraphs 52–53 of PCAOB Auditing Standard No. 12. Consider how a revenue recognition fraud might occur under Enron's strategy in the late 1990s. Next, identify an internal control procedure that would prevent, detect, or deter such a fraudulent scheme.

Case

3.2

The Baptist Foundation of Arizona: Related Party Transactions

Synopsis

The Baptist Foundation of Arizona (BFA) was organized as an Arizona nonprofit organization primarily to help provide financial support for various Southern Baptist causes. Under William Crotts's leadership, the foundation engaged in a major strategic shift in its operations. BFA began to invest heavily in the Arizona real estate market and also accelerated its efforts to sell investment agreements and mortgage-backed securities to church members.

Two of BFA's most significant affiliates were ALO and New Church Ventures. It was later revealed that BFA had set up these affiliates to facilitate the sale of its real estate investments at prices significantly above fair market value. In so doing, BFA's management perpetrated a fraudulent scheme that cost at least 13,000 investors more than $590 million. In fact, Arizona Attorney General Janet Napolitano called the BFA collapse the largest bankruptcy of a religious nonprofit in the history of the United States.[1]

Background

The Baptist Foundation of Arizona (BFA) was an Arizona religious nonprofit 501(c)(3) organization that was incorporated in 1948 to provide financial support for Southern Baptist causes. It was formed under the direction of the Arizona Southern Baptist Convention, which required BFA to be a profitable, self-sustaining independent entity (that is, it could not accept money from any other source). In BFA's early days, it focused its attention on funding church start-ups and providing aid for children and elderly people. In 1962 Pastor Glen Crotts became its first president and was succeeded in 1984 by his son, William P. Crotts.

[1] Terry Greene Sterling, "Arthur Andersen and the Baptists," *Salon.com Technology*, February 7, 2002.

Under William Crotts's leadership, BFA began to invest heavily in the Arizona real estate market, and also accelerated its efforts to sell investments to church members. Although Arizona real estate prices skyrocketed in the early 1980s, the upward trend did not continue, and property values declined substantially in 1989. Soon after this decline, management decided to establish a number of related affiliates. These affiliates were controlled by individuals with close ties to BFA, such as former board members. In addition, BFA gained approval to operate a trust department that would serve as a nonbank passive trustee for individual retirement accounts (IRAs). To do so, BFA had to meet certain regulatory requirements, which included minimum net worth guidelines.

Related Parties

Two of BFA's most significant affiliates were ALO and New Church Ventures. A former BFA director incorporated both of these nonprofit entities. The entities had no employees of their own, and both organizations paid BFA substantial management fees to provide accounting, marketing, and administrative services. As a result, both ALO and New Church Ventures owed BFA significant amounts by the end of 1995. Overall BFA, New Church Ventures, and ALO had a combined negative net worth of $83.2 million at year-end 1995, $102.3 million at year-end 1996, and $124.0 million at year-end 1997.[2]

New Church Ventures

Although the stated purpose of New Church Ventures was to finance new Southern Baptist churches in Arizona, its major investment activities were similar to those of BFA. That is, New Church Ventures raised most of its funds through the sale of investment agreements and mortgage-backed securities, and then invested most of those funds in real estate loans to ALO. Thus the majority of New Church Ventures' assets were receivables from ALO. New Church Ventures' two main sources of funding were BFA's marketing of its investment products to IRA investors and loans it received from BFA.[3]

ALO

Contrary to its intended purpose to invest and develop real estate, one of ALO's primary activities in the 1990s was to buy and hold BFA's nonproducing and overvalued investments in real estate so that BFA could avoid recording losses

[2] Notice of Public Hearing and Complaint No. 98.230-ACY, Before the Arizona State Board of Accountancy, pp. 3–4.
[3] Notice of Public Hearing and Complaint No. 98.230-ACY, Before the Arizona State Board of Accountancy, pp. 8–9.

(write-downs) on its real estate. In fact, ALO owned many of the real estate investments that were utilized as collateral for IRA investor loans. However, BFA's 1991 through 1997 financial statements did not include a set of summarized financial statements for ALO. ALO incurred operating losses each year since its inception in 1988. By the end of 1997, ALO's total liabilities of $275.6 million were over two times its assets, leaving a negative net worth of $138.9 million. In total, ALO owed New Church Ventures $173.6 million and BFA $70.3 million, respectively.[4]

BFA's Religious Exemptions

BFA operated in a manner similar to a bank in many respects. Its investment products were similar to those sold by financial institutions. Its trust department, which was fully authorized by the federal government to serve as a passive trustee of IRAs, was similar to a trust department at a bank. BFA also made real estate loans in a manner similar to a bank. Because of its banklike operations and products, BFA faced several risk factors that affect banks and other savings institutions, such as interest rate risk and liquidity risk.[5]

Yet because of its status as a religious organization, BFA's product offerings were not subject to the same regulatory scrutiny as a bank's products.[6] That is, although BFA underwrote its own securities offerings and used its staff to sell the investment instruments (like a bank), it was able to claim a religious exemption from Arizona statutes that regulate such activities. BFA also claimed exemption from Arizona banking regulations on the basis that its investment products did not constitute deposits as defined by Arizona banking laws.[7]

Passive Trustee Operation

BFA gained approval to operate a trust department that would serve as a nonbank passive trustee for IRAs. To operate a trust department, BFA had to comply with certain regulatory requirements, such as maintaining an appropriate minimum net worth. In addition to the minimum net worth requirement, treasury regulations also required BFA to conduct its affairs as a fiduciary; that is, it could not manage or direct the investment of IRA funds. In addition, BFA had to subject itself to an audit that would detect any failures to meet these regulatory requirements. In cases where the minimum net worth was not achieved, treasury regulations prohibited a trustee from accepting new IRA accounts and required the relinquishment of existing accounts.[8]

---

[4] Ibid.

[5] Ibid., pp. 4–5.

[6] Notice of Public Hearing and Complaint No. 98.230-ACY, Before the Arizona State Board of Accountancy, p. 5.

[7] Ibid., pp. 4–5.

[8] Ibid., pp. 15–20.

Case Questions

1. Consult Paragraphs 5–8 of PCAOB Auditing Standard No. 8 and Paragraphs 7–10 of PCAOB Auditing Standard No. 12. Based on your understanding of inherent risk assessment, identify three specific factors about BFA that might cause you to elevate inherent risk. Briefly provide your rationale for each factor that you identify.

2. Consult Paragraphs .04–.06 of AU Section 334. Comment on why the existence of related parties (such as ALO and New Church Ventures) presents additional risks to an auditor. Do you believe that related party transactions deserve special attention from auditors? Why or why not?

3. Assume you are an investor in BFA. As an investor, what type of information would you be interested in reviewing before making an investment in BFA? Do you believe that BFA should have been exempt from Arizona banking laws? Why or why not?

4. Consult Paragraph 7 of PCOAB Auditing Standard No. 9. Consider the planning phase for the audit of BFA's trust department operations. As an auditor, what type of evidence would you want to collect and examine to determine whether BFA was meeting the U.S. Treasury regulations for nonbank passive trustees of IRA accounts?

Case 3.3

WorldCom: Significant Business Acquisitions

Synopsis

On June 25, 2002, WorldCom announced that it would be restating its financial statements for 2001 and the first quarter of 2002. Less than one month later, on July 21, 2002, WorldCom announced that it had filed for bankruptcy. It was later revealed that WorldCom had engaged in improper accounting that took two major forms: overstatement of revenue by at least $958 million and understatement of line costs, its largest category of expenses, by over $7 billion. Several executives pled guilty to charges of fraud and were sentenced to prison terms, including CFO Scott Sullivan (five years) and Controller David Myers (one year and one day). Convicted of fraud in 2005, CEO Bernie Ebbers was the first to receive his prison sentence: 25 years.

Growth through Acquisitions

WorldCom started as a long distance telephone provider named Long Distance Discount Services (LDDS), which had annual revenues of approximately $1.5 billion by the end of 1993. LDDS connected calls between the local telephone company of a caller and the local telephone company of the call's recipient by reselling long distance capacity it purchased from major long distance carriers (such as AT&T, MCI, and Sprint) on a wholesale basis.[1] LDDS was renamed WorldCom in 1995.

A change in industry regulation was the primary catalyst for WorldCom's growth. That is, the Telecommunications Act of 1996 allowed long distance telephone service providers to enter the market for local telephone services and other telecommunications services, such as Internet-related services. Like many players in the industry, WorldCom turned to acquisitions to expand into these markets.

[1] Board of Directors' Special Investigative Committee Report, June 9, 2003, pp. 44–45.

WorldCom's revenues grew rapidly as it embarked on these acquisitions. Between the first quarter of 1994 and the third quarter of 1999, WorldCom's year-over-year revenue growth was over 50 percent in 16 of the 23 quarters; the growth rate was less than 20 percent in only 3 of the quarters. WorldCom's stock price experienced rapid growth as well, from $8.17 at the beginning of January 1994 to $47.91 at the end of September 1999 (adjusted for stock splits). Importantly, its stock performance exceeded those of its largest industry competitors, AT&T and Sprint.[2]

MFS and Subsidiary UUNET

In late 1996 WorldCom acquired MFS, which provided local telephone services, for $12.4 billion. In that transaction, WorldCom also gained an important part of the Internet backbone through MFS's recently acquired subsidiary, UUNET.[3]

Brooks Fiber Properties, CompuServe Corporation, and ANS Communications

In 1998 WorldCom purchased Brooks Fiber Properties for approximately $2.0 billion and CompuServe Corporation and ANS Communications (a three-way transaction valued at approximately $1.4 billion that included a five-year service commitment to America Online). Each of these companies expanded WorldCom's presence in the Internet arena.

MCI

In September 1998 WorldCom acquired MCI, using approximately 1.13 billion of its common shares and $7.0 billion cash as consideration, for a total price approaching $40 billion. MCI's annual revenues of $19.7 billion in 1997 far exceeded WorldCom's 1997 annual revenues of $7.4 billion. As a result of this merger, WorldCom became the second largest telecommunications provider in the United States.

SkyTel Communications and Sprint

In October 1999 WorldCom purchased SkyTel Communications, adding wireless communications to its service offerings, for $1.8 billion. A few days after its Sky-Tel acquisition, WorldCom announced that it would merge with Sprint in a deal valued at $115 billion. In the proposed deal, WorldCom would gain Sprint's PCS wireless business, in addition to its long distance and local calling operations.[4]

Challenges

By 2000, WorldCom started to face some difficult challenges. For starters, World-Com faced fierce competition in its industry. In addition, WorldCom's proposed merger with Sprint failed to receive approval from the Antitrust Division of the

---

[2] Ibid., p. 48.
[3] Ibid., p. 46.
[4] Ibid., pp. 47–48.

U.S. Department of Justice. As a result, the companies officially terminated their merger discussions on July 13, 2000.[5]

Although WorldCom's revenue continued to grow, its rate of growth slowed. On November 1, 2000, WorldCom announced the formation of two tracking stocks: one—called WorldCom Group—to capture the growth of its data business, and the other—called MCI—to capture the cash generation of its voice business, which experienced a lower growth rate. WorldCom also announced reduced expectations for revenue growth of the consolidated company, from its previous expectation of 12 percent to between 7 percent and 9 percent in the fourth quarter of 2000 and all of 2001. By the close of market on the day of its announcement, WorldCom's stock price had fallen by 20.3 percent, from $23.75 on October 31, 2000, to $18.94.[6]

Industry conditions worsened in 2001. Both the local telephone services and Internet segments experienced downturns in demand. The impact of the downturn in the Internet segment was particularly severe because of the industry's increased investment in network capacity (supply). Many competitors found themselves mired in long-term contracts that they had entered to obtain the capacity to meet anticipated customer demand. As the ratio of their expenses to revenues was increasing, industry revenues and stock prices plummeted. For example, the stock prices of WorldCom, AT&T, and Sprint lost at least 75 percent of their share price values between January 2000 and June 25, 2002.[7]

[5] Ibid., pp. 48–49.
[6] Ibid., p. 50.
[7] Ibid., pp. 51–55.

Case Questions

1. Consult Paragraphs 7–10 of PCAOB Auditing Standard No. 12. Based on your understanding of risk assessment and the case information, identify three specific factors about WorldCom's strategy that might cause you to elevate the risk of material misstatement.
2. Consult Paragraphs 5–7 of PCAOB Auditing Standard No. 13. Comment about how your understanding of the risks identified at WorldCom (in Question 1) would influence the nature, timing, and extent of your audit work at WorldCom.
3. Consult Paragraph 33 and Paragraph B10 (in Appendix B) of PCAOB Auditing Standard No. 5. If you were conducting an internal control audit of WorldCom, comment about how WorldCom's acquisition strategy would impact the nature, timing, and extent of your audit work at WorldCom.
4. Consult Paragraphs 65–66 of PCAOB Auditing Standard No. 12. Based on your understanding of fraud risk assessment, what three conditions are likely to be present when a fraud occurs (that is, the fraud triangle)? Based on the information provided in the case, which of these three conditions appears to be the most prevalent, and why?

Case 3.4

Sunbeam: Incentives and Pressure to Commit Fraud

Synopsis

In April 1996 Sunbeam named Albert J. Dunlap as its CEO and chair. Formerly with Scott Paper Co., Dunlap was known as a turnaround specialist and was nicknamed "Chainsaw Al" because of the cost-cutting measures he typically employed. Almost immediately, Dunlap began replacing nearly all of the upper management team and led the company into an aggressive corporate restructuring that included the elimination of half of its 12,000 employees and the elimination of 87 percent of Sunbeam's products.

Unfortunately, in May 1998 Sunbeam disappointed investors with its announcement that it had earned a worse-than-expected loss of $44.6 million in the first quarter of 1998.[1] CEO and Chair Dunlap was fired in June 1998. In October 1998 Sunbeam announced that it would need to restate its financial statements for 1996, 1997, and 1998.[2]

Sunbeam's History[3]

The early beginnings of Sunbeam Corporation can be traced back to the Chicago Flexible Shaft Company, founded by John Stewart and Thomas Clark in 1897. Although the company did not change its name to Sunbeam until 1946, it adopted the name Sunbeam in its advertising shortly after it expanded into manufacturing electrical appliances in 1910.

Successful products in the 1930s included the Sunbeam Mixmaster, a stationary food mixer; the Sunbeam Shavemaster Shaver; the first automatic coffeemaker; and the first pop-up electric toaster. Later appliances included the hair

[1] Robert Frank and Joann S. Lublin. "Dunlap's Ax Falls—6,000 Times—at Sunbeam," *The Wall Street Journal,* November 13, 1996, p. B1.

[2] Much of this section is based on information from GAO-03-138, Appendix XVII "Sunbeam Corporation," p. 201.

[3] Hoovers Online.

dryer (1949), humidifiers (1950), ice crushers (1950), a knife sharpener (1950), the Sunbeam Egg Cooker (1950), the Sunbeam Controlled Heat fry pan (1953), and the electric blanket (1955). The company acquired rival household appliance maker Oster in 1960.

In 1981 Sunbeam was acquired by industrial conglomerate Allegheny International, which fell into bankruptcy in 1988 due to economic difficulties in its other divisions. Michael Price, Michael Steinhardt, and Paul Kazarian bought Allegheny from its creditors in 1990 and named the company Sunbeam-Oster. Kazarian assumed the positions of CEO and chair. Under his leadership the company paid off its debt, reorganized operations, and cut its workforce dramatically.[4]

The company went public in 1992. Kazarian was forced out in 1993 and replaced by Roger Schipke, a former manager of General Electric's appliance division. Kazarian was subsequently awarded $160 million in a lawsuit he filed for being forced out. The company was renamed Sunbeam in 1995. That year, the company faced stagnant product prices and other difficult industry conditions, such as the growth of discount chains. In the face of these conditions, Sunbeam introduced new product lines, made acquisitions, and invested in greater production capacity.[5] After several quarters of disappointing sales and earnings results, Schipke tendered his resignation in April 1996. The company named Albert J. Dunlap, chief of Scott Paper Co., as Schipke's successor.

Sunbeam in 1996

Sunbeam Corporation had five major product lines in its domestic operations: household appliances, health care products, personal care and comfort products, outdoor cooking products, and "away from home" business. It also had international sales that accounted for approximately 19 percent of its total net sales.[6]

Household appliances (29 percent of 1996 domestic net sales) included blenders, food steamers, bread makers, rice cookers, coffeemakers, toasters, and irons. Examples of health care products (11 percent) were vaporizers, humidifiers, air cleaners, massagers, and blood pressure monitors. Its line of personal care and comfort products (21 percent) included shower massagers, hair clippers and trimmers, and electric warming blankets. Some of its major outdoor cooking products (29 percent) were electric, gas, and charcoal grills, as well as grill accessories. Its "away from home" business (5 percent) marketed clippers and related products for the professional and veterinarian trade as well as products for commercial and institutional channels.

---

[4] Robert Frank and Joann S. Lublin, "Dunlap's Ax Falls—6,000 Times—at Sunbeam," *The Wall Street Journal,* November 13, 1996.

[5] Ibid.

[6] 1996 10K filing to SEC, Item 1 ("Business").

Executive Leadership

Chair and CEO Albert J. Dunlap assumed leadership in 1996 and promptly invested $3 million of his own money in Sunbeam shares. "If I make a lot of money here [at Sunbeam]—which I certainly intend to do—then the shareholders will make a lot. . . . I'm in lockstep with the shareholders."[7]

Dunlap immediately hired Russell Kersh as Sunbeam's chief financial officer. Dunlap and Kersh both entered lucrative three-year employment agreements that gave them strong financial incentives to raise the share price of the company. Dunlap then replaced almost all of top management, and the replacements were each provided with strong financial incentives to improve the company's share price.[8]

Corporate Restructuring and Plans for Growth

Under Dunlap's reign, Sunbeam embarked on an aggressive restructuring that would involve eliminating half of the company's 12,000 employees; the sale or consolidation of 39 of its 53 facilities; the divestiture of several lines of businesses, such as its furniture business; the elimination of 87 percent of Sunbeam's product list; and the replacement of six regional headquarters in favor of a single office in Delray Beach, Florida. "We planned this like the invasion of Normandy. . . . We attacked every aspect of the business," said Dunlap.[9]

Dunlap publicly predicted that as a result of the restructuring, the company would attain operating margins of 20 percent of sales in 1997 and increase its sales by 20 percent, 30 percent, and 35 percent, respectively, in 1997, 1998, and 1999. This meant that the company would have to double its sales to $2 billion by 1999.[10] Other goals were to introduce 30 new products each year domestically and to triple international sales to $600 million by 1999.[11]

Times of Trouble

After the first quarter of 1997, Dunlap heralded the success of the company's turnaround efforts:

> The impressive growth in both revenues and earnings is proof that the revitalization of Sunbeam is working. In fact, the sales growth in the first quarter is

---

[7] Joann S. Lublin and Martha Brannigan, "Sunbeam Names Albert Dunlap as Chief, Betting He Can Pull Off a Turnaround," *The Wall Street Journal,* July 19, 1996, p. B2.

[8] "Complaint for Civil Injunction and Civil Penalties," *SEC v. Albert J. Dunlap, Russell A. Kersh, Robert J. Gluck, Donald R. Uzzi, Lee B. Griffith, and Phillip E. Harlow,* pp. 7–8.

[9] Robert Frank and Joann S. Lublin. "Dunlap's Ax Falls—6,000 Times—at Sunbeam," *The Wall Street Journal,* November 13, 1996, p. B1.

[10] *SEC v. Albert J. Dunlap, Russell A. Kersh, Robert J. Gluck, Donald R. Uzzi, Lee B. Griffith, and Phillip E. Harlow,* pp. 10–11.

[11] 1996 10K filing to SEC, Item 1 ("Business").

the highest level achieved without acquisitions since Sunbeam became public in 1992. . . . The substantially higher earnings in the quarter from ongoing operations were due to increased sales coupled with the successful implementation of our restructuring efforts.[12]

Yet by the fourth quarter of 1997, Sunbeam's results had fallen below expectations. Its first-quarter results in 1998 earned a worse-than-expected loss of $44.6 million.[13] CEO and Chair Dunlap was fired in June 1998. In October 1998 Sunbeam announced that the audit committee of its board of directors had determined that the company would need to restate its prior financial statements, as follows: to reduce the 1996 net loss by $20 million (9 percent of reported losses); to reduce 1997 net income by $71 million (65 percent of reported earnings); and to increase 1998 earnings by $10 million (21 percent of reported losses).[14]

Sunbeam filed for Chapter 11 bankruptcy protection in February 2001. In May 2001 the U.S. Securities and Exchange Commission (SEC) brought charges of fraud against several former Sunbeam officials. At the end of 2002 the company emerged from Chapter 11 and changed its name to American Household. In early 2005 it was acquired by Jarden to be part of its consumer solutions division.

[12] *SEC v. Albert J. Dunlap, Russell A. Kersh, Robert J. Gluck, Donald R. Uzzi, Lee B. Griffith, and Phillip E. Harlow,* p. 20.

[13] Robert Frank and Joann S. Lublin. "Dunlap's Ax Falls—6,000 Times—at Sunbeam," *The Wall Street Journal,* November 13, 1996, p. B1.

[14] GAO-03-138, Appendix XVII "Sunbeam Corporation," p. 201.

Case Questions

1. Consult Paragraphs 5–8 of PCAOB Auditing Standard No. 8 and Paragraphs 7–10 of PCAOB Auditing Standard No. 12. Based on your understanding of inherent risk assessment and the case information, identify three specific factors about Sunbeam that might cause you to elevate inherent risk.

2. Consult Paragraphs 8–10 of PCAOB Auditing Standard No. 13. Comment about how your understanding of the inherent risks identified at Sunbeam (in Question 1) would influence the nature, timing, and extent of your audit work at Sunbeam.

3. Consult Paragraphs 29 and 32 of PCAOB Auditing Standard No. 5. Next briefly identify the types of revenue earned by Sunbeam. Do you believe that any of the different types of revenue earned by Sunbeam "might be subject to significantly differing" levels of inherent risk? Why or why not?

4. Consult Paragraphs 52–53 of PCOAB Auditing Standard No. 12. For one of Sunbeam's revenue types (please choose one), brainstorm about how a fraud might occur. Next identify an internal control procedure that would prevent, detect, or deter such a fraudulent scheme.

Case 3.5

Qwest: Understanding the Client's Business and Industry

Synopsis

When Joseph Nacchio became Qwest's CEO in January 1997, the company's existing strategy began to shift from building a nationwide fiber-optic network to include increasing communications services. By the time it released earnings in 1998, Nacchio proclaimed Qwest's successful transition from a network construction company to a communications services provider. "We successfully transitioned Qwest . . . into a leading Internet protocol-based multimedia company focused on the convergence of data, video, and voice services."[1]

During 1999 and 2000, Qwest consistently met its aggressive revenue targets and became a darling to its investors. Yet, when the company announced its intention to restate revenues in August 2002, its stock price plunged to a low of $1.11 per share in August 2002, from a high of $55 per share in July 2000.[2] Civil and criminal charges related to fraudulent activitity were brought against several Qwest executives, including CEO Joseph Nacchio. Nacchio was convicted on 19 counts of illegal insider trading, and was sentenced to six years in prison in July 2007. He was also ordered to pay a $19 million fine and forfeit $52 million that he gained in illegal stock sales.[3]

[1] SEC v. Joseph P. Nacchio, Robert S. Woodruff, Robin R. Szeliga, Afshin Mohebbi, Gregory M. Casey, James J. Kozlowski, Frank T. Noyes, Defendants, Civil Action No. 05-MK-480 (OES), pp. 11–14.

[2] SEC v. Qwest, pp. 1–2.

[3] Dionne Searcey, "Qwest Ex-Chief Gets 6 Years in Prison for Insider Trading," *The Wall Street Journal*, July 28, 2007, p. A3.

Strategic Direction

In the mid-1990s Qwest Communications International embarked on building a fiber-optic network across major cities within the United States. The network would consist of a series of cables that contained strands of pure glass that could transmit data by using light and the appropriate equipment. Qwest's initial strategy was to build the network of fiber cable and sell it in the form of an indefeasible right of use (IRU), an irrevocable right to use a specific amount of fiber for a specified time period.

However, when Joseph Nacchio became Qwest's CEO in January 1997, the strategy of the company shifted toward communications services. Nacchio envisioned that Qwest had the potential of becoming a major telecommunications company that offered Internet and multimedia services over its fiber-optic network, in addition to offering traditional voice communications services.[4]

Qwest's Construction Services Business

A fiber-optic network consists of a series of cables that contain strands of pure glass and allow transmission of data between any two connected points using beams of light. While each cable of the fiber-optic network typically contains at least 96 strands of fiber, Qwest intended to use 48 of the fiber strands for its own use and to sell the remaining strands to help finance the cost of construction of the network.[5] Total revenue from its construction services business was approximately $224.5 million, $688.4 million, and $581.4 million in 1999, 1998, and 1997, respectively.[6]

Competition

As of 1999, Qwest faced competition in the construction services segment from three other principal facilities-based long distance fiber optic networks: AT&T, Sprint, and MCI WorldCom. In its 1999 annual filing with the SEC, Qwest warned investors that others—including Global Crossing, GTE, Broadwing, and Williams Communications—were building or planning networks that could employ advanced technology similar to Qwest's network. Yet Qwest assured investors that it was at a significant advantage because its network would be completed in mid-1999, at least a year ahead of the planned completion of other networks, and it could extend and expand the capacity of its network using the additional fibers that it had retained.[7]

---

[4] *SEC v. Joseph P. Nacchio, Robert S. Woodruff, Robin R. Szeliga, Afshin Mohebbi, Gregory M. Casey, James J. Kozlowski, Frank T. Noyes, Defendants,* Civil Action No. 05-MK-480 (OES), pp. 11–14.

[5] 1997 10-K, p. 10.

[6] 1999 10-K, p. 12.

[7] 1999 10-K, p. 13.

Qwest's Communications Services Business

As part of its communications services business, Qwest provided traditional voice communications services, as well as Internet and multimedia services to business customers, governmental agencies, and consumers in domestic and international markets. Qwest also provided wholesale services to other communications providers, including Internet service providers (ISPs) and other data service companies. Total revenue from its communications services business was approximately $3,703.1 million, $1,554.3 million, and $115.3 million in 1999, 1998, and 1997, respectively.[8]

Regulation

The impact of regulatory change was significant in the highly regulated telecommunications industry. The Telecommunications Act of 1996 increased competition in the long distance market by allowing the entry of local exchange carriers and others. Indeed, Qwest warned investors in its 1999 annual filing with the SEC that its costs of providing long distance services could be affected by changes in the rules controlling the form and amount of "access charges" long distance carriers had to pay local exchange carriers to use the local networks they needed to provide the local portions of long distance calls.[9]

Competition

Qwest's primary competitors in its communications services business included AT&T, Sprint, and MCI WorldCom, all of which had extensive experience in the traditional long distance market. In addition, the industry faced continuing consolidation, such as the merger of MCI and WorldCom.

In the markets for Internet and multimedia services, Qwest competed with a wide range of companies that provided Web hosting, Internet access, and other Internet Protocol (IP) products and services. Significant competitors included GTE, UUNET (a subsidiary of MCI WorldCom), Digex, AboveNet, Intel, and Exodus.[10]

Qwest's Mergers and Acquisitions

Like its competition, Qwest pursued several mergers and acquisitions to strengthen its service offerings. From October 1997 to December 1998 it acquired SuperNet, Inc., a regional ISP in the Rocky Mountain region; in March 1998 it acquired Phoenix Network, Inc., a reseller of long distance services; in

---

[8] 1999 10-K, p. 10.
[9] 1999 10-K, pp. 14–17.
[10] 1999 10-K, p. 13.

April 1998 it acquired EUnet International Limited, a leading European ISP; in June 1998 it purchased LCI International, Inc., a provider of long distance telephone services; and in December 1998 it acquired Icon CMT Corp., a leading Internet solutions provider.[11] In many of these acquisitions, Qwest used its own company stock as the tender to acquire the companies.

Qwest's string of acquisitions culminated during 1999 when it entered into a merger agreement with telecommunications company US West on July 18, 1999. The merger agreement required Qwest to issue $69 worth of its common stock for each share of US West stock, and it gave US West the option to terminate the agreement if the average price of Qwest stock was below $22 per share or the closing price was below $22 per share for 20 consecutive trading days. Less than a month after the merger announcement, Qwest's stock price had dropped from $34 to $26 per share.

---

[11] 1998 10-K, p. 5.

Case Questions

1. Consult Paragraphs 65–66 of PCAOB Auditing Standard No. 12. Based on your understanding of fraud risk assessment, what three conditions are likely to be present when a fraud occurs (the fraud triangle)? Based on the information provided in the case, which of these three conditions appears to be the most prevalent, and why?

2. Consult Paragraphs 5–8 of PCAOB Auditing Standard No. 8 and Paragraphs 7–10 of PCAOB Auditing Standard No. 12. Based on your understanding of inherent risk assessment and the case information, identify three specific factors about Qwest's business model that might cause you to elevate inherent risk if you were conducting an audit at Qwest.

3. Consult Paragraphs 8–10 of PCAOB Auditing Standard No. 13. Comment on how your understanding of the inherent risks identified at Qwest (in Question 2) would influence the nature, timing, and extent of your audit work at Qwest.

4. Consult Paragraphs 29 and 32 of PCAOB Auditing Standard No. 5. Next consider revenue earned in the construction services and the communication services businesses. Do you believe that any of the different types of revenue earned by Qwest might be subject to significantly differing levels of inherent risk? Why or why not?

Case 3.6

Bernard L. Madoff Investment and Securities: Understanding the Client's Business and Industry

Synopsis

During 2008, Bernie Madoff became famous for a Ponzi scheme that defrauded investors out of as much as $65 billion. To satisfy his clients' expectations of earning returns greater than the market average, Madoff falsely asserted that he used an innovative "split-strike conversion strategy," which provided the appearance that he was achieving extraordinary results. In reality, he was a fraudster. Madoff was arrested on December 11, 2008, and convicted in 2009 on 11 counts of fraud, perjury, and money laundering. As a result, Madoff was sentenced to 150 years in prison.

Not a Typical Hedge Fund

In 2001 Madoff Securities had 600 major brokerage clients and over $7 billion in assets under management in its hedge fund portfolio.[1] By the end of 2005 the company had assets under management estimated at $20 billion.[2] Interestingly, Madoff had not registered with the SEC as an investment advisor until September 2006, following an SEC investigation into his business.[3]

[1] Michael Ocrant, "Madoff Tops Charts; Skeptics Ask How," MARHedge magazine, May 2001.

[2] Harry Markopolos, Submission to the SEC on Madoff Securities, December 22, 2005.

[3] Greg N. Gregoriou and Francois-Serge Lhabitant, "Madoff: A Flock of Red Flags," *The Journal of Wealth Management,* Summer 2009.

Unlike a typical hedge fund, Madoff Securities did not charge a fee on the money it managed. It only earned money by charging commissions on trades executed for the accounts of its third party hedge funds. "We're perfectly happy to just earn commissions on the trades," said Madoff in an interview in 2001.[4] In so doing, Madoff Securities was operating differently than largely all other hedge funds. To some observers, it was shocking that "Madoff was voluntarily giving up huge profits. Nobody anybody of us ever knew in the industry voluntarily left money on the table - except for Bernie."[5]

In addition, while the third party hedge funds (referred to as "feeder funds") obtained the investors, 100% of the money raised was actually managed by Madoff. Interestingly, investors were unaware that Madoff was actually managing the funds. In fact, the feeder funds were not allowed to name Madoff as the actual money manager in their marketing literature or performance summaries.[6]

A typical hedge fund uses a network of third-party providers, including an investment manager, one or several brokers to execute trades, and some custodians to hold the investment positions. Typically, these providers are independent of one another to reduce the risk for fraud. In Madoff's firm, all of these functions were performed internally with no independent oversight by any third-party provider.

Instead of providing electronic access to their accounts, Madoff mailed his feeder funds paper statements showing account activity. Sometimes, the

How money was invested with Bernie Madoff

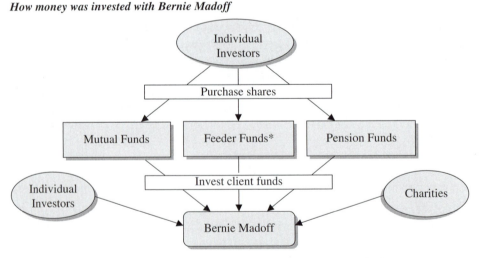

*Feeder funds are funds investing nearly exclusively with a master fund, in this case the master fund was Bernard L. Madoff Investment and Securities.

---

[4] "What We Wrote About Madoff," *Barron's*, December 22, 2008.

[5] Harry Markopolis, No One Would Listen (Hoboken NJ: John Wiley & sons, 2010, 131.

[6] Harry Markopolos, Submission to the SEC on Madoff Securities, December 22, 2005.

statements had no time stamps. It was later proven that these statements were fabricated, and the employees involved with creating these statements were brought up on criminal charges. Enrica Cotellessa-Pitz, the firm's Controller, was one of the employees who admitted to falsifying records, including the firm's general ledger and reports for the SEC. "Although I now know the crimes I committed helped to cover up and perpetuate Bernard Madoff's fraudulent Ponzi scheme, at the time I did not know that Madoff and others were stealing investors' money," said Cotellessa-Pitz who pled guilty to four charges and faces a maximum of 50 years in prison.[7]

The returns that were passed along to the third party investors were consistently high. From 1990 to 2005, 12-month returns ranged from a low of 6.23% to a high of 19.98%, with an average 12 month return during that time period of 12%.[8] When Madoff was asked about how he accomplished these returns in an interview in *Barron's* in 2001, he responded, "It's a proprietary strategy. I can't go into it in great detail."[9] According to his son Andrew, in an interview on *60 Minutes,* Madoff was highly secretive and access to the floor that the investment advisory business was on was extremely restricted.

The Fraud Revealed and Aftermath for the Madoff Family

During 2008, the United States began to experience an economic crisis, and the stock market was in decline. In response, many investors began to liquidate their holdings in the stock market and funds like Madoff's. Subsequently, in December 2008 Madoff was struggling to meet the requests from clients for approximately $7 billion in redemptions from his fund. He told his sons that he wanted to pay bonuses to employees of the firm in December, instead of in February, when bonuses were usually paid. When pressed by sons, he suggested that that they speak at his apartment rather than at the office. Shortly after, Madoff confessed to his brother, sons, and wife that the investment advisory business was "all just one big lie" and was "basically, a giant Ponzi scheme." His sons turned him in to the authorities.

Three months after his confession, Madoff pled guilty; in 2009, he was convicted on 11 counts of fraud, perjury, and money laundering and sentenced to 150 years in prison. Madoff insisted to prosecutors that he had acted alone in the fraudulent activity. Yet 13 others have since been brought up on criminal charges, including his brother Peter.

Peter Madoff agreed to serve 10 years in prison and to forfeit all of his assets, admitting to crimes including tax evasion and submitting false filings to securities regulators. Peter maintains that he knew nothing about his brother's

---

[7] "Madoff's Ex-Controller Pleads Guilty in NYC," Wall Street Journal Online, December 19, 2011.
[8] Ibid.
[9] "What We Wrote About Madoff," *Barron's,* December 22, 2008.

Ponzi scheme, however. In his guilty plea, Peter admitted that he helped his brother send out $300 million to employees, family, and friends after his brother confessed about the Ponzi scheme to him. "I did as my brother said, as I'd consistently done for decades," Peter told the judge.[10]

Madoff's oldest son Mark, committed suicide in 2010. His younger son Andrew, who maintains his innocence, faces no criminal charges, but faces a $198 million lawsuit brought by the court-appointed trustee in charge of recovering assets for the victims.

Madoff's wife Ruth, who also says she was unaware of the fraud, was allowed to keep $2.5 million in cash in an agreement with federal prosecutors that involved her giving up her claims to about $80 million in assets held in her name.[11] Like her son Andrew, Ruth has also been named in a multi-million dollar lawsuit brought by the court-appointed trustee, as are Madoff's nephew and niece.

[10] Peter Lattman and Ben Protess, "In Guilty Plea, Peter Madoff Says He Didn't Know About the Fraud," The New York Times, June 29, 2012.

[11] Jamie Heller and Joanna Chung, "The Madoff Fraud: Lives in Limbo, Two Years After Scheme Revealed," The Wall Street Journal, December 13, 2010.

Case Questions

1. As stated in the case, until an investigation into his company in 2006, Madoff had not registered as an investment advisor with the SEC. Please refer to the SEC website (www.sec.gov). Are all investment advisors required to register with the SEC? How can the investing public discover whether an investment advisor has violated SEC regulations?

2. Consult Paragraphs 5–8 of PCAOB Auditing Standard No. 8 and Paragraphs 7–10 of PCAOB Auditing Standard No. 12. Based on your understanding of inherent risk assessment and the case information, identify three specific factors about Madoff Securities' business model that might cause you to elevate inherent risk if you were conducting an audit at Madoff Securities.

3. Consider the Dodd-Frank Wall Street Reform and Consumer Protection Act of 2010. Explain the changes brought upon by this act to the hedge fund industry. Do you believe that the Act went far enough? Why or why not?

4. In August 2011 an appeals court ruled that Madoff's customers were eligible to recover only the money that they had invested (estimated at $17.3 billion), not the fake profits that Madoff had promised (which totaled $52 billion). Do you agree with this decision? Why or why not?

Case 3.7

Waste Management: Understanding the Client's Business and Industry

Synopsis

In February 1998 Waste Management announced that it was restating the financial statements it had issued for the years 1993 through 1996. In its restatement, Waste Management said that it had materially overstated its reported pretax earnings by $1.43 billion. After the announcement, the company's stock dropped by more than 33 percent and shareholders lost over $6 billion.

The SEC brought charges against the company's founder, Dean Buntrock, and other former top officers. The charges alleged that management had made repeated changes to depreciation-related estimates to reduce expenses and had employed several improper accounting practices related to capitalization policies, also designed to reduce expenses.[1] In its final judgment, the SEC permanently barred Buntrock and three other executives from acting as officers or directors of public companies and required payment from them of $30.8 million in penalties.[2]

History

In 1956 Dean Buntrock took control of Ace Scavenger, a garbage collector that was owned by his then father-in-law who had recently died. After merging Ace with several waste companies, Buntrock founded Waste Management in 1968.[3] Under Buntrock's reign as its CEO, the company went public in 1971

[1] SEC, Accounting and Auditing Enforcement Release No. 1532, March 26, 2002.
[2] SEC, Accounting and Auditing Enforcement Release No. 2298, August 29, 2005.
[3] "Waste Management: Change with the Market or Die," *Fortune,* January 13, 1992.

and expanded during the 1970s and 1980s through several acquisitions of local waste hauling companies and landfill operators. At one point the company was performing close to 200 acquisitions a year.[4]

From 1971 to 1991 Waste Management enjoyed 36 percent average annual revenue growth and 36 percent average annual net income growth. By 1991 it had become the largest waste removal business in the world, with revenue of more than $7.5 billion.[5] Despite a recession, Buntrock and other executives at Waste Management continued to set aggressive goals for growth. For example, in 1992 the company forecast that revenue and net income would increase by 26.1 percent and 16.5 percent, respectively, over 1991's figures.[6]

Waste Management's Core Operations

Waste Management's core solid waste management operations in North America consisted of the following major processes: collection, transfer, and disposal.

Collection

Solid waste collection from commercial and industrial customers was generally performed under one- to three-year service agreements. Most of its residential solid waste collection services were performed under contracts with—or franchises granted by—municipalities giving it exclusive rights to service all or a portion of the homes in their respective jurisdictions. These contracts or franchises usually lasted from one to five years. Factors that contributed to the determination of fees collected from industrial and commercial customers were market conditions, collection frequency, type of equipment furnished, length of service agreement, type and volume or weight of the waste collected, distance to the disposal facility, and cost of disposal. Similar factors determined the fees collected in the residential market.[7]

Transfer

As of 1995, Waste Management operated 151 solid waste transfer stations—facilities where solid waste was received from collection vehicles and was then transferred to trailers for transportation to disposal facilities. In most instances, several collection companies used the services of these facilities, which were provided to municipalities or counties. Market factors, the type and volume or weight of the waste transferred, the extent of processing of recyclable materials, the transport distance involved, and the cost of disposal were the major factors that determined the fees collected.[8]

---

[4] *SEC v. Dean L. Buntrock, Phillip B. Rooney, James E. Koenig, Thomas C. Hau, Herbert A. Getz, and Bruce D. Tobecksen,* Complaint No. 02C 2180 (Judge Manning).

[5] Ibid.

[6] Ibid.

[7] Waste Management, 1995 10-K.

[8] 1995 10-K.

Disposal

As of 1995, Waste Management operated 133 solid waste sanitary landfill facilities, 103 of which were owned by the company. All of the sanitary landfill facilities were subject to governmental regulation aimed at limiting the possibility of water pollution. In addition to governmental regulation, land scarcity and local resident opposition also conspired to make it difficult to obtain permission to operate and expand landfill facilities in certain areas. The development of a new facility also required significant up-front capital investment and a lengthy amount of time, with the added risk that the necessary permit might not be ultimately issued by the municipality or county. In 1993, 1994, and 1995, approximately 52 percent, 55 percent, and 57 percent, respectively, of the solid waste collected by Waste Management was disposed of in sanitary landfill facilities operated by it. These facilities were typically also used by other companies and government agencies on a noncontract basis for fees determined by market factors and the type and volume or weight of the waste.[9]

Corporate Expansion

As the company grew, it expanded its international operations and into new industries, including hazardous waste management, waste to energy, and environmental engineering businesses. By the mid-1990s, Waste Management had five major business groups that provided the following services: solid waste management; hazardous waste management; engineering and industrial services; trash to energy, water treatment, and air quality services; and international waste management. Table 3.7.1 describes the primary services these groups provided and the revenues recorded in 1993, 1994, and 1995.

Challenges

By the mid-1990s, the company's core North American solid waste business was suffering from intense competition and excess landfill capacity in some of its markets. New environmental regulations also added to the cost of operating a landfill and made it more difficult and expensive for Waste Management to obtain permits for constructing new landfills or to expand old ones.[10]

Several of its other businesses (including its hazardous waste management business and several international operations) were also performing poorly. After a strategic review that began in 1994, the company was reorganized into four global lines of business: waste services, clean energy, clean water, and environmental and infrastructure engineering and consulting.[11]

---

[9] Ibid.

[10] SEC, Accounting and Auditing Enforcement Release No. 1532, March 26, 2002.

[11] 1995 10-K.

TABLE 3.7.1 Waste Management's Major Business Groups

Business Group	Services	Revenues (In thousands)		
		1993	1994	1995
Solid waste management	Garbage collection, transfer, resource recovery, and disposal for commercial, industrial, municipal, and residential customers, as well as for other waste management companies. Included recycling of paper, glass, plastic, and metal; removal of methane gas from sanitary landfill facilities for use in electricity generation; and medical and infectious waste management services to hospitals and other health care and related facilities.	$4,702,166	5,117,871	5,642,857
Hazardous waste management	Chemical waste treatment, storage, disposal, and related services provided to commercial and industrial customers, governmental entities, and other waste management companies by Waste Management and Chemical Waste Management (CWM), a wholly owned subsidiary; onsite integrated hazardous waste management services provided by Advanced Environmental Technical Services (AETS), a 60 percent owned subsidiary; and low-level radioactive waste disposal services provided by subsidiary Chem-Nuclear Systems.	$ 661,860	649,581	613,883
Engineering and industrial	Through Rust International, a 60 percent owned subsidiary, provides environmental and infrastructure engineering and consulting services, primarily to clients in government and in the chemical, petrochemical, nuclear energy, utility, pulp and paper, manufacturing, environmental services, and other industries.	$1,035,004	1,140,294	1,027,430

Trash to energy, water treatment, air quality	Through Wheelabrator Technologies Inc. (WTI), a 58 percent owned subsidiary, develops, arranges financing for, operates, and owns facilities that dispose of trash and other waste materials by recycling them into electrical or steam energy. Also designs, fabricates, and installs technologically advanced air pollution control, and systems and equipment. WTI's clean water group is principally involved in design, manufacture, operation, and ownership of facilities and systems used to purify water, to treat municipal and industrial wastewater, and to recycle organic wastes into compost material usable for horticultural and agricultural purposes.	$1,142,219	1,324,567	1,451,675
International waste management	Solid and hazardous waste management and related environ-mental services in 10 European countries along with Argentina, Australia, Brazil, Brunei, Hong Kong, Indonesia, Israel, Malaysia, New Zealand, Taiwan, and Thailand. Also has 20 percent interest in Wessex Water Plc, an English publicly traded company providing water treatment, water distribution, wastewater treatment, and sewerage services.	$1,411,211	1,710,862	1,865,081
Consolidated revenue*		$8,636,116	9,554,705	10,274,617

*Intercompany revenue eliminations in 1993, 1994, and 1995, respectively, were as follows: ($316,344), ($388,470), ($353,309).

Case Questions

1. Consult Paragraphs 5–8 of PCAOB Auditing Standard No. 8 and Paragraphs 7–10 of PCAOB Auditing Standard No. 12. Based on your understanding of inherent risk assessment and the case information, identify three specific factors about Waste Management that might cause you to elevate inherent risk. When identifying each factor, indicate the financial statement account that is likely to be most affected (and briefly discuss why it is most affected).

2. Consult Paragraphs 29 and 32 of PCAOB Auditing Standard No. 5. Identify the types of revenue earned (a brief description will do) by Waste Management. Do you believe that any of the different types of revenue earned by Waste Management might be subject to significantly differing levels of inherent risk? Why or why not?

3. Consult Paragraphs 8–10 of PCAOB Auditing Standard No. 13. Comment on how your understanding of the different types of revenue earned (in Question 2) would influence the nature, timing, and extent of your audit work at Waste Management.

4. Consult Paragraphs 52–53 of PCAOB Auditing Standard No. 12. For one of Waste Management's revenue sources (please choose one), brainstorm about how a fraud might occur. Next identify an internal control procedure that would prevent, detect, or deter such a fraudulent scheme.

Internal Control Systems: Entity-Level Control Cases

Since 2004 audit firms have been required to express an opinion on the effectiveness of the internal control system over financial reporting for all public companies. In May 2007 the Public Company Accounting Oversight Board (PCAOB) issued Auditing Standard No. 5, "An Audit of Internal Control over Financial Reporting Performed in Conjunction with an Audit of Financial Statements." Auditing Standard No. 5 (AS 5) provides the primary technical guidance to be followed by auditors in completing their internal control audits at public companies.

AS 5 makes it clear that the internal control audit process employed by CPA firms when auditing public companies must take a "top-down" approach. To execute a top-down approach, an auditor must first evaluate the entity-level controls, including all pervasive controls, before considering internal control activities at the business process, application, or transaction level. The cases in this section are designed to illustrate the importance of entity-level controls and other pervasive controls to the effective design and operation of an internal control system.

The case readings have been developed solely as a basis for class discussion. The case readings are not intended to serve as a source of primary data or as an illustration of effective or ineffective auditing.

Case 4.1

Enron: The Control Environment

Synopsis

In its 2000 annual report Enron prided itself on having "metamorphosed from an asset-based pipeline and power generating company to a marketing and logistics company whose biggest assets are its well-established business approach and its innovative people."[1] Enron's strategy seemed to pay off: In 2000 it was the seventh largest company on the Fortune 500, with assets of $65 billion and sales revenues of $100 billion.[2] From 1996 to 2000 Enron's revenues had increased by more than 750 percent which was unprecedented in any industry.[3] Yet just a year later, in December 2001, Enron filed for bankruptcy, and billions of shareholder and retirement savings dollars were lost.

Executive Incentives

At Enron, executives had incentives to achieve high-revenue growth because their salary increases and cash bonus amounts were linked to reported revenues. In the proxy statement filed in 1997, Enron wrote that "base salaries are targeted at the median of a competitor group that includes peer group companies . . . and general industry companies similar in size to Enron."[4] In the proxy statement

---

[1] Enron 2000 annual report, p. 7.

[2] Joseph F. Berardino, remarks to U.S. House of Representatives Committee on Financial Services, December 12, 2001.

[3] Bala G. Dharan and William R. Bufkins, "Red Flags in Enron's Reporting of Revenues and Key Financial Measures," March 2003, prepublication draft (www.ruf.rice.edu/~bala/files/dharan-bufkins_enron_red_flags_041003.pdf), p. 4.

[4] Bala G. Dharan and William R. Bufkins, "Red Flags in Enron's Reporting of Revenues and Key Financial Measures," March 2003, prepublication draft (www.ruf.rice.edu/~bala/files/dharan-bufkins_enron_red_flags_041003.pdf), p. 6.

filed in 2001, Enron wrote, "The [Compensation] Committee determined the amount of the annual incentive award taking into consideration the competitive pay level for a CEO of a company with comparable revenue size, and competitive bonus levels for CEOs [*sic*] in specific high performing companies."[5]

Employees also had incentives to achieve high revenues and earnings targets because of the shares of stock they held. Enron made significant use of stock options as a further means of providing incentives for its executives to achieve growth. For example, Enron noted in its 2001 proxy statement that the following stock option awards would become exercisable as of February 15, 2001: 5,285,542 shares for Chair Kenneth Lay, 824,038 shares for President Jeffrey Skilling, and 12,611,385 shares for all officers and directors combined.[6] In fact, as of December 31, 2000, Enron had dedicated 96 million of its outstanding shares (almost 13 percent of its common shares outstanding) to stock option plans.[7]

Enron's Performance Review Committee

Enron's performance review committee (PRC) determined the salaries and bonuses of employees on a semiannual basis. The PRC was initially instituted in the gas services business during the early 1990s after the merger between Houston Natural Gas and InterNorth. One Enron employee said, "At the time, it was a great tool. . . . When we started the ranking process, we were trying to weed out the lower 5 or 6 percent of the company. We had some old dinosaurs, and we had some younger people who needed incentives."[8] The PRC was gradually instituted companywide when Jeffrey Skilling, a former McKinsey & Co. consultant who joined Enron in 1990 as the chief executive of the Enron finance division, was promoted to president and COO.

The PRC made its determinations based on feedback reports that assessed the performance of employees on a scale from 1 to 5. Those who received ratings of 1 received large bonuses, and a rating of 2 or 3 could cost a vice president a six-figure sum.[9] Those who ranked in the bottom 10 percent of the review had until the next semiannual review to improve or they would be fired. Those in categories 2 and 3 were also given notice that they could be fired within the next year.[10]

---

[5] Ibid.

[6] Paul M. Healy and Krishna G. Palepu, "The Fall of Enron," *Journal of Economic Perspectives* 17, no. 2 (Spring 2003), p. 13.

[7] Ibid.

[8] Robert Bryce, *Pipe Dreams: Greed, Ego, and the Death of Enron* (New York: Perseus Book Group, 2002), p. 127.

[9] Bethany McLean and Peter Elkind, *The Smartest Guys in the Room: The Amazing Rise and Scandalous Fall of Enron* (Penguin Group, 2003), pp. 63–64.

[10] Peter C. Fuasaro and Ross M. Miller, *What Went Wrong at Enron* (Hoboken, New Jersey: John Wiley & Sons, Inc., 2002), pp. 51–52.

Enron's Changes to Accounting Procedures

During the 1990s Enron made significant changes to several of its accounting procedures designed to improve reported earnings and financial position. For example, Enron began using mark-to-market (MTM) accounting for its trading business, which allowed the present value of a stream of *future* inflows and outflows under a contract to be recognized as revenues and expenses, respectively, once the contract was signed. Enron was the first company outside the financial services industry to use MTM accounting.[11] Enron also began establishing several special-purpose entities, which were formed to accomplish specific tasks such as building gas pipelines. If an SPE satisfied certain conditions, it did not have to be consolidated with the financial statements of the sponsoring company. Thus an SPE could be utilized by a company hoping to achieve certain accounting purposes, such as hiding debt.

---

[11] Bala G. Dharan and William R. Bufkins, "Red Flags in Enron's Reporting of Revenues and Key Financial Measures," March 2003, prepublication draft (www.ruf.rice.edu/~bala/files/dharan-bufkins_enron_red_flags_041003.pdf), pp. 7–11.

Case Questions

1. Consult Paragraphs 65–69 of PCAOB Auditing Standard No. 12. Based on your understanding of fraud risk assessment, what three conditions are likely to be present when a fraud occurs (the fraud triangle)? Based on the information provided in the case, which of these three conditions appears to have been the most prevalent at Enron, and why?

2. Consult Paragraph 25 of PCAOB Auditing Standard No. 5. Define what is meant by *control environment*. Why is the control environment so important to effective internal control over financial reporting at an audit client like Enron?

3. Consult Paragraphs 21–22 of PCAOB Auditing Standard No. 5. Comment on how your understanding of Enron's control environment and other entity-level controls would help you implement a top-down approach for an internal control audit at Enron.

4. Consult Sections 204 and 301 of SARBOX. What is the role of the audit committee in the financial reporting process? Do you believe that an audit committee can be effective in providing oversight of a management team like Enron's?

5. Consult Sections 302 and 305 and Title IX of SARBOX. Do you believe that these provisions could help deter fraudulent financial reporting by an upper management group? Why or why not?

Case 4.2

Waste Management: General Computing Controls

Synopsis

In February 1998 Waste Management announced that it was restating its financial statements for the years 1993 through 1996. In its restatement, it said that it had materially overstated its reported pretax earnings by $1.43 billion. After the announcement, the company's stock dropped by more than 33 percent and shareholders lost over $6 billion.

The SEC brought charges against the company's founder, Dean Buntrock, and other former top officers. The charges alleged that management had made repeated changes to depreciation-related estimates to reduce expenses and had employed several improper accounting practices related to capitalization policies, also designed to reduce expenses.[1] In its final judgment, the SEC permanently barred Buntrock and three other executives from acting as officers or directors of public companies and required payment from them of $30.8 million in penalties.[2]

Merger with USA Waste Service[3]

Shortly after the announcement that Waste Management had overstated reported pretax earnings by $1.43 billion for the years 1993 through 1996, the company entered into a merger agreement with USA Waste Service, which was also in the business of collecting, transporting, and disposing of solid waste.

[1] SEC, Accounting and Auditing Enforcement Release No 1532, March 26, 2002.
[2] SEC, Accounting and Auditing Enforcement Release No. 2298, August 29, 2005.
[3] SEC Accounting and Auditing Enforcement, Release No. 1277, June 21, 2000.

The newly merged entity, named Waste Management Incorporated (WMI), forecast 1999 earnings per share in the range of $2.90 to $3.05, which took into account anticipated synergies as a result of the merger.

WMI's Accounting and Billing Systems[4]

On July 29, 1998, less than two weeks after the merger closed, WMI reiterated the 1999 earnings forecast. WMI also introduced its senior management team on this date. Interestingly, although almost 80 percent of the regions and districts were staffed primarily by former Waste Management personnel, all of the senior managers at the corporate level were from USA Waste Service.

The success of the merger's transition was highly dependent on the successful conversion of the accounting and billing systems of the operating entities that were part of Waste Management to the systems of USA Waste Service. The company completed tests of the accounting and billing systems conversions in the fall of 1998 and hoped to complete its full-scale conversion of these systems by the end of the first quarter of 1999.

Problems with Consolidated Accounting System

In the early months of 1999, however, USA Waste Service experienced numerous problems with its newly consolidated accounting system. In particular, the system did not provide the company's field and corporate management with access to timely financial management information, needed to monitor the company's operations. To address this issue, USA Waste Service developed an additional management information system to provide such financial reports. But this system was not linked to the enterprisewide general ledger system. As a result, a significant offline entry and reconciliation process had to be completed at each level of the company's operations. Thus the information in the enterprisewide system was often incomplete or inaccurate, and it required extensive and time-consuming manual reconciliations. Meanwhile the conversion of the old Waste Management operating entities' billing system to the USA Waste Service system led to delayed and sometimes erroneous billing of customers.

So to estimate second-quarter operating results, corporate financial personnel collected estimates from each of the five domestic operating areas. The results showed an estimated revenue shortfall from its target of more than $200 million and an earnings per share shortfall of $.11 for the second quarter of 1999. Throughout the month of June, management received additional information suggesting potential problems with second-quarter results. Yet in discussions with analysts and other members of the public at the 1999 Waste Expo conference from June 7 to 9, 1999, one of the largest waste industry trade meetings, WMI maintained its second-quarter-earnings guidance of $.78 to $.81 per share.

---

[4] Ibid.

Following the June 9 Waste Expo, the company received a steady stream of adverse information. Therefore, WMI issued a press release on July 6, 1999, reporting a $250 million projected revenue shortfall from target levels and earnings per share forecasts in the range of $.67–$.70 for the second quarter of 1999 and $2.65–$2.70 for the year (1999). By the close of trading on July 7, the company's share price had fallen from more than $53.50 per share to below $34 per share.

Following the July 6 announcement, the company's board of directors appointed a three-member executive committee of independent members of the board to oversee the management of the company. During July and August 1999 the executive committee and the board requested and accepted the resignation of the company's CFO, general counsel, COO, and CEO. The board also ordered the creation of an updated and more effective financial system. After a detailed review of the company's accounting records, the company recognized $1.23 billion in after-tax charges and adjustments to expenses.

Case Questions

1. What is the difference between an information technology general control and an automated application control? Provide an example of each in your response.
2. Consult Paragraphs B1–B6 (in Appendix B) of PCAOB Auditing Standard No. 12. Do you believe that information technology general controls have a pervasive effect on the reliability of financial reporting at an audit client like WMI? Why or why not? Please be specific.
3. Consult Paragraphs B28–B31 (in Appendix B) of PCAOB Auditing Standard No. 5. Define what is meant by a *benchmarking strategy*. Based on the case information, do you believe that a benchmarking strategy would have been appropriate during the first year audit at WMI? Why or why not?
4. Consult Paragraph A4 (in Appendix A) of PCAOB Auditing Standard No. 5. Given the PCAOB's view, do you believe that the audit firm should be providing assurance on the information contained in public company press releases? Why or why not?

4.3

The Baptist Foundation of Arizona: The Whistleblower Hotline

Synopsis

The Baptist Foundation of Arizona (BFA) was organized as an Arizona nonprofit organization primarily to help provide financial support for various Southern Baptist causes. Under William Crotts's leadership, the foundation engaged in a major strategic shift in its operations. BFA began to invest heavily in the Arizona real estate market and also accelerated its efforts to sell investment agreements and mortgage-backed securities to church members.

Two of BFA's most significant affiliates were ALO and New Church Ventures. It was later revealed that BFA had set up these affiliates to facilitate the sale of its real estate investments at prices significantly above fair market value. In so doing, BFA's management perpetrated a fraudulent scheme that cost at least 13,000 investors more than $590 million. In fact, Arizona Attorney General Janet Napolitano called the BFA collapse the largest bankruptcy of a religious nonprofit in the history of the United States.[1]

Background

Soon after the precipitous decline of Arizona's real estate market in 1989, BFA management decided to establish a number of related affiliates. These affiliates were controlled by individuals with close ties to BFA, such as former board members. Two of BFA's most significant affiliates were ALO and New Church Ventures. A former BFA director incorporated both of these nonprofit entities. The entities had no employees of their own, and both organizations paid BFA substantial

[1] Terry Greene Sterling, "Arthur Andersen and the Baptists," *Salon.com Technology,* February 7, 2002.

management fees to provide accounting, marketing, and administrative services. As a result, both ALO and New Church Ventures owed BFA significant amounts by the end of 1995. On an overall basis, BFA, New Church Ventures, and ALO had a combined negative net worth (deficiency in assets) of $83.2 million at year-end 1995, $102.3 million at year-end 1996, and $124.0 million at year-end 1997.[2]

It was later revealed that BFA had sold real estate to both ALO and New Church Ventures at book value (or at a profit), even though the fair market value of the assets was actually significantly lower than the amounts recorded on BFA's books. In addition, ALO had borrowed money from BFA and its related entities to provide the down payments necessary to execute the purchase transactions with BFA. As a result, ALO's debt increased each year from 1989 to 1997, and its deficit from operations also increased each year.

BFA's Independent Auditors

From 1984 to 1998 BFA engaged Arthur Andersen as its independent auditor. Arthur Andersen was also hired by BFA or BFA's attorneys to perform other accounting and auditing, management consulting, and tax services. From 1984 to 1997 Arthur Andersen issued unqualified audit opinions on BFA's combined financial statements.

From 1992 to 1998 Jay Steven Ozer was the Arthur Andersen engagement partner with the ultimate responsibility for the BFA audits, including the review of all audit work performed, resolution of all accounting issues, evaluating the results of all audit procedures, and signing the final audit opinions. Ann McGrath was an auditor on the BFA engagement from 1988 to 1998. In 1991 she began her role as manager on the audit engagements. For audit years 1991 to 1998 McGrath had primary responsibility for all audit planning and field work, which included assessing areas of inherent and control risk, supervising the audit team, and reviewing all audit workpapers.[3]

Employees' Concerns over ALO's Deficit

In April 1996 several of BFA's accountants and one attorney were sufficiently concerned about ALO's deficit situation and related financial viability issues to confront BFA's senior management team. The response was perceived as inadequate by the employees. Due to their concerns about the lack of response by the BFA senior management team, most of these employees resigned during 1996, citing their concerns in their letters of resignation. One of BFA's accountants who showed concern was Karen Paetz.

---

[2] Notice of Public Hearing and Complaint No. 98.230-ACY, Before the Arizona State Board of Accountancy, pp. 3–4.

[3] Ibid.

Karen Paetz's Concerns

Karen Paetz was familiar with the financial condition of ALO and the inter-relationships among ALO, New Church Ventures, and BFA because one of her responsibilities had been to supervise the preparation of the financial statements of New Church Ventures and ALO. In 1994, at the request of BFA President Crotts, Paetz produced a detailed analysis of the fair market value of ALO's assets compared to the cost basis of its assets. Her analysis revealed a $70.1 million negative net worth.[4] Paetz's misgivings about ALO, New Church Ventures, and BFA prompted her to resign as a BFA accountant in July 1996.

During the seven years Paetz was employed by BFA, she interacted frequently with the Arthur Andersen auditors during each year's audit. In February 1997, during the field work for Arthur Andersen's 1996 audit of BFA, Paetz decided to contact Arthur Andersen auditor Ann McGrath and set up a lunch meeting with McGrath to voice her concerns. At the meeting, Paetz expressed her concern about ALO's deficit, which was in excess of $100 million, and ALO's monthly losses, which were approximately $2.5 million. In addition, Paetz noted that the money from BFA and New Church Ventures was being used to service ALO's substantial debt to BFA. Paetz specifically advised McGrath to ask BFA, during the 1996 audit, for detailed financial statements for both ALO and New Church Ventures.

Arthur Andersen's Response to Concerns

McGrath reported her meeting with Paetz to the engagement partner, Ozer. However, Arthur Andersen's audit workpapers, and its analysis of fraud risk, did not refer to the Paetz meeting in February 1997 because McGrath and Ozer considered the meeting to be a "nonevent."[5] Arthur Andersen did, however, expand its audit procedures for the 1996 audit and requested from BFA the detailed financial statements of ALO and New Church Ventures. However, BFA refused to make the detailed financial statements of ALO and New Church Ventures available to McGrath and Ozer.

McGrath and Ozer decided not to insist that ALO's financial statements be provided, although the financial statements were necessary to properly assess ALO's ability to repay its loans to BFA and affiliate New Church Ventures. Fortunately, the financial statements of ALO were a matter of public record and part of a four-page annual disclosure statement that ALO had filed with the Arizona Corporation Commission on March 19, 1997, during Arthur Andersen's field work for the 1996 audit. This four-page annual report showed a $116.5 million negative net worth as of year-end 1996, and a $22 million net loss for the year.[6] New Church

---

[4] Ibid., pp. 29–30.

[5] Notice of Public Hearing and Complaint No. 98.230-ACY, Before the Arizona State Board of Accountancy, pp. 50–51.

[6] Notice of Public Hearing and Complaint No. 98.230-ACY, Before the Arizona State Board of Accountancy, pp. 30–31.

Ventures' unaudited detailed financial statements were available for years 1995, 1996, and 1997. These financial statements revealed that substantially all of New Church Ventures' notes receivable were from ALO.[7]

Disclosure of ALO and New Church Ventures in 1996 Financial Statements

Footnote 3 to BFA's combined financial statements as of December 31, 1996, included an unaudited condensed balance sheet for New Church Ventures (identified only as "a company associated with Southern Baptist causes") as of year-end 1996, which reported net assets of $2.5 million and total assets of $192.5 million. The footnote did not disclose ALO's financial position or that approximately 81 percent of New Church Ventures' assets were notes receivable from ALO. Of course, to the extent that New Church Ventures' receivables from ALO were uncollectible due to ALO's negative net worth, New Church Ventures would not be able to meet its liabilities, which included liabilities to IRA holders by year-end 1996 that totaled $74.7 million.[8]

[7] Ibid., pp. 30–32.
[8] Ibid., pp. 31–32.

Case Questions

1. Consult Paragraphs 23–25 of PCAOB Auditing Standard No. 12. Define what is meant by *control environment*. Based on the information provided in the case, explain why the control environment is so important to effective internal control over financial reporting at an audit client like the Baptist Foundation of Arizona (BFA).

2. Consult Sections 204 and 301 of SARBOX. What is the role of the audit committee in the financial reporting process? Can you provide an example of how the audit committee might have been helpful in the BFA situation?

3. Consult Paragraph 56 of PCAOB Auditing Standard No. 12. What is meant by the term *whistleblower* within the context of the financial reporting process? Do you think that all whistleblower complaints should go directly to the audit committee? Why or why not? Do you think that a whistleblower program would have been helpful at BFA? Why or why not?

4. Consult Paragraph 5 of PCAOB Auditing Standard No. 10. Do you believe the Arthur Andersen auditors responded appropriately to the information received from BFA's former accountant, Karen Paetz? Why or why not?

5. Consult Section 401 of SARBOX. How would Section 401 apply to the BFA audit? Do you believe that Section 401 would have improved the presentation of BFA's financial statements?

Case

4.4

WorldCom: The Internal Audit Function

Synopsis

On June 25, 2002, WorldCom announced that it would be restating its financial statements for 2001 and the first quarter of 2002. Less than one month later, on July 21, 2002, WorldCom announced that it had filed for bankruptcy. It was later revealed that WorldCom had engaged in improper accounting that took two major forms: overstatement of revenue by at least $958 million and understatement of line costs, its largest category of expenses, by over $7 billion. Several executives pled guilty to charges of fraud and were sentenced to prison terms, including CFO Scott Sullivan (five years) and Controller David Myers (one year and one day). Convicted of fraud in 2005, CEO Bernie Ebbers was the first to receive his prison sentence: 25 years.

Internal Audit Department Deficiencies

The audit committee of the board of directors at WorldCom had ultimate responsibility for ensuring that the company's systems of internal controls were effective. The internal audit department periodically gathered information relating to aspects of the company's operational and financial controls and reported its findings and recommendations directly to the audit committee. Dick Thornburgh, WorldCom's bankruptcy court examiner, wrote in his second interim report released on June 9, 2003, that "the members of the Audit Committee and the internal audit department personnel appear to have taken their jobs seriously and worked to fulfill their responsibilities within certain limits."[1]

However, the bankruptcy court examiner also wrote that he found a number of deficiencies in both the internal audit department and the audit committee. Among the issues the bankruptcy court examiner noted in the internal audit department were as follows: its relationship with management, lack of budgetary resources, lack of substantive interaction with the external auditors, and its restricted access

[1] Second interim report of Dick Thornburgh, bankruptcy court examiner, June 9, 2003, p. 12.

to relevant information.[2] The bankruptcy court examiner found that WorldCom's internal audit department focused its audits primarily on the areas that were expected to yield cost savings or result in additional revenues.[3] In planning its audits, the department did not seem to conduct any quantifiable risk assessment of the weaknesses or strengths of the company's internal control system. In addition, the examiner found that the department's lack of consultation with WorldCom's external auditor, Arthur Andersen, resulted in even further audit coverage gaps.[4]

Internal Audit Department's Relationship with Management

The SEC's investigation revealed that management's influence over the activities of the internal audit department may have superseded those of the audit committee. It appeared that management was able to direct the internal audit department to work on audits not previously approved by the audit committee and away from other audits that were originally scheduled. At most, it appears that the audit committee was advised of such changes after the fact.[5]

Although the audit committee annually approved the audit plans of the internal audit department, it seemed to have had little input into the development of the scope of each audit or the disposition of any findings and/or recommendations. The audit committee also did not seem to play any role in determining the day-to-day activities of the internal audit department. Rather, the CFO appeared to provide direction over the development of the scope of the department's audit plans, the conduct of its audits, and the issuance of its conclusions and recommendations. The CFO also oversaw all personnel actions for the department, such as promotions and increases in salaries, bonuses, and stock options granted.[6]

The internal audit department distributed preliminary drafts of its internal audit reports to CFO Scott Sullivan and at times to CEO Bernie Ebbers. The internal audit department also distributed preliminary drafts of its reports to the management that was affected by a particular report. All people on the distribution list provided their input on the conclusions and recommendations made in the reports. In contrast, the audit committee did not receive any preliminary drafts of the internal audit reports.[7]

It was also found that CFO Sullivan or CEO Ebbers had assigned certain special projects to the internal audit department. Some of these projects were not audit-related, and the audit committee did not appear to have been consulted about such assignments.[8]

---

[2] Ibid., pp. 174–176.
[3] Ibid., pp. 186–187.
[4] Ibid., pp. 194–195.
[5] Ibid.
[6] Ibid., pp. 190–191.
[7] Ibid., pp. 195–197.
[8] Ibid., pp. 190–191.

Impact of Lack of Budgetary Resources

According to the 2002 global auditing information network (GAIN) peer study conducted by the Institute of Internal Auditors, WorldCom's internal audit department (at a staff of 27 by 2002) was half the size of the internal audit departments of peer telecommunications companies. The head of the internal audit department, Cynthia Cooper (a vice president), presented the results of the GAIN study to the audit committee in May 2002. She advised them that her department was understaffed as well as underpaid. The minutes reflect that she advised the committee that the average cost (including salary and benefits) of each of their internal auditors was $87,000 annually, well below the peer group average of $161,000.[9]

The budgetary resources allocated to the department seemed particularly inadequate given the international breadth and scope of the company's operations and the challenges posed by the company's various mergers and acquisitions over a relatively short period. For example, budget constraints restricted travel by internal audit staffers outside Mississippi, where most of the internal audit staff was located. Such a restriction made managing and conducting audits of company units located outside Mississippi, and particularly international audits, far more difficult.[10]

Lack of Substantive Interaction with External Auditors

Arthur Andersen's annual statement to the audit committee noted no serious internal control weaknesses found as part of its annual audit of the company's financial statements. Yet in the same year, the internal audit department identified a number of seemingly important internal control weaknesses as part of its operational audits that impacted financial systems and the reporting of revenue. It appears that no communication occurred between the internal and external auditors to ensure awareness about all of the internal control weaknesses that were discovered. In fact, after 1997, internal audit department had few substantive interactions with the company's external auditors other than at the quarterly meetings of the audit committee, where both groups made presentations.[11]

Restricted Access to Information

Support of the internal audit department was not universal throughout the company. There were allegedly many instances when management refused to answer or dodged certain questions asked by internal audit personnel. In several cases, internal audit personnel had to make repeated requests for

[9] Ibid., pp. 192–193.
[10] Ibid.
[11] Ibid., pp. 193–194.

information, and the answer to their requests were not always furnished in a timely manner.[12]

In addition, the internal audit department had limited access to the company's computerized accounting systems. Although the internal audit charter provided that internal audit had "full, free, and unrestricted access to all company functions, records, property, and personnel," few internal audit staff personnel had full systems access to the company's reporting system and the company's general ledgers.[13]

---

[12] Ibid., pp. 195–197.
[13] Ibid.

Case Questions

1. Consult Paragraph A5 (in Appendix A) of PCAOB Auditing Standard No. 5. Based on your understanding of WorldCom's internal audit department, do you believe that the department could have been helpful in the internal control process at WorldCom? Why or why not?

2. Consult Paragraph 56 of PCAOB Auditing Standard No. 12 and Sections 204 and 301 of SARBOX. Based on the case information, do you believe that WorldCom's audit committee was effective in its management of the internal audit department? Why or why not?

3. Consult Paragraphs .04–.08 of AU Section 322. Do you believe that auditors should be allowed to use the work of other professionals as evidence to support their own internal control audit opinion? Why or why not?

4. Consult Paragraphs 18–19 of PCAOB Auditing Standard No. 5. What factors must the external auditor consider before using the work of other professionals as evidence to support an internal control opinion? Please be specific.

Case 4.5

Waste Management: Top-Side Adjusting Journal Entries

Synopsis

In February 1998 Waste Management announced that it was restating its financial statements for the years 1993 through 1996. In its restatement, Waste Management said that it had materially overstated its reported pre-tax earnings by $1.43 billion. After the announcement, the company's stock dropped by more than 33 percent, and shareholders lost over $6 billion.

The SEC brought charges against the company's founder, Dean Buntrock, and five other former top officers. The charges alleged that management had made repeated changes to depreciation-related estimates to reduce expenses and had employed several improper accounting practices related to capitalization policies, also designed to reduce expenses.[1] In its final judgment, the SEC permanently barred Buntrock and three other executives from acting as officers or directors of public companies and required payment from them of $30.8 million in penalties.[2]

Top-Side Adjusting Journal Entries[3]

Top-side adjusting journal entries are typically made by upper managers at the very end of the reporting process, usually at corporate headquarters. Because these journal entries are typically not generated at the level of the business process (such as Internet sales) or at the business unit level (such as the North American

---

[1] SEC, Accounting and Auditing Enforcement Release No. 1532, March 26, 2002.

[2] SEC, Accounting and Auditing Enforcement No. 2298, August 29, 2005.

[3] SEC v. Dean L. Buntrock, Phillip B. Rooney, James E. Koenig, Thomas C. Hau, Herbert A. Getz, and Bruce D. Tobecksen, Complaint No. 02C 2180 (Judge Manning).

division), they can be used by upper managers to circumvent the internal control system and perpetrate fraud.

According to the SEC, management at Waste Management allegedly used top-side adjusting journal entries in the process of consolidating the results reported by their operating groups. Upper management allegedly employed top-side adjusting journal entries to intentionally hide the fraud from both their operating groups and the investing public.

It was not uncommon for Waste Management to use top-side adjusting entries when consolidating the results of several of its business units to prepare its annual and quarterly financial statements. Indeed, Waste Management's use of several unbudgeted and unsupported top-side adjustments in the early 1990s caused observers (including Arthur Andersen) to question whether management had employed these adjustments as tools to help "manage" their reported earnings.

Waste Management set earnings targets during an annual budget process. The company followed a top-down budgeting process whereby the CEO (Buntrock until 1996 and Rooney after Buntrock's retirement until early 1997) set goals for earnings growth, and the operating units would, in turn, determine their budgets based on the goals set at the top. The budgets were then consolidated to arrive at the budgeted consolidated earnings. At this time, the upper managers also set budgets for the anticipated top-side adjustments, which were based on the existing accounting assumptions used.

Closing the Gap[4]

As operating results were recorded by Waste Management's operating units at the end of each quarter, upper management monitored the gaps between the results and the goals. Management then made a number of different types of unbudgeted top-side adjusting entries in the financial statements in an effort to close these gaps. For example, a top-side adjustment might have been used to (1) reduce the allowance for doubtful accounts (or another reserve account); (2) extend the useful lives of trucks by two years; or (3) double the salvage values of trucks, depending on the nature and size of the budget gap.

Management did not disclose to investors the impact of the top-side adjustments on the company's earnings. In fact, management did not inform its own internal operating units about the top-side adjusting entries that were made and their resulting impact on reported net income.

As early as 1992, the company's auditor Arthur Andersen advised management against the use of top-side adjusting entries in a postaudit letter recommending accounting changes. Andersen auditors wrote that "individual decisions are not being evaluated on the true results of their operations" as a result of the extensive use of top-side adjustments. Andersen recommended that "all such corporate adjustments should be passed back to the respective" divisions. Instead

---

[4] Ibid.

of following this recommendation, top management seemed to increase the budget for the top-side adjustments from 1992 to 1997, and each year the actual adjustments made exceeded the budgeted adjustments. From the first quarter of 1992 through the first quarter of 1997, top management allegedly used unsupported top-side adjustments in 14 of the 21 quarters to achieve reported results within the range of the company's public earnings projections.

Case Questions

1. Consult Paragraphs 14–15 of PCAOB Auditing Standard No. 13. If you were auditing Waste Management, what type of documentary evidence would you require to evaluate the propriety of a top-side adjusting journal entry?

2. Consult Paragraph 14 of PCAOB Auditing Standard No. 5. Based on the case information, do you think this paragraph relates to the use of top-side adjusting journal entries at an audit client like Waste Management in any way? Why or why not?

3. Consult Paragraphs 26–27 of PCAOB Auditing Standard No. 5. Do you believe that the period-end financial reporting process should always be evaluated by auditors as a significant and material process during an audit of internal control? Why or why not?

4. Consult Paragraphs 71–72 of PCAOB Auditing Standard No. 12. Identify one specific control procedure that could be designed to prevent or detect a misstatement related to a top-side adjusting journal entry.

Internal Control Systems: Control Activity Cases

In formulating its post-Sarbanes technical audit guidance, the PCAOB has made it clear that the relevant financial statement assertions must be the focal point of the integrated audit process. Of course, if designed and operating effectively, a company's internal control system should prevent or detect fraud related to management's relevant assertions about the financial statements. As a result, it is absolutely essential for auditors to understand the relationship between a company's internal control system and the financial statement assertions.

In this spirit, the cases in this section help illustrate the explicit linkage between internal control activities and the financial statement assertions being supported using different examples of economic transaction activity.

The case readings have been developed solely as a basis for class discussion. The case readings are not intended to serve as a source of primary data or as an illustration of effective or ineffective auditing.

Case 5.1

The Fund of Funds: Valuation of Investments

Synopsis

As total assets reached $617 million in 1967, the Fund of Funds (FOF) was the most successful of the mutual funds offered by the Investor Overseas Services, Limited. In the late 1960s FOF diversified into natural resource asset investments. To do so, it formed a relationship with John King, a Denver oil, gas, and mineral investor and developer, whereby FOF would purchase oil and gas properties directly from his company, King Resources. By the 1970s FOF was forced into bankruptcy.

It was later uncovered that King Resources had dramatically overcharged FOF for the properties that it sold to FOF. FOF's bankruptcy trustee sued Arthur Andersen for failing to inform FOF that it was being defrauded by King Resources. Arthur Andersen was ultimately found liable and forced to pay around $70 million in civil damages, while John King was charged and convicted for masterminding the fraud against FOF.

Background

FOF incorporated FOF Proprietary Funds, Ltd. (FOF Prop) as an umbrella for its specialized investment accounts that were managed by outside investment advisers. Each investment adviser had a duty to act in FOF's best interests and to avoid conflicts of interest. Advisers were compensated based on the realized and unrealized (paper) appreciation of their investment portfolios.[1]

In a presentation at a meeting of the FOF board of directors in Acapulco, Mexico, on April 5, 1968, John King suggested that FOF establish a proprietary account with an initial allocation of $10 million that would be invested in a minimum of

[1] *The Fund of Funds, Limited, F.O.F. Proprietary Funds, Ltd., and IOS Growth Fund, Limited, A/K/A Transglobal Growth Fund, Limited, Plaintiffs, v. Arthur Andersen & Co., Arthur Andersen & Co. (Switzerland), and Arthur Andersen & Co., S.A., Defendants,* No. 75 Civ. 540 (CES), United States District Court for the Southern District of New York, 545 F. Supp. 1314; 1982 U.S. Dist. Lexis 9570; Fed. Sec. L. Rep. (Cch) P98,751, July 16, 1982. Available from LexisNexis Academic.

40 properties. King described the role of King Resources as follows: "that of a vendor of properties to the proprietary account, with such properties to be sold on an arms-length basis at prices no less favorable to the proprietary account than the prices charged by King to its 200-odd industrial and other purchasers." The board approved the idea, and the National Resources Fund Account (NRFA) was established.

Although no formal written agreement established the King Resources Corporation (KRC) as the investment adviser for the NRFA, FOF's clear intent was to use KRC's expertise to locate and purchase speculative natural resource investments. FOF had no means of valuing the assets proposed for investment by NRFA and did not possess the industry expertise to do so.

Independent Audit Relationships

KRC, NRFA, and FOF were all audited by the same independent auditor, Arthur Andersen. Andersen's Denver office performed the KRC audits, as well as performing substantial work on the NRFA. The partner in charge and the manager of the KRC audit held the same respective positions on the NRFA audit. Many aspects of the NRFA audit were completed by using the records of KRC, and sometimes Andersen staffers would even work on both the KRC and NRFA audits contemporaneously. Finally, Arthur Andersen also audited various third parties to which KRC sold assets in order to ultimately determine the valuations of those assets.

FOF's Natural Interest Purchases[2]

Beginning immediately after the board of directors' meeting where NRFA was established, on April 5, 1968, it began to purchase oil, gas, and mineral interests from KRC. King reported to the FOF board of directors on August 2, 1968, that $3 million of the initial authorization of $10 million was committed. For the year-end 1968 audit of FOF by Andersen, the Denver office prepared a series of comparisons of prices charged by the King group to FOF, other King affiliates, and other knowledgeable industry purchasers. The "Summary of 1968 Sales" shows the following with respect to sales to the King affiliates:

	Current Sales	Current Cost [to KRC]	Current Profit	Profit as a Percentage of Sales
Sales to IAMC	$ 9,876,271	$8,220,324	$1,655,947	16.8%
Sales to Royal	6,566,491	4,085,544	2,480,947	37.8%
Sales to IOS	11,325,386	4,307,583	7,017,803	62.0%

[2] Ibid.

In the same document, Andersen also computed the comparative profits for KRC, excluding interests sold to Royal and to IOS (which was essentially FOF). After subtracting those sales with higher markups, KRC's profits as percentages of sales on its sales to its affiliates, Royal and IAMC, were substantially smaller than the profits on its sales to FOF.

In fact, KRC's "Consolidated Sales to Industry," dated September 30, 1969, illustrated that KRC's profits on sales to FOF were 68.2 percent, as compared with average profits on all sales of nearly 36 percent. In comparing only the seven industry customers that purchased over $1 million of interests from KRC, FOF had the highest profit/sales ratio, at 68.2 percent. After FOF, the next highest profit/sales ratio earned by KRC on sales to such customers was 24.4 percent; the lowest profit/sales ratio was 5 percent.

Andersen's Knowledge of the Purchases[3]

By Andersen's account, "the earliest date when anyone employed by Andersen would have become aware of KRC's 1968 sales to FOF was in early 1969." At the same time, evidence exists that some FOF–KRC transactions were reviewed for the 1968 year-end audit in Andersen's Denver office before January 28, 1969. Andersen auditors from its Denver office also testified that they did some "information gathering" on the NRFA for the FOF Prop audit as of December 31, 1968. They also testified that they obtained documents related to the FOF audit from KRC. Andersen's auditors contended that their duty of confidentiality to KRC would prohibit it from having disclosed to FOF any relevant knowledge it may have had related to KRC's costs.

---

[3] Ibid.

Case Questions

1. Consult Paragraphs 4–8 of PCAOB Auditing Standard No. 15. Based on your understanding of audit evidence, did Arthur Andersen rely on sufficient appropriate audit evidence in auditing the valuation assertion related to FOF's natural resources assets? Why or why not?

2. Consult Paragraph 10 of PCAOB Auditing Standard No. 15. Next, consider the series of comparisons prepared by the Denver office of Arthur Andersen of prices charged by the King group to FOF, King affiliates, and other knowledgeable industry purchasers. Can you think of any additional evidence that would have strengthened the "Summary of 1968 Sales"?

3. Consult Paragraphs 24–27 of PCAOB Auditing Standard No. 14. Based on the case information presented, do you believe that the management of FOF exhibited bias in their estimates? Why or why not? Next, if they did exhibit bias, please identify two steps that you would take if you were auditing FOF.

4. Do you believe Andersen had a duty of client confidentiality to KRC that would prohibit the firm from disclosing to FOF any relevant knowledge it may have had related to KRC's costs? Why or why not?

Case 5.2

Enron: Presentation and Disclosure of Special Purpose Entities

Synopsis

In its 2000 annual report, Enron prided itself on having "metamorphosed from an asset-based pipeline and power generating company to a marketing and logistics company whose biggest assets are its well-established business approach and its innovative people."[1] Enron's strategy seemed to pay off; in 2000 it was the seventh largest company on the Fortune 500, with assets of $65 billion and sales revenues of $100 billion.[2] From 1996 to 2000 its revenues had increased by more than 750 percent, which was unprecedented in any industry.[3] Yet just a year later, in December 2001, Enron filed for bankruptcy, and billions of shareholder and retirement savings dollars were lost.

Background

Enron was created in 1985 by the merger of two gas pipeline companies: Houston Natural Gas and InterNorth. Enron's mission was to become the leading natural gas pipeline company in North America. As it adapted to changes in the natural gas industry, Enron changed its mission, expanding into natural gas trading and financing and into other markets, such as electricity and other commodity markets.

---

[1] Enron 2000 annual report, p. 7.

[2] Joseph F. Berardino, remarks to U.S. House of Representatives Committee on Financial Services, December 12, 2001.

[3] Bala G. Dharan and William R. Bufkins, "Red Flags in Enron's Reporting of Revenues and Key Financial Measures," March 2003, prepublication draft (www.ruf.rice.edu/~bala/files/dharan-bufkins_enron_red_flags_041003.pdf), p. 4.

In the process Enron also made significant changes to several of its accounting procedures. For example, Enron began establishing several special purpose entities in many aspects of its business. A special purpose entity (SPE) is an entity—partnership, corporation, trust, or joint venture—created for a limited purpose, with limited activities and a limited life. A company forms an SPE so that outside investors are assured they will be exposed only to the risk of the SPE and its particular purpose, such as building a gas pipeline, and not to the risks associated with the entire company. In addition, the SPE also protects the investment of outside investors by giving them control over its activities.

Conditions for Nonconsolidation of SPEs

A company is *not* required to consolidate the assets and liabilities of an SPE into those contained on its own balance sheet, and it may record gains and losses on transactions with an SPE if two conditions are met:

1. An owner independent of the company must own a "substantive" equity interest (at least 3 percent of the SPE's assets, and that 3 percent must remain at risk throughout the transaction).
2. The independent owner must exercise control of the SPE.

The requirement of 3 percent minimum equity owned by outside investors was created in 1990 by EITF 90–15 and formalized by FASB Statements No. 125 and No. 140. This standard represented a major departure from typical consolidation rules, which generally required an entity to be consolidated if a company owned (directly or indirectly) 50 percent or more of the entity.[4] Consolidation rules for SPEs were also controversial because a company could potentially use an SPE for fraudulent purposes, such as keeping debt or nonperforming assets off its own consolidated balance sheet.

JEDI and Chewco

In 1993 Enron and the California Public Employees Retirement System (CalPERS) formed an SPE: a $500 million 50–50 partnership they called Joint Energy Development Investments Limited (JEDI).[5] Enron was not required to consolidate the partnership within Enron's financial statements because it did not own more than 50 percent of the venture.

In 1997 Enron offered to buy out CalPERS's interest in JEDI. To maintain JEDI as an unconsolidated entity, Enron needed to identify a new limited partner.

---

[4] Bala G. Dharan, "Enron's Accounting Issues—What Can We Learn to Prevent Future Enrons," Prepared Testimony Presented to the U.S. House Energy and Commerce Committee's Hearings on Enron Accounting, February 6, 2002, pp. 11–12.

[5] JEDI was also a sly nod to the *Star Wars* films; CFO Andy Fastow, who devised the partnership, was a *Star Wars* fan.

Enron's CFO Andrew Fastow proposed that Enron form another SPE named Chewco Investments (after *Star Wars* character Chewbacca), the bulk of whose equity investment would come from third-party investors, to buy out CalPERS's JEDI interest.[6]

Chewco's Capital Structure

Unsuccessful in obtaining outside equity, Enron created a capital structure for Chewco that had three elements:

1. A $240 million unsecured subordinated loan to Chewco from Barclays Bank (Enron would guarantee the loan).
2. A $132 million advance from JEDI to Chewco under a revolving credit agreement.
3. $11.5 million in equity (representing approximately 3 percent of total capital) from Chewco's general and limited partners.[7]

Chewco's Partners

Michael Kopper, an Enron employee who reported to CFO Fastow, was the general partner of Chewco. The limited partner of Chewco was an entity called Big River Funding LLC, whose sole member was an entity named Little River Funding LLC. Kopper had invested $115,000 in Big River and $10,000 in Little River but transferred these investments to William Dodson (who allegedly may have been Kopper's domestic partner). As such, Kopper technically had no ownership interest in Chewco's limited partner. The remaining $11.4 million was provided by Barclays Bank in the form of equity loans to Big River and Little River.

Barclays required Big River and Little River to establish cash reserve accounts of $6.6 million and required that the reserve accounts be fully pledged to secure repayment of the $11.4 million. JEDI, of which Enron still owned 50 percent, made a special $16.6 million distribution to Chewco, out of which $6.6 million could be used to fund the cash reserve accounts.[8] (See Figure 5.2.1 for a visual depiction of the Chewco transaction.)

---

[6] William C. Powers, Jr., Raymond S. Troubh, Herbert S. Winokur, Jr, *Report of Investigation by the Special Investigative Committee of the Board of Directors of Enron Corp.*, February 1, 2002, p. 43.

[7] William C. Powers, Jr., Raymond S. Troubh, Herbert S. Winokur, Jr, *Report of Investigation by the Special Investigative Committee of the Board of Directors of Enron Corp.*, February 1, 2002, p. 49.

[8] William C. Powers, Jr., Raymond S. Troubh, Herbert S. Winokur, Jr, *Report of Investigation by the Special Investigative Committee of the Board of Directors of Enron Corp.*, February 1, 2002, pp. 48–51.

FIGURE 5.2.1 Chewco Transaction

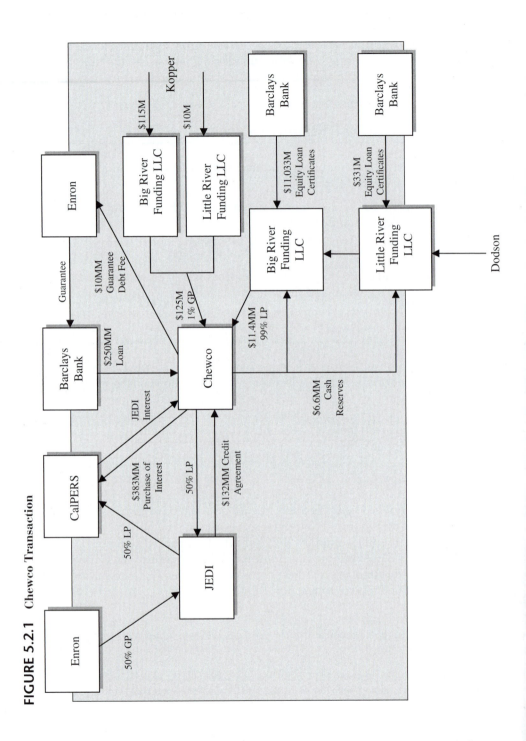

Andersen's Audit of the Chewco Transaction

Enron's auditor Arthur Andersen requested that Enron provide all of the documentation in its possession relating to the Chewco transaction. In its audit of the transaction, Andersen allegedly reviewed the following:[9]

- The minutes of Enron's executive committee of the board of directors approving the transaction.
- The $132 million loan agreement between JEDI and Chewco.
- Enron's guarantee agreement of a $240 million loan from Barclays to Chewco.
- An amended JEDI partnership agreement.
- A representation letter from Enron and a representation letter from JEDI, each of which stated that the related party transactions had been disclosed, and all financial records and related data had been made available to Andersen.

Andersen received confirmation regarding the loan agreement from a Chewco representative. Andersen also requested that Enron provide documents relating to Chewco's formation and structure. However, Enron allegedly told Andersen that it did not have these documents and could not obtain them because Chewco was a third party with its own legal counsel and ownership independent of Enron.[10] Andersen allegedly accepted this explanation and relied only on the evidence it had been given.

When the Chewco transaction was reviewed closely in late October and early November 2001, Enron and Andersen concluded that Chewco was an SPE without sufficient outside equity and that it should have been consolidated into Enron's financial statements. The retroactive consolidation of Chewco and the investment partnership in which Chewco was a limited partner decreased Enron's reported net income by $28 million (out of $105 million total) in 1997, by $133 million (out of $703 million total) in 1998, by $153 million (out of $893 million total) in 1999, and by $91 million (out of $979 million total) in 2000. It also increased Enron's reported debt by $711 million in 1997, by $561 million in 1998, by $685 million in 1999, and by $628 million in 2000.[11]

---

[9] Thomas H. Bauer, Prepared Witness Testimony at Subcommittee on Oversight and Investigations related to "Financial Collapse of Enron Corp," February 7, 2002.

[10] Ibid.

[11] William C. Powers, Jr., Raymond S. Troubh, Herbert S. Winokur, Jr, *Report of Investigation by the Special Investigative Committee of the Board of Directors of Enron Corp.*, February 1, 2002, p. 42.

Case Questions

1. Based on your understanding of the information presented in the case, how did Enron's Chewco SPE fail to meet the outside equity requirement for non-consolidation? Did Enron meet the control requirement for nonconsolidation?

2. Consult Paragraphs 4–8 of PCAOB Auditing Standard No. 15. Based on your understanding of audit evidence, did Arthur Andersen rely on sufficient appropriate audit evidence in its audit of the Chewco transaction? Why or why not?

3. Consult Section 401 of SARBOX. How would Section 401 apply to the Enron audit? Do you think Section 401 would have improved the presentation of Enron's financial statements? Why or why not?

4. Consult Paragraphs 28–30 of PCAOB Auditing Standard No. 5. Identify one or more relevant financial statement assertions about at least one financial statement account related to the Chewco transaction. Provide adequate support for your answer.

Case 5.3

Sunbeam: Completeness of the Restructuring Reserve

Synopsis

In April 1996 Sunbeam named Albert J. Dunlap as its CEO and chair. For-merly with Scott Paper Co., Dunlap was known as a turnaround specialist and was nicknamed "Chainsaw Al" because of the cost-cutting measures he typically employed. Almost immediately, Dunlap began replacing nearly all of the upper management team and led the company into an aggressive corporate restructuring that included the elimination of half of its 12,000 employees and the elimination of 87 percent of Sunbeam's products.

Unfortunately, in May 1998 Sunbeam disappointed investors with its announcement that it had earned a worse-than-expected loss of $44.6 million in the first quarter of 1998.[1] CEO and Chair Dunlap was fired in June 1998. In October 1998 Sunbeam announced that it would need to restate its financial statements for 1996, 1997, and 1998.[2]

Background

In its 1996 financial results, Sunbeam reported restructuring costs that did not comply with GAAP because they included amounts for items that benefited future activities.[3] These costs lowered Sunbeam's reported 1996 net income. One possible motivation for executives to report higher costs in a given year is to make a company's net income for the following year appear better by compari-son. Executives have also been known to report higher reserve levels in a given year and then use these reserves to increase income in a year that follows.[4]

---

[1] Robert Frank and Joann S. Lublin. "Dunlap's Ax Falls—6,000 Times—at Sunbeam," *The Wall Street Journal,* November 13, 1996, p. B1.

[2] GAO-03-138, Appendix XVII "Sunbeam Corporation," p. 201.

[3] SEC Accounting and Auditing Enforcement Release No. 1706, January 27, 2003.

[4] Ibid.

Sunbeam's Reported Restructuring Charge in 1996

Associated with its operational restructuring, Sunbeam's 1996 results included a pretax charge to earnings of $337.6 million, which was allocated as follows:[5]

Restructuring, impairment, and other costs	$154.9 million
Cost of goods sold	$ 92.3 million
Selling, general, and administrative (SG&A)	$ 42.5 million
Estimated loss from discontinued operations	$ 47.9 million
Total	$337.6 million

Restructuring, Impairment, and Other Costs

The "restructuring, impairment, and other costs" category included the following cash items: severance and other employee costs ($43.0 million), lease obligations and other exit costs associated with facility closures ($12.6 million), back office outsourcing start-up costs, and other costs related to the implementation of the restructuring and growth plan ($7.5 million). Noncash items in this category ($91.8 million) were related to asset write-downs for disposals of excess facilities and equipment, and noncore product lines; write-offs of redundant computer systems from the administrative back office consolidations and outsourcing initiatives; and intangible, packaging, and other asset write-downs related to exited product lines and SKU reductions.

Importantly, this amount also included approximately $18.7 million of items that benefited future activities, such as costs of redesigning product packaging, costs of relocating employees and equipment, and certain consulting fees.[6] Inclusion of these items was not allowed under GAAP because these costs related to activities that benefited future periods.

Cost of Goods Sold, SG&A, and Estimated Loss from Discontinued Operations

As part of its operational restructuring, Sunbeam sold the inventory of its eliminated products to liquidators at a substantial discount. As such, the cost of goods sold portion of the restructuring charge related principally to inventory write-downs and costs of inventory liquidation programs.

The SG&A portion of the restructuring charge related principally to increases in environmental, litigation, and other reserves. The litigation reserve was created for a lawsuit alleging Sunbeam's potential obligation to cover a portion of the cleanup costs for a hazardous waste site. To establish a litigation reserve

[5] 1996 10K filing to SEC. Also see 1997 10K SEC filing, Note 8 ("Restructuring, Impairment, and Other Costs").

[6] SEC Accounting and Auditing Enforcement Release No. 1706, January 27, 2003.

under GAAP, management must determine that the reserved amount reflects a loss that is probable and able to be reasonably estimated. However, the SEC found that the amount of Sunbeam's reserve was improbable to be incurred.[7] Finally, the estimated loss from the discontinued operations portion of the restructuring reserve related to the divestiture of the company's furniture business.[8]

Using Excess Reserves to Offset Current Expenses

Initially, during the first quarter of 1997, Sunbeam used $4.3 million of these restructuring reserves to offset against costs incurred in that period. Essentially this reserve was set up as a "cookie jar" in 1996 that allowed Sunbeam's 1997 income to improve by approximately 13 percent. Sunbeam failed to disclose this "infrequent item" in its quarterly filing. In the second quarter of 1997, Sunbeam offset $8.2 million in second-quarter costs against the restructuring and other reserves created at year-end 1996 without making the appropriate disclosures. It made similar offsets of current period expenses in the third and fourth quarters of 1997: $2.9 million and $1.5 million, respectively.[9]

Restatement of Restructuring Charge

In November 1998 Sunbeam ultimately restated the pretax restructuring charge from $337.6 million to $239.2 million, which was allocated as follows:[10]

Restructuring, impairment, and other costs	$110.1 million
Cost of goods sold	$ 60.8 million
Selling, general, and administrative (SG&A)	$ 10.1 million
Estimated loss from discontinued operations	$ 58.2 million
Total	$239.2 million

Restructuring, Impairment, and Other Costs

Restructuring, impairment, and other costs were restated as follows: severance and other employee costs of $24.7 million; lease obligations and other exit costs associated with facility closures of $16.7 million. Noncash items totaled $68.7 million—related to asset write-downs for disposals of excess facilities, and equipment and noncore product lines; write-offs of redundant computer

---

[7] Ibid.

[8] 1996 10K filed with the SEC.

[9] SEC Accounting and Auditing Enforcement Release No. 1393, May 15, 2001.

[10] Amended 1997 10K filed with the SEC.

systems from the administrative back office consolidations and outsourcing initiatives; and intangible, packaging, and other asset write-downs related to exited product lines and SKU reductions.[11]

Cost of Goods Sold, SG&A, and Estimated Loss from Discontinued Operations

Contributing to the company's need to restate its cost of goods sold expense related to restructuring was the fact that in estimating its year-end inventory of household products, management failed to distinguish excess and obsolete inventory from inventory that was part of its continuing product lines. Thus the value of Sunbeam's inventory from its continuing household product lines had been understated by $2.1 million on its balance sheet. In addition, its restatement of its SG&A included a revision of a $12 million litigation reserve that initially was improperly overstated by at least $6 million.[12]

[11] Amended 1997 10K filed with the SEC.
[12] SEC Accounting and Auditing Enforcement Release No. 1393, May 15, 2001.

Case Questions

1. Consult Paragraphs 13–21 of PCAOB Auditing Standard No. 15. What is meant by a *restructuring reserve?* As an auditor, what type of evidence would you want to examine to determine whether a company was inappropriately accounting for its restructuring reserve?

2. Consult Paragraphs 29 and 32 of PCAOB Auditing Standard No. 5. As an auditor, do you believe that the different components of the restructuring reserve might be subject to significantly differing levels of inherent risk? Why or why not?

3. Consult Paragraphs 28–30 of PCAOB Auditing Standard No. 5. Identify at least one relevant financial statement assertion related to the restructuring reserve account. Why is it relevant?

4. This case describes a situation where a company overstated its recorded expenses in 1996 (as compared to understating recorded expenses). Why would a company choose to overstate its expenses and understate its net income?

Case 5.4

Qwest: Occurrence of Revenue

Synopsis

When Joseph Nacchio became Qwest's CEO in January 1997, its existing strategy began to shift from just building a nationwide fiber-optic network toward increased communications services as well. By the time it released earnings in 1998, Nacchio proclaimed Qwest's successful transition from a network construction company to a communications services provider. "We successfully transitioned Qwest . . . into a leading Internet protocol-based multimedia company focused on the convergence of data, video, and voice services."[1]

During 1999 and 2000, Qwest consistently met its aggressive revenue targets and became a darling to its investors. Yet, when the company announced its intention to restate revenues in August 2002, its stock price plunged to a low of $1.11 per share in August 2002, from a high of $55 per share in July 2000.[2] Civil and criminal charges related to fraudulent activitity were brought against several Qwest executives, including CEO Joseph Nacchio. Nacchio was convicted on 19 counts of illegal insider trading, and was sentenced to six years in prison in July 2007. He was also ordered to pay a $19 million fine and forfeit $52 million that he gained in illegal stock sales.[3]

---

[1] SEC v. Joseph P. Nacchio, Robert S. Woodruff, Robin R. Szeliga, Afshin Mohebbi, Gregory M. Casey, James J. Kozlowski, Frank T. Noyes, Defendants, Civil Action No. 05-MK-480 (OES), pp. 11–14.

[2] SEC v. Qwest, pp. 1–2.

[3] Dionne Searcey, "Qwest Ex-Chief Gets 6 Years in Prison for Insider Trading," The Wall Street Journal, July 28, 2007, p. A3.

Background

An IRU is an irrevocable right to use specific fiber-optic cable or fiber capacity for a specified period. Qwest treated IRU sales as sales-type leases, which allow a seller to treat a lease transaction as a sale of an asset with complete, up-front revenue recognition. According to GAAP, this type of up-front revenue recognition required (1) completion of the earnings process; (2) that the assets sold remain fixed and unchanged; (3) full transfer of ownership, with no continuing involvement by the seller; and (4) an assessment of fair market value of the revenue components. In addition, as part of the completion of the earnings process, the assets being sold had to be explicitly and specifically identified.

Portability

Qwest generally allowed customers of IRUs the ability to *port*, or exchange, IRUs purchased for other IRUs. By mid-2001 Qwest had ported at least 10 percent of assets sold as IRUs. Portability was not uncommon in the telecommunications industry because companies needed the flexibility to change their networks as demand changed.[4]

However, Qwest salespeople often granted customers the right to port through secret side agreements or verbal assurances—allegedly due to the fact that the practice of porting jeopardized Qwest's ability to recognize revenue on IRUs up front. For example, in the fourth quarter 2000 Qwest sold to Cable & Wireless $109 million of capacity in the United States (and recognized $108 million in up-front revenue) by providing a secret side agreement, which guaranteed that Cable & Wireless could exchange the specific capacity it purchased at a later date.[5]

As another example, in the first quarter of 2001 Qwest sold IRU capacity to Global Crossing and recognized $102 million of up-front revenue after it gave secret verbal assurances to Global Crossing that Qwest would agree to exchange the capacity when the IRU capacity that Global Crossing actually wanted became available.[6]

Ownership Transfer

Qwest also allegedly had a significant continuing involvement with all IRUs sold in the form of ongoing administrative, operating, and maintenance activities. Although Qwest's IRU sales agreements generally provided for title transfer at the end of the lease terms, conditions also allegedly existed requiring that in reality the title remain with Qwest.[7] Interestingly, there was no statutory title

[4] *SEC v. Qwest*, p. 20.

[5] *SEC v. Qwest*, pp. 26–27.

[6] Ibid.

[7] *SEC v. Qwest*, pp. 22–23.

transfer system for IRUs that is comparable to what exists for real property. In addition, some of Qwest's "right of way" agreements on the underlying IRUs actually expired prior to the end of the IRU terms. Further, some of the underlying IRU agreements (concerning IRUs that Qwest purchased from a third party and then resold) did not allow Qwest to sublease its "rights of way" or did not provide title to Qwest. Thus Qwest could not legally provide those rights to a third party.[8]

The SEC found evidence that in some IRU contracts, Qwest specifically stated that the purchaser did not receive any ownership interest in the fiber. Similarly, there was also evidence that in many contracts Qwest prohibited purchasers from assigning, selling, or transferring the fiber-optic capacity without Qwest's prior written consent. For example, on March 31, 2000, Qwest entered into a $9.6 million IRU transaction with Cable & Wireless in which Qwest included a clause preventing assignment, sale, or transfer without Qwest's consent.[9]

Other Characteristics That Failed to Comply with GAAP

Qwest's up-front revenue recognition of IRUs was also premature because Qwest routinely neglected to specify the assets it was selling. For example, in the first quarter ended March 31, 2001, Qwest sold $105 million of fiber-optic capacity to Global Crossing and recognized approximately $102 million in revenue on the sale. This was done despite the fact that the majority of the capacity was not specified in the contract by the end of the quarter. Rather, the contract exhibit intended to list the assets sold simply stated "to be identified." Further, Global Crossing and Qwest did not identify the geographic termination points of some of the capacity purchased by Qwest until June 2001—three months after Qwest recognized the revenue on the sale transaction.[10] In addition, to circumvent problems on its network or to optimize the network's efficiency, Qwest often moved IRUs previously sold, without customer consent, to different wavelengths and different routes as required. This process was known as *grooming*. During the third and fourth quarters of 2001, Qwest senior management allegedly knew of numerous IRUs that had been rerouted on different fibers. Qwest personnel allegedly informed senior management that the IRUs could not be restored to their original routes and advised senior management to reverse the revenue recognized from the IRU sales. Qwest senior management, however, allegedly rejected the employees' recommendations. From the fourth quarter of 2001 through early 2002, Qwest continued to reroute IRU fibers as necessary.[11]

---

[8] *SEC v. Qwest*, p. 22.

[9] Ibid.

[10] *SEC v. Qwest*, p. 28.

[11] *SEC v. Qwest*, p. 21.

Independent Auditor Arthur Andersen and the SEC

The SEC brought charges against Mark Iwan, the global managing partner at Arthur Andersen—the outside auditor for Qwest from 1999 to 2002—alleging that Iwan "unreasonably relied on management's false representations that certain revenue recognition criteria for immediate revenue recognition on IRUs were met." On account of these charges and others, the SEC ordered that Iwan be denied the privilege of appearing or practicing before the SEC as an accountant for a minimum of five years.

Specifically, the SEC found that Iwan learned that Qwest's porting of capacity had risen to approximately 10 percent of the capacity sold by mid-2001. Although Iwan required Qwest to stop the practice of porting, he allegedly did not go back and ensure that the prior revenue recognition was in conformity with GAAP. Rather, Iwan exclusively relied on management's representations that "Qwest had made no commitments to allow its customers to port capacity, that it was never Qwest's intention to allow customers to port capacity, and that Qwest would not honor any future request to port capacity."[12]

The SEC also found that Iwan relied on representations from Qwest's management and legal counsel that title did actually transfer on IRUs. In fact, Iwan allegedly knew by early 2000 that Qwest senior tax personnel believed there were "significant uncertainties as to whether title transfer would occur," and thus Qwest would treat IRUs as operating leases for tax purposes. Surprisingly, Iwan failed to reconcile Qwest's position on title transfer for IRUs for income tax reporting purposes with its different position for financial reporting purposes under GAAP.[13]

In 2001 Iwan required Qwest to obtain an outside legal opinion that Qwest had the ability to transfer title to the IRUs it sold over the past three years. Qwest provided to Iwan an abridged summary of the legal opinion that contained significant assumptions, qualifications, ambiguities, and limitations that were critical to evaluating whether Qwest met the ownership transfer requirements. Yet Iwan continued to rely on the representations of management and legal counsel in this regard.[14]

[12] A.A.E.R. No. 2220, pp. 3–4.
[13] Ibid.
[14] Ibid.

Case Questions

1. Describe specifically why the up-front revenue recognition practice for sales of IRUs by Qwest was not appropriate under Generally Accepted Accounting Principles (GAAP).
2. Consult Paragraphs 4–6 of PCAOB Auditing Standard No. 15. Based on your understanding of audit evidence, did Arthur Andersen rely on sufficient appropriate audit evidence in its audit of Qwest's up-front revenue recognition processes? Why or why not?

3. Consult Paragraphs 28–30 of PCAOB Auditing Standard No. 5. Identify one relevant financial statement assertion related to revenue recognized for IRU sales by Qwest. Why is it relevant?

4. Consult Paragraphs 39–41 and Paragraph A5 (in Appendix A) of PCAOB Auditing Standard No. 5. For the assertion identified in Question 3, identify a specific internal control activity that would help prevent or detect a misstatement related to the practice of up-front revenue recognition of IRUs by Qwest.

5.5

The Baptist Foundation of Arizona: Presentation and Disclosure of Related Parties

Synopsis

The Baptist Foundation of Arizona (BFA) was organized as an Arizona non-profit organization primarily to help provide financial support for various Southern Baptist causes. Under William Crotts's leadership, the foundation engaged in a major strategic shift in its operations. BFA began to invest heavily in the Arizona real estate market and also accelerated its efforts to sell investment agreements and mortgage-backed securities to church members.

Two of BFA's most significant affiliates were ALO and New Church Ventures. It was later revealed that BFA had set up these affiliates to facilitate the sale of its real estate investments at prices significantly above fair market value. In so doing, BFA's management perpetrated a fraudulent scheme that cost at least 13,000 investors more than $590 million. In fact, Arizona Attorney General Janet Napolitano called the BFA collapse the largest bankruptcy of a religious nonprofit in the history of the United States.[1]

Background

ALO and New Church Ventures had no employees of their own, and both organizations paid BFA substantial management fees to provide accounting, marketing, and administrative services. As a result, both ALO and New Church Ventures

[1] Terry Greene Sterling, "Arthur Andersen and the Baptists," *Salon.com,* February 7, 2002.

owed BFA significant amounts by the end of 1995. Overall BFA, New Church Ventures, and ALO had a combined negative net worth of $83.2 million at year-end 1995, $102.3 million at year-end 1996, and $124.0 million at year-end 1997.[2]

Related Parties Disclosure (1991–1994)

In addition to its affiliates, BFA's related parties included its subsidiaries, BFA senior management, and their immediate families, as well as any former or current members of the board of directors. Yet except for information provided about New Church Ventures in its 1994 financial statements, the transactions and balances due from the following individuals and companies were *not* disclosed as related parties in the financial statements for the years 1991 through 1994:

• Dwain Hoover, BFA board member.
• Harold Friend, former BFA board member.
• Jalma Hunsinger, owner of ALO, former BFA board member and New Church Ventures board member.
• ALO and its subsidiaries and affiliates.
• New Church Ventures and its subsidiaries and affiliates.[3]

Related Parties Disclosure (1995)

In the footnotes to BFA's 1995 financial statements, rather than using their names, BFA described its related parties according to their titles or roles in the business. This practice made it far more difficult and time-consuming for users to identify the true related parties. For example, BFA disclosed its related parties as follows: "Director A [Dwain Hoover] and his companies"; "Benefactor A [Harold Friend] and his companies"; and "Benefactor B [Jalma Hunsinger] and his companies." ALO was a Benefactor B company, and New Church Ventures was "a company associated with Southern Baptist causes."[4]

Related Party Pseudonyms

• Director A = Dwain Hoover.
• Benefactor A = Harold Friend.
• Benefactor B = Jalma Hunsinger.
• ALO = a Benefactor B company.
• New Church Ventures = a company associated with Southern Baptist causes.

[2] Notice of Public Hearing and Complaint No. 98.230-ACY, Before the Arizona State Board of Accountancy, pp. 3–4.

[3] Notice of Public Hearing and Complaint No. 98.230-ACY, Before the Arizona State Board of Accountancy, pp. 16–17.

[4] Notice of Public Hearing and Complaint No. 98.230-ACY, Before the Arizona State Board of Accountancy, p. 21.

BFA disclosed in Footnote 13 of its 1995 financial statements, titled "Related Parties," that "a substantial portion of BFA's transactions involve individuals or companies associated with Southern Baptist causes."[5] In Footnote 13 it described "some of the more significant transactions involving related parties," including notes receivable from "Director A, Benefactor A, and Benefactor B or their companies" totaling $8,825,063, $2,400,000, and $53,797,827 (notes owed from ALO). Footnote 13 did not include an additional $37,400,000 in notes receivable owed to BFA from New Church Ventures, which was discussed in Footnote 3 titled "Notes Receivable."[6]

The footnotes to the 1995 financial statements did not disclose the material nature of the total notes receivable owed to BFA from related parties ALO and New Church Ventures, which accounted for 63 percent of BFA's total notes receivable—or 30 percent of BFA's total assets and more than 10 times as much as BFA's total net assets. This substantial concentration of credit given to ALO and New Church Ventures was also not disclosed in Footnote 2 in a subsection titled "Concentration of Credit Risk," which stated, "Concentration of credit risk with respect to notes receivable are limited due to the fact that BFA requires notes receivable to be adequately collateralized."[7]

Related Parties Disclosure (1996–1997)[8]

In connection with its 1996 audit of BFA, Arthur Andersen commented in a memorandum on internal control structure on BFA's lack of review, analysis, and proper documentation of related party transactions.

Andersen also criticized the fact that the collateral on related party notes receivable was not adequately monitored. It noted that "certain of the notes receivable from individuals and companies affiliated with Southern Baptist causes had outstanding balances in excess of the current value of the underlying collateral." Yet Arthur Andersen did not require BFA to take a reserve or write-down on its notes receivable. Rather, in BFA's 1996 financial statements, a footnote merely stated that "certain of the notes have outstanding balances that may be in excess of underlying collateral."

Again, for year-end 1997 Arthur Andersen assessed BFA's internal controls and criticized BFA for lack of review, analysis, and proper documentation of related party transactions and for failing to adequately monitor collateral on related party notes receivable. The criticisms stated in the 1997 internal control

---

[5] Ibid.

[6] Notice of Public Hearing and Complaint No. 98.230-ACY, Before the Arizona State Board of Accountancy, pp. 20–22.

[7] Notice of Public Hearing and Complaint No. 98.230-ACY, Before the Arizona State Board of Accountancy, pp. 22–23.

[8] Notice of Public Hearing and Complaint No. 98.230-ACY, Before the Arizona State Board of Accountancy, pp. 40–41.

memorandum were practically identical to those voiced by Andersen in 1996. In fact, in the 1997 memorandum Arthur Andersen noted that its 1996 audit recommendations regarding related parties had not been fully implemented and encouraged management to do so.

The 1997 memorandum repeated, almost verbatim, Arthur Andersen's observation "that certain of the notes receivable from individuals and companies affiliated with Southern Baptist causes had outstanding balances, which appeared to be in excess of the current value of the underlying collateral."

As it had in 1996, Arthur Andersen issued an unqualified opinion on BFA's 1997 financial statements, without requiring adequate disclosures regarding the concentration of credit risk with related parties and the nature of the relationships with ALO and New Church Ventures. The footnote disclosures regarding the amounts due from related parties also appeared to be inadequate and misleading to financial statement users.

Case Questions

1. Consult Paragraphs .04–.06 of AU Section 334. Explain why gains recorded on transactions with related parties would have greater inherent risk of being overstated in the financial statements.

2. Consult Paragraphs 23–25 of PCAOB Auditing Standard No. 12. Define what is meant by a company's *control environment*. Comment on the impact that BFA's related party disclosure practices would have on an auditor's assessment of BFA's control environment.

3. Consult Paragraphs 28–30 of PCAOB Auditing Standard No. 5. What is the most relevant financial statement assertion(s) about the related party transaction activity at BFA? Why? Please provide support for your answer.

4. Consult Paragraphs 39–41 and Paragraph A5 (in Appendix A) of PCAOB Auditing Standard No. 5. For the assertion identified in Question 3, identify a specific internal control activity that would help prevent or detect a misstatement connected to the related party transaction activity at BFA.

5.6

Waste Management: Valuation of Fixed Assets

Synopsis

In February 1998 Waste Management announced that it was restating its financial statements for 1993 through 1996. In its restatement, Waste Management said that it had materially overstated its reported pretax earnings by $1.43 billion. After the announcement, the company's stock dropped by more than 33 percent, and shareholders lost over $6 billion.

The SEC brought charges against the company's founder, Dean Buntrock, and other former top officers. The charges alleged that management had made repeated changes to depreciation-related estimates to reduce expenses and had employed several improper accounting practices related to capitalization policies, also designed to reduce expenses.[1] In its final judgment, the SEC permanently barred Buntrock and three other executives from acting as officers or directors of public companies and required payment from them of $30.8 million in penalties.[2]

Upper Management Turnover

In the summer of 1996 Dean Buntrock, who founded Waste Management in 1968, retired as CEO, but he continued to serve as chair of the board of directors. Buntrock was initially replaced as CEO by Phillip Rooney, who had started working at Waste Management in 1969. By early 1997 Rooney resigned as director and CEO because of mounting shareholder discontent.

After a new five-month search, Waste Management chose Ronald LeMay, the president and COO of Sprint, to assume its post of chair and CEO. Surprisingly, just three months into his new role, LeMay quit to return to his former job at Sprint.

[1] SEC, Accounting and Auditing Enforcement Release No. 1532, March 26, 2002.
[2] SEC, Accounting and Auditing Enforcement Release No. 2298, August 29, 2005.

In addition, several other key executives who, unlike LeMay, had worked for Waste Management for several years—including CFO James Koenig, Corporate Controller Thomas Hau, and Vice President of Finance Bruce Tobecksen—also resigned by the end of 1997.

Alleged Fraudulent Activities

In February 1998 Waste Management announced that it was restating its financial statements for 1993 through 1996. Although shareholders lost billions of dollars, management had already collected salaries and bonuses based on the inflated earnings and the resulting stock options. The SEC brought charges against founder Buntrock and five other former top officers on charges of fraud. The SEC alleged that top management had made several top-side adjustments in the process of consolidating the results reported by each of the operating groups and intentionally hid these adjustments from the operating groups themselves. These entries were routinely posted at the corporate offices and frequently lacked adequate supporting documentation.

In addition, the SEC charged that upper management had employed several other improper accounting practices designed to reduce expenses and artificially inflate earnings.[3] Specifically, to help conceal the intentional understatement of expenses, top management allegedly used a practice known as *netting*, whereby one-time gains realized on the sale or exchange of assets were used to eliminate unrelated current period operating expenses, as well as accounting misstatements that had accumulated from prior periods. It was also alleged that management made use of *geography* entries, which involved moving millions of dollars to different line items on the income statement. Essentially, these entries made it harder for auditors to compare operating results over time, a key audit procedure used by Arthur Andersen. Finally, top management allegedly made or authorized several false and misleading disclosures in financial statements.[4] The company's auditor had proposed a series of action steps in early 1994 to help adjust the improper accounting. However, rather than following these steps, top management at Waste Management allegedly continued to manipulate results in 1994, 1995, and 1996.

Senior Executives Charged with Fraudulent Activity

A complete profile of the senior executives accused of fraud by the SEC is provided in Table 5.6.1. Top management profited from the fraudulent accounting in at least two ways. First, bonuses were based on the fraudulently inflated net income amounts. And stock options increased in value as the share price increased based on the news of inflated net income amounts. In total, the SEC brought charges of fraud against six former top executives and calculated their ill-gotten gains, based on their bonuses, retirement benefits, trading, and charitable giving alone.

---

[3] *SEC v. Dean L. Buntrock, Phillip B. Rooney, James E. Koenig, Thomas C. Hau, Herbert A. Getz, and Bruce D. Tobecksen,* Complaint No. 02C 2180 (Judge Manning).

[4] Ibid.

TABLE 5.6.1 Ill-Gotten Gains Alleged by SEC

Executive	Title	Profile	Alleged Ill-Gotten Gains
Dean Buntrock	Founder, chair of the board of directors, and CEO.	Founded Waste Management in 1968. In June 1996 he retired as CEO but continued to serve as chairman of the board of directors. Also served as CEO on an interim basis from February 1997 until July 1997 and continued to serve on the board until his resignation on December 31, 1997.	$16,917,761
Phillip Rooney	President, COO, director, and CEO.	Started working at Waste Management in March 1969 and first became an officer in 1971. Became chairman of Waste Management's largest subsidiary, Waste Management of North America, in October 1993. In June 1996 Rooney replaced Buntrock as CEO of the company. In February 1997 he resigned as director and CEO.	$ 9,286,124
James Koenig	Executive vice president and CFO of Waste Management.	Began employment with the company in July 1977. Like every CFO who preceded him, Koenig worked as an auditor at Arthur Andersen. In January 1997 Koenig was fired from the CFO position because of shareholder discontent, but he continued to have responsibility for financial, accounting, and reporting matters.	$ 951,005

(*Continued*)

TABLE 5.6.1 *(Continued)*

Executive	Title	Profile	Alleged Ill-Gotten Gains
Thomas Hau	Vice president, corporate controller, and CAO.	Served as vice president, corporate controller, and CAO from September 1990 to October 1997. Remained vice president until his retirement on April 3, 1998. Like every CAO that preceded him, Hau worked as an auditor at Arthur Andersen, where he was a partner for 30 years. While at AA, Hau was the partner in charge of the Waste Management audit from 1976 to 1983, and later he became head of the AA audit division that handled the Waste Management account. Hau was again slotted to become engagement partner for the Waste Management audit in 1990, but he resigned from AA after Buntrock invited him to join Waste Management.	$ 640,100
Herbert Getz	Senior vice president, general counsel, and secretary.	Began employment with the company in 1983; retired from the company in late 1998. Prior to coming to Waste Management, Getz was a lawyer at the firm that had served as outside counsel to Waste Management and its officers since 1968.	$ 472,500
Bruce Tobecksen	Vice president of finance.	Vice president of finance until December 1997, when he was asked to leave by the new CFO of Waste Management. Prior to holding that position, from 1987 to February 1993, Tobecksen was CFO of Chemical Waste Management, a subsidiary of Waste Management. Before joining Waste Management in 1979, Tobecksen worked as an audit manager at AA, and during a portion of that time, he worked on the Waste Management audit.	$ 403,779

Case Questions

1. Consult Paragraphs 65–69 of PCAOB Auditing Standard No. 12. Based on your understanding of fraud risk assessment, what three conditions are likely to be present when a fraud occurs (i.e., the fraud triangle)? Based on the information provided in the case, which of these three conditions was most prevalent at Waste Management, and why?

2. Consult Paragraphs 26–27 of PCAOB Auditing Standard No. 5 and Paragraph 41 of PCAOB Auditing Standard No. 13. Do you believe that the period-end financial reporting process deserves special attention from auditors? Why or why not?

3. Consult Sections 204 and 301 of SARBOX. What is the role of the audit committee in the financial reporting process? Do you believe that an audit committee can be effective in providing oversight of the management team at Waste Management?

4. Consult Sections 302 and 305 and Title IX of SARBOX. Do you believe that these provisions will help deter fraudulent financial reporting by a top management group such as that of Waste Management? Why or why not?

Case 5.7

Qwest: Occurrence of Revenue

Synopsis

When Joseph Nacchio became Qwest's CEO in January 1997, the company's existing strategy began to shift from building only a nationwide fiber-optic network to include increasing communications services. By the time it released earnings in 1998, Nacchio proclaimed Qwest's successful transition from a network construction company to a communications services provider. "We successfully transitioned Qwest . . . into a leading Internet protocol-based multimedia company focused on the convergence of data, video, and voice services."[1]

During 1999 and 2000, Qwest consistently met its aggressive revenue targets and became a darling to its investors. Yet, when the company announced its intention to restate revenues in August 2002, its stock price plunged to a low of $1.11 per share in August 2002, from a high of $55 per share in July 2000.[2] Civil and criminal charges related to fraudulent activity were brought against several Qwest executives, including CEO Joseph Nacchio. Nacchio was convicted on 19 counts of illegal insider trading, and was sentenced to six years in prison in July 2007. He was also ordered to pay a $19 million fine and forfeit $52 million that he gained in illegal stock sales.[3]

[1] *SEC v. Joseph P. Nacchio, Robert S. Woodruff, Robin R. Szeliga, Afshin Mohebbi, Gregory M. Casey, James J. Kozlowski, Frank T. Noyes, Defendants,* Civil Action No. 05-MK-480 (OES), pp. 11–14.

[2] *SEC v. Qwest,* pp. 1–2.

[3] Dionne Searcey, "Qwest Ex-Chief Gets 6 Years in Prison for Insider Trading," *The Wall Street Journal,* July 28, 2007, p. A3.

Background

An IRU is an irrevocable right to use specific fiber-optic cable or fiber capacity for a specified period. In Qwest's IRU swap transactions, Qwest sold IRUs to customers in exchange for purchasing fiber or capacity in similar dollar amounts from those same customers. Under GAAP, no revenue should be recognized in this type of swap transaction unless Qwest had a legitimate business need to purchase the IRU capacity simultaneously from the other telecommunications company. Unfortunately, based on the available evidence, it seemed that many of Qwest's IRU swap transactions failed to meet the requirement to recognize revenue. In addition, in some cases, Qwest's executives backdated documents for IRU swap transactions to enable earlier revenue recognition.

Business Need for Assets Purchased in IRU Swap Transactions

Beginning in 1999, Qwest found it increasingly difficult to sell IRUs to customers unless it purchased fiber or capacity in similar dollar amounts from those same customers in swap transactions. As an example, in the third quarter of 2001, Qwest agreed to purchase $67.2 million of capacity in Pan America from Global Crossing in a swap transaction because Global Crossing could deliver the capacity by the close of the third quarter, a necessary element for booking revenue on Qwest's simultaneous sale to Global Crossing.[4] In fact, many of the assets Qwest purchased in swap transactions seemingly did not have a legitimate business purpose besides their role in the completion of a swap transaction.

Qwest's Failure to Use Assets Purchased in Swap Transactions

In most cases Qwest did not use the assets it purchased. For example, on September 29, 2000, Qwest purchased from Global Crossing $20.8 million in capacity across the Pacific Ocean as part of a swap transaction. Qwest never activated the capacity and, six months later, returned the $20.8 million in capacity as a credit toward the purchase of different capacity from Global Crossing.[5] In fact, members of Qwest's senior management directed and established quotas for the IRU sales teams to resell capacity that Qwest "[took] on as a result of trades with other carriers that we do not intend to use."[6]

---

[4] *SEC v. Qwest,* p. 31.

[5] *SEC v. Qwest,* p. 32.

[6] *SEC v. Qwest,* p. 30.

Qwest's Purchase of Assets That Duplicated Other Assets It Owned

Many of the routes Qwest purchased in IRU swaps duplicated network assets that Qwest already possessed. For example, Qwest purchased similar East Asia capacity during 2001 in four swap transactions with Cable & Wireless, Global Crossing, Flag Telecom, and TyCom Networks. Because the routes were redundant, Qwest did not have a business use for at least three of the four routes. In another example, Qwest engaged in a swap with Enron on December 21, 1999, whereby it bought fiber between Denver and Dallas for $39.2 million. However, Qwest had already built and completed a route between those cities that had excess capacity and the ability to be expanded.[7]

Interaction of IRU Sales Staff with the Network Planning Department

Although Qwest's network planning department was responsible for determining what capacity was needed to expand or develop Qwest's fiber-optic network, Qwest's IRU salespeople did not generally consult with the network planning department before purchasing assets in a swap.[8] In those few instances when Qwest's network planning department was consulted, it recommended against the purchase of capacity because Qwest had little or no need for the IRU.[9] For example, prior to the purchase of a large amount of fiber from Enron in a third quarter 2001 swap, in which Qwest recognized $85.5 million in revenue on the sale, Qwest's network planning group allegedly made it clear that the Qwest network had no need for the majority of Enron's fiber route and other assets.[10]

Study of Use of International Capacity Purchased in IRU Swaps

In late 2001 through early 2002, Qwest conducted a study to determine how to use the international capacity it had purchased in IRU swaps. The study concluded that Qwest could possibly use or resell only one-third of the capacity it had purchased in the swaps. The remaining two-thirds of the capacity purchased was not needed by Qwest, could not be resold, and was therefore worthless.[11]

---

[7] *SEC v. Qwest*, pp. 32–33.

[8] *SEC v. Qwest*, p. 31.

[9] Ibid.

[10] Ibid.

[11] *SEC v. Qwest*, p. 30.

Accounting for Swap Transactions

In accounting for swaps, Qwest recognized large amounts of revenue immediately, which was an aggressive method relative to the rest of the telecommunications industry. Yet Qwest capitalized its costs related to purchasing capacity from others as long-term assets that were amortized over the 20- to 25-year terms of the IRUs.[12]

During 2000 and 2001 the frequency, dollar amount, and number of swap transactions grew as Qwest tried to meet its aggressive revenue targets in the face of declining demand for fiber-optic assets. Internally some Qwest managers and employees referred to these transactions using the acronym of SLUTS, which stood for simultaneous, legally unrelated transactions. In fact, most of Qwest's swaps were completed as directed by members of senior management in the waning days and hours of each quarter in desperate attempts to achieve previously stated revenue targets.[13]

Pressure from senior management allegedly motivated employees to backdate contracts to falsely demonstrate that a contract was completed by the end of a quarter. For example, the company recorded revenue of $69.8 million in the first quarter of 2001 on a swap transaction with Cable & Wireless that had not closed until after the quarter (on April 12, 2001) by backdating the contract to March 30, 2001. In another example of backdating, in the third quarter of 2001 Qwest recognized $85.5 million of revenue on the sale of IRU capacity in a swap with Enron. The parties' agreements, which were dated September 30, 2001, were not executed until October 1, 2001, after the close of the quarter.[14]

[12] *SEC v. Qwest*, p. 24.
[13] Ibid.
[14] *SEC v. Qwest*, pp. 28–29.

Case Questions

1. Describe why the recognition of revenue from IRU swaps for fiber-optic assets that were not actually needed by Qwest is inappropriate under GAAP. As an auditor, what type of evidence would allow you to determine whether the recognition of this revenue would be appropriate under GAAP?

2. Consult Paragraphs 28–30 of PCAOB Auditing Standard No. 5. Identify one relevant financial statement assertion related to the revenue account that is impacted by an IRU swap. Why is it relevant?

3. Consult Paragraphs 39–41 and Paragraph A5 (in Appendix A) of PCAOB Auditing Standard No. 5. For the assertion identified in Question 2, identify a specific internal control activity that would help *prevent* a misstatement related to the recognition of revenue for IRU swaps.

4. Next, for the assertion identified in Question 2, identify a specific internal control activity that would help *detect* a misstatement related to the recognition of revenue for IRU swaps.

Section

6

Comprehensive Company Cases

The case readings have been developed solely as a basis for class discussion. The case readings are not intended to serve as a source of primary data or as an illustration of effective or ineffective auditing.

Case 6.1

Enron

Synopsis

In its 2000 annual report, Enron prided itself on having "metamorphosed from an asset-based pipeline and power generating company to a marketing and logistics company whose biggest assets are its well-established business approach and its innovative people."[1] Enron's strategy seemed to pay off; in 2000 it was the seventh largest company on the Fortune 500, with assets of $65 billion and sales revenues of $100 billion.[2] From 1996 to 2000 Enron's revenues had increased by more than 750 percent, which was unprecedented in any industry.[3] Yet just a year later, in December 2001, Enron filed for bankruptcy, and billions of shareholder and retirement savings dollars were lost.

Enron's First Few Years

In 1985 Enron had assets along the three major stages of the supply chain of natural gas: production, transmission, and distribution. Natural gas was produced from deposits found underground. The natural gas was transmitted via pipelines, or networks, of underground pipes, and sold directly either to industrial customers or to regional gas utilities, which then distributed the gas to smaller businesses and customers. Some companies in the industry had assets related to specific activities within the supply chain. For example, some companies owned pipelines but did not produce their own gas. These companies often entered into

---

[1] Enron 2000 annual report, p. 7.

[2] Joseph F. Berardino, remarks to U.S. House of Representatives Committee on Financial Services, December 12, 2001.

[3] Bala G. Dharan and William R. Bufkins, "Red Flags in Enron's Reporting of Revenues and Key Financial Measures," March 2003, prepublication draft (www.ruf.rice.edu/~bala/files/dharan-bufkins_enron_red_flags_041003.pdf), p. 4.

long-term "take or pay" contracts, whereby they paid for minimum volumes in the future at prearranged prices to protect against supply shortages.

In early 1986 Enron reported a loss of $14 million for its first year. As a result, the company employed a series of cost-cutting measures, including layoffs and pay freezes for top executives. Enron also started selling off assets to reduce its debt. Nevertheless, Enron's financial situation was still bleak in 1987. That year Moody's downgraded its credit rating to junk bond status.[4]

Impact of Significant Industry Change on Enron

Enron faced significant change in its industry environment due to the government's decision in the mid-1980s to deregulate the once highly regulated industry. The government, which had dictated the prices pipeline companies paid for gas and the prices they could charge their customers, decided to allow the market forces of supply and demand to dictate prices and volumes sold. As part of this process, the government required that pipeline companies provide "open access" to their pipelines to other companies wanting to transport natural gas, so that pipeline companies would not have an unfair competitive advantage.[5]

Enron's Natural Gas Pipeline Business

Enron adapted by providing open access to its pipelines—that is, charging other firms for the right to use them. It also took advantage of the ability to gain open access to pipelines owned by other companies. For example, in 1988 Enron signed a 15-year contract with Brooklyn Union to supply gas to a plant being built in New York. Because Brooklyn Union was not connected to Enron's pipeline system, Enron needed to contract with another pipeline company to transport the gas to Brooklyn Union. Enron was therefore assuming added risks related to the transportation of the gas. The long-term nature of the contract was also risky because prices could rise to a level that would make the contract unprofitable.[6]

Enron Expands into Natural Gas Trading and Financing

Enron capitalized on the introduction of market forces into the industry by becoming involved in natural gas trading and financing. Enron served as an intermediary among producers that contracted to sell their gas to Enron and gas customers that contracted to purchase gas from Enron. Enron collected as

---

[4] Bethany McLean and Peter Elkind, *The Smartest Guys in the Room: The Amazing Rise and Scandalous Fall of Enron* (New York: Penguin Group, 2003), p. 14.

[5] Paul M. Healy and Krishna Palepu, "Governance and Intermediation Problems in Capital Markets: Evidence from the Fall of Enron," Harvard NOM Research Paper No. 02–27, August 2002, p. 7.

[6] Bethany McLean and Peter Elkind, *The Smartest Guys in the Room: The Amazing Rise and Scandalous Fall of Enron* (New York: Penguin Group, 2003), p. 34.

profits the differences between the prices at which it sold and purchased the gas. Enron's physical market presence (owning the pipelines and charging a price for distribution that was proportional to the spot price of gas it might purchase) helped mitigate the risk of a price increase of the gas it was purchasing.[7]

In response to the problem of getting producers to sign long-term contracts to supply gas, Enron started giving such producers cash up front instead of payment over the life of the contracts. Enron then allowed the natural gas contracts it devised—which were quite complex and variable, depending on different pricing, capacity, and transportation parameters—to be traded.

Enron Expands beyond Natural Gas

Enron decided to apply its gas trading model to other markets, branching out into electricity and other commodity markets, such as paper and chemicals. To accomplish its expansion strategy, Enron sought to pursue an "asset-light" strategy. Enron's goal was to achieve the advantages of a presence in the physical market without the disadvantages of huge fixed capital expenditures. For example, in natural gas, Enron divested its assets related to pumping gas at the wellhead or selling gas to customers, and then set out to acquire assets related to midstream activities, such as transportation, storage, and distribution.[8] By late 2000 Enron owned 5,000 fewer miles of natural gas pipeline than when it was founded in 1985; in fact, its gas transactions represented 20 times its existing pipeline capacity.[9]

In addition, Enron undertook international projects involving the construction and management of energy facilities outside the United States—in the United Kingdom, Eastern Europe, Africa, the Middle East, India, China, and Central and South America. Established in 1993, the Enron international division did not adhere to the asset-light strategy pursued by other divisions. Enron also expanded aggressively into broadband, the use of fiber optics to transmit audio and video. Among its goals in that business were to deploy the largest open global broadband network in the world.[10]

Enron's Changes to Accounting Procedures

As a result of its change in business strategy, Enron made significant changes to several of its accounting procedures. For example, Enron began establishing several special purpose entities in many aspects of its business. A special purpose

---

[7] Christopher L. Culp and Steve H. Hanke, "Empire of the Sun: An Economic Interpretation of Enron's Energy Business," *Policy Analysis* 470 (February 20, 2003), p. 6.

[8] Christopher L. Culp and Steve H. Hanke, "Empire of the Sun: An Economic Interpretation of Enron's Energy Business," *Policy Analysis* 470 (February 20, 2003), p. 7.

[9] Paul M. Healy and Krishna Palepu, "Governance and Intermediation Problems in Capital Markets: Evidence from the Fall of Enron," Harvard NOM Research Paper No. 02–27, August 2002, pp. 9–10.

[10] Christopher L. Culp and Steve H. Hanke, "Empire of the Sun: An Economic Interpretation of Enron's Energy Business," *Policy Analysis* 470 (February 20, 2003), p. 4.

entity (SPE) is an entity—partnership, corporation, trust, or joint venture—created for a limited purpose, with limited activities and a limited life. A company forms an SPE so outside investors are assured that they will be exposed to only the risk of the SPE and its particular purpose, such as building a gas pipeline, and not the risks associated with the entire company. In addition, the SPE also protects the investment of outside investors by giving them control over its activities. If an SPE satisfies certain conditions, it does not have to be consolidated with the sponsoring company.

Conditions for Nonconsolidation of SPEs

A company was *not* required to consolidate both assets and liabilities of the SPE into those contained on its own balance sheet, and it could record gains and losses on transactions with the SPE, if two conditions were met:

1. An owner independent of the company had to own a "substantive" equity interest (at least 3 percent of the SPE's assets, and that 3 percent remain at risk throughout the transaction).
2. The independent owner had to exercise control of the SPE.

The requirement of 3 percent minimum equity being owned by outside investors was created in 1990 by EITF 90–15 and formalized by FASB Statements No. 125 and 140. This standard represented a major departure from typical consolidation rules, which generally required an entity to be consolidated if a company owned (directly or indirectly) 50 percent or more of the entity.[11] Consolidation rules for SPEs were also controversial because a company could potentially use an SPE for fraudulent purposes, such as hiding debt or nonperforming assets by keeping these items off its own consolidated balance sheet.

JEDI and Chewco

In 1993 Enron and the California Public Employees Retirement System (CalPERS) formed an SPE: a $500 million 50–50 partnership they called Joint Energy Development Investments Limited (JEDI).[12] Enron was not required to consolidate the partnership within Enron's financial statements because it did not own more than 50 percent of the venture.

In 1997 Enron offered to buy out CalPERS's interest in JEDI. To maintain JEDI as an unconsolidated entity, Enron needed to identify a new limited partner.

[11] Bala G. Dharan, "Enron's Accounting Issues—What Can We Learn to Prevent Future Enrons," prepared testimony presented to the U.S. House Energy and Commerce Committee's Hearings on Enron Accounting, February 6, 2002, pp. 11–12.

[12] JEDI was also a sly nod to the *Star Wars* films; CFO Andy Fastow, who devised the partnership, was a *Star Wars* fan.

Enron's CFO Andrew Fastow proposed that Enron form another SPE named Chewco Investments (after *Star Wars* character Chewbacca), the bulk of whose equity investment would come from third-party investors, to buy out CalPERS's JEDI interest.[13]

Chewco's Capital Structure

Unsuccessful in obtaining outside equity, Enron created a capital structure for Chewco that had three elements:

1. A $250 million unsecured subordinated loan to Chewco from Barclays Bank (Enron would guarantee the loan).
2. A $132 million advance from JEDI to Chewco under a revolving credit agreement.
3. $11.5 million in equity (representing approximately 3 percent of total capital) from Chewco's general and limited partners.[14]

Chewco's Partners

Michael Kopper, an Enron employee who reported to CFO Fastow, was the general partner of Chewco. The limited partner of Chewco was an entity called Big River Funding LLC, whose sole member was an entity called Little River Funding LLC. Kopper had invested $115,000 in Big River and $10,000 in Little River but transferred these investments to William Dodson (who allegedly may have been Kopper's domestic partner). As such, Kopper technically had no ownership interest in Chewco's limited partner. The remaining $11.4 million was provided by Barclays Bank in the form of equity loans to Big River and Little River.

Barclays required that Big River and Little River establish cash reserve accounts of $6.6 million and that the reserve accounts be fully pledged to secure repayment of the $11.4 million. JEDI, of which Enron still owned 50 percent, made a special $16.6 million distribution to Chewco, out of which $6.6 million could be used to fund the cash reserve accounts.[15] (Refer to Figure 5.2.1 in Section 5, on page 146, for a visual depiction of the Chewco transaction.)

---

[13] William C. Powers, Jr., Raymond S. Troubh, and Herbert S. Winokur, Jr., *Report of Investigation by the Special Investigative Committee of the Board of Directors of Enron Corp.*, February 1, 2002, p. 43.

[14] William C. Powers, Jr., Raymond S. Troubh, and Herbert S. Winokur, Jr., *Report of Investigation by the Special Investigative Committee of the Board of Directors of Enron Corp.*, February 1, 2002, p. 49.

[15] William C. Powers, Jr., Raymond S. Winokur, Jr., *Report of Investigation by the Special Investigative Committee of the Board of Directors of Enron Corp.*, February 1, 2002, pp. 48–51.

Andersen's Audit of the Chewco Transaction

Enron's auditor Arthur Andersen requested that Enron provide all the documentation in its possession relating to the Chewco transaction. In its audit of the transaction, Andersen reviewed the following:[16]

- The minutes of Enron's executive committee of the board of directors approving the transaction.
- The $132 million loan agreement between JEDI and Chewco.
- Enron's guarantee agreement of a $240 million loan from Barclays to Chewco.
- An amended JEDI partnership agreement.
- A representation letter from Enron and a representation letter from JEDI, each of which stated that related party transactions had been disclosed and that all financial records and related data had been made available to Andersen.

Andersen received confirmation regarding the loan agreement from a Chewco representative. Andersen also requested that Enron provide documents relating to Chewco's formation and structure. However, Enron told Andersen that it did not have these documents and could not obtain them because Chewco was a third party with its own legal counsel and ownership independent of Enron.[17] Andersen allegedly accepted this explanation and relied only on the evidence it had been given.

When the Chewco transaction was reviewed closely in late October and early November 2001, Enron and Andersen concluded that Chewco was an SPE without sufficient outside equity and that it should have been consolidated into Enron's financial statements. The retroactive consolidation of Chewco and the investment partnership in which Chewco was a limited partner decreased Enron's reported net income by $28 million (out of $105 million total) in 1997, by $133 million (out of $703 million total) in 1998, by $153 million (out of $893 million total) in 1999, and by $91 million (out of $979 million total) in 2000. It also increased Enron's reported debt by $711 million in 1997, by $561 million in 1998, by $685 million in 1999, and by $628 million in 2000.[18]

Enron's Use of Mark-to-Market Accounting

Enron also lobbied the SEC about the use of mark-to-market (MTM) accounting for its trading business, which allowed the present value (rather than the actual value, which was used in its original natural gas business) of a stream of

---

[16] Thomas H. Bauer, prepared witness testimony at Subcommittee on Oversight and Investigations related to Financial Collapse of Enron Corp., February 7, 2002.

[17] Ibid.

[18] William C. Powers, Jr., Raymond S. Troubh, and Herbert S. Winokur, Jr., *Report of Investigation by the Special Investigative Committee of the Board of Directors of Enron Corp.*, February 1, 2002, p. 42.

future inflows and expenses under a contract to be recognized as revenues and expenses, respectively, once the contract was signed.

In 1992 the SEC's chief accountant, Walter Scheutz, granted Enron permission to use MTM during the first quarter of its fiscal year ended December 31, 1992. However, he also said that MTM could be used *only* in Enron's natural gas trading business.[19] Enron's chief financial officer, Jack Tompkin, wrote back to Scheutz informing him that "Enron has changed its method of accounting for its energy-related, price-risk management activities effective January 1, 1991 ... the cumulative effect of initial adoption of mark-to-market accounting, as well as the impact on 1991 earnings is not material."[20] Enron was the first company outside the financial services industry to use MTM accounting.[21]

While the values of stock portfolios varied directly with changes in stock prices, the values of natural gas contracts were harder to assess. They often required complex valuation formulas with multiple assumptions for the formulas' variables, such as interest rates, customers, costs, and prices. These assumptions have a major impact on value and are related to long time periods—in some cases as long as 20 years.

Early Application of MTM Accounting: Sithe Energies Agreement

One of the earliest contracts for which Enron employed MTM accounting was an agreement for Enron to supply Sithe Energies with 195 million cubic feet of gas per day for 20 years for a plant that Sithe was planning to build in New York. The estimated value of the gas to be supplied was $3.5 to $4 billion. Using MTM, Enron was able to book profits from the contract even before the plant started operating.[22]

Before MTM, Enron would have recognized the *actual* costs of supplying the gas and *actual* revenues received from selling the gas in each time period. Using MTM meant that as soon as a long-term contract was signed, the *present value* of the stream of future inflows under the contract was recognized as revenues, and the *present value* of the expected costs of fulfilling the contract was expensed.[23] Changes in value were recognized as additional income or losses (with corresponding changes to the relevant balance sheet accounts) in subsequent periods.[24]

---

[19] Robert Bryce, *Pipe Dreams: Greed, Ego, and the Death of Enron* (New York: Perseus Book Group, 2002), p. 67.

[20] Ibid.

[21] Bala G. Dharan and William R. Bufkins, "Red Flags in Enron's Reporting of Revenues and Key Financial Measures," March 2003, prepublication draft (www.ruf.rice.edu/ bala/~files/dharan-bufkins_ enron_red_flags_041003.pdf), pp. 7–11.

[22] Bethany McLean and Peter Elkind, *The Smartest Guys in the Room: The Amazing Rise and Scandalous Fall of Enron* (New York: Penguin Group, 2003), pp. 60–61.

[23] Bala G. Dharan and William R. Bufkins, "Red Flags in Enron's Reporting of Revenues and Key Financial Measures," March 2003, prepublication draft (http://www.ruf.rice.edu/~bala/files/ dharan-bufkins_enron_red_flags_041003.pdf), pp. 7–11.

[24] Bethany McLean and Peter Elkind, *The Smartest Guys in the Room: The Amazing Rise and Scandalous Fall of Enron* (New York: Penguin Group, 2003), p. 39.

Enron's Expanded Use of MTM Accounting

Although the SEC had initially given approval for Enron to use MTM in the accounting of natural gas futures contracts, Enron quietly began using MTM for electric power contracts and trades as well.[25] In one example, Enron signed a 15-year $1.3 billion contract to supply electricity to Eli Lilly. Enron calculated the present value of the contract as more than $500 million and recognized this amount as revenue. It also reported estimates for the costs associated with servicing the contract. At the time, Indiana had not yet deregulated electricity. Thus Enron needed to predict when Indiana would deregulate, as well as the impact of the deregulation on the costs related to the deal.[26]

Enron also extended MTM accounting to other businesses. In another example, Enron signed a 20-year agreement with Blockbuster Video in July 2000 to introduce entertainment on demand. Enron set up pilot projects in Portland, Seattle, and Salt Lake City to store the entertainment and distribute it over its broadband network. Based on these pilot projects, Enron recognized estimated profits of more than $110 million for the Blockbuster deal. Technical viability and market demand were difficult to predict in these initial stages.[27] Canceled in March 2001, the Blockbuster deal never reached past the pilot stage; yet significant profits were recognized by Enron on the deal.

Enron's Relationship with Auditor Arthur Andersen

Enron paid Arthur Andersen $46.8 million in fees for auditing, business consulting, and tax work for the fiscal year ended August 31, 1999; $58 million in 2000; and more than $50 million in 2001.[28] Andersen was collecting $1 million a week from Enron in the year before Enron's crash. It was one of Andersen's largest clients.

More than half of that amount was for fees that were charged for nonaudit services.[29] In 2000, for example, Enron paid Andersen $25 million for audit services and $27 million for consulting and other services, such as internal audit services.[30]

Andersen had performed Enron's internal audit function since 1993. That year Andersen had hired 40 Enron personnel, including the vice president of

[25] Bethany McLean and Peter Elkind, *The Smartest Guys in the Room: The Amazing Rise and Scandalous Fall of Enron* (New York: Penguin Group, 2003), p. 127.

[26] Paul M. Healy and Krishna Palepu, "The Fall of Enron," *Journal of Economic Perspectives* 17, no. 2 (Spring 2003), p. 10.

[27] Ibid.

[28] Anita Raghavan, "Accountable: How a Bright Star at Andersen Fell Along with Enron," *The Wall Street Journal,* May 15, 2002. Accessed from Factiva (February 25, 2005).

[29] Jane Mayer, "The Accountants' War," *New Yorker,* April 22, 2002. Accessed from LexisNexis Academic (February 25, 2005).

[30] Nanette Byrnes, "Accounting in Crisis," *BusinessWeek,* January 28, 2002. Accessed from LexisNexis Academic (February 25, 2005).

internal audit, to be part of Andersen's team providing internal audit services.[31] In 2000, as SEC Chair Arthur Levitt was trying to reform the industry practice of an audit firm also offering consulting services to audit clients, Enron's Chair and CEO Ken Lay sent a letter to Levitt (the letter was secretly coauthored by Andersen partner David Duncan), in which he wrote,

> While the agreement Enron has with its independent auditors displaces a significant portion of the activities previously performed by internal resources, it is structured to ensure that Enron management maintains appropriate audit plan design, results assessment, and overall monitoring and oversight responsibilities. . . . Enron has found its "integrated audit" arrangement to be more efficient and cost-effective than the more traditional roles of separate internal and external auditing functions.[32]

At Andersen, an audit partner's individual compensation depended on his or her ability to sell other services (in addition to auditing) to clients.[33] Therefore, the nonaudit services provided to Enron had a big impact on the salary of the lead Andersen partner on the Enron engagement, David Duncan, who was earning around $1 million a year.[34] After graduating from Texas A&M University, Duncan joined Andersen in 1981, was made partner in 1995, and was named the lead partner for Enron two years later. Duncan developed a close personal relationship with Enron's Chief Accounting Officer (CAO) Richard Causey, who himself had worked at Arthur Andersen for almost nine years. Duncan and Causey often went to lunch together, and their families had even taken vacations together.[35]

Causey, who came to Enron in 1991, was appointed CAO in 1997. Causey was responsible for recruiting many Andersen alumni to work at Enron. Over the years, Enron hired at least 86 Andersen accountants.[36] Several were in senior executive positions, including Jeffrey McMahon, who had served as Enron's treasurer and president, and Vice President Sherron Watkins.

Although Andersen had separate offices in downtown Houston, Duncan and up to a hundred Andersen managers had a whole floor available to them within Enron's headquarters in Houston.[37] Duncan once remarked that he liked having the office space there because it "enhanced our ability to serve" and to

---

[31] Thaddeus Herrick and Alexei Barrionuevo, "Were Auditor and Client Too Close-Knit?" *The Wall Street Journal,* January 21, 2002. Accessed from ProQuest Research Library (February 26, 2005).

[32] "Letter from Kenneth Lay," Bigger Than Enron transcript, *Frontline,* Aired on Public Broadcasting Service on June 20, 2002 (www.pbs.org/wgbh/pages/frontline/shows/regulation/congress/lay.html).

[33] Jane Mayer, "The Accountants' War," *New Yorker,* April 22, 2002. Accessed from LexisNexis Academic (February 25, 2005).

[34] Bethany McLean and Peter Elkind, *The Smartest Guys in the Room: The Amazing Rise and Scandalous Fall of Enron* (New York: Penguin Group, 2003), pp. 146–147.

[35] Susan E. Squires, Cynthia J. Smith, Lorna McDougal, and William R. Yeack, *Inside Arthur Andersen* (Upper Saddle River, NJ: Prentice Hall, 2003), p. 2.

[36] Bethany McLean and Peter Elkind, *The Smartest Guys in the Room: The Amazing Rise and Scandalous Fall of Enron* (New York: Penguin Group, 2003), p. 145.

[37] Susan E. Squires, Cynthia J. Smith, Lorna McDougal, and William R. Yeack, *Inside Arthur Andersen* (Upper Saddle River, NJ: Prentice Hall, 2003), p. 126.

"generate additional work."[38] Andersen boasted about the closeness of their relationship in a promotional video. "We basically do the same types of things. . . . We're trying to kinda cross lines and trying to, you know, become more of just a business person here at Enron," said one accountant. Another spoke about the advantage of being located in Enron's building: "Being here full-time year-round day-to-day gives us a chance to chase the deals with them and participate in the deal making process."[39]

In fact, Andersen and Enron employees went on ski trips and took annual golf vacations together. They played fantasy football against each other on their office computers and took turns buying each other margaritas at a local Mexican restaurant chain. One former senior audit manager at Andersen said that it was "like these bright geeks at Andersen suddenly got invited to this really cool, macho frat party."[40]

PSG's Disapproval of Special Purpose Entities and the Audit Team's Response

In 1999 Enron's CFO, Andrew Fastow, spoke to David Duncan about Enron's plan to set up a special purpose entity (later called LJM), a financing vehicle used to access capital or increase leverage without adding debt to a firm's balance sheet. After the discussion with Fastow, Duncan asked for the advice of the professional standards group (PSG).

A member of the PSG, Benjamin Neuhausen, represented the group's disapproval in an e-mail message written to Duncan on May 28, 1999: "Setting aside the accounting, (the) idea of a venture equity managed by CFO is terrible from a business point of view. . . . Conflicts of interest galore. Why would any director in his or her right mind ever approve such a scheme?" he wrote.[41]

In addition, the PSG was firmly against the idea of Enron's recording gains on the sales of assets (or immediate gains on any transactions) to the Fastow-controlled special purpose entity. In response to the recording of gains, Duncan wrote in a June e-mail message, "I'm not saying I'm in love with this either. . . . But I'll need all the ammo I can get to take that issue on . . . on your point 1 (i.e., the whole thing is a bad idea), I really couldn't agree more." Yet Duncan later told Fastow that Andersen would sign off on the transaction, under a few

---

[38] Rebecca Smith and John R. Emshwiller, *24 Days: How Two Wall Street Journal Reporters Uncovered the Lies That Destroyed Faith in Corporate America* (New York: HarperBusiness, 2003), p. 289.

[39] Bethany McLean and Peter Elkind, *The Smartest Guys in the Room: The Amazing Rise and Scandalous Fall of Enron* (Penguin Group, 2003), p. 146.

[40] Flynn McRoberts, "Ties to Enron Blinded Andersen," *Chicago Tribune*, September 3, 2002. Accessed from Factiva (February 3, 2004).

[41] Anita Raghavan, "Accountable: How a Bright Star at Andersen Fell Along with Enron," *The Wall Street Journal*, May 15, 2002. Accessed from Factiva (February 25, 2005).

conditions, one of which was that Fastow obtain the approval of Enron's chief executive and its board of directors.[42]

Shortly after, Carl Bass, who was promoted to the PSG in December 1999, raised concerns over the sale of some equity options within the LJM special purpose entity. Bass wrote to his boss John Stewart in an e-mail message, "This is a big item and the team apparently does not want to go back to the client on this. I think at a minimum the Practice Director needs to be made aware of this history and our opposition to the accounting."[43] However, the memo Duncan's team prepared to document the deal indicated that Bass "concurred with our conclusions."[44]

Bass continued to object to the LJM transaction, writing via e-mail to Stewart (Bass's boss) in February 2000, "This whole deal looks like there is no substance. The only money at risk here is $1.8 million in a bankrupt-proof SPE. All of the money here appears to be provided by Enron."[45] Duncan's team did not address Bass's concerns and in fact continued to misrepresent his views to the client.

In late 2000 Duncan asked Bass for more advice on how best to account for four Enron SPEs known as Raptors. Enron wanted to lump together the financial results for all the entities, so that the more profitable ones could offset losses being garnered by others. Bass opposed the idea. Nevertheless, Duncan later decided that Andersen would "accept the client's position" with some modifications.[46]

In February 2001 Andersen held a routine annual risk assessment meeting to determine whether to keep Enron as a client. Some partners raised concerns relating to how much debt Enron was *not* putting on its balance sheet, Fastow's conflict of interest, and the lack of disclosure in the company's financial footnotes.[47] Duncan reassured his fellow partners.

Carl Bass was removed from the Enron account in March 2001. Bass wrote to Stewart (Bass's boss) in an e-mail message, "Apparently, part of the process issue stems from the client (Enron) knowing all that goes on within our walls on our discussions with respect to their issues. . . . We should not be communicating with the client that so and so said this and I could not get this past so and so in the PSG. . . . I have first hand experience on this because at a recent EITF meeting some lower level Enron employee who was with someone else from Enron introduced herself to me by saying she had heard my name a lot—'so you are the one that will not let us do something. . . .' I have also noted a trend

[42] Ibid.

[43] Carl E. Bass, internal e-mail to John E. Stewart, "Subject: Enron Option," December 18, 1999.

[44] Mike McNamee, "Out of Control at Andersen," *BusinessWeek Online*, March 29, 2002. Accessed from Business Source Premier database (December 31, 2004).

[45] Carl E. Bass, internal e-mail to John E. Stewart, "Subject: Enron Transaction," February 1, 2000.

[46] Anita Raghavan, "Accountable: How a Bright Star at Andersen Fell Along with Enron," *The Wall Street Journal*, May 15, 2002. Accessed from Factiva (February 25, 2005).

[47] Mimi Swartz, *Power Failure: The Inside Story of the Collapse of Enron* (New York: Doubleday, 2003), pp. 235–236.

on this engagement that the question is usually couched along the lines 'will the PSG support this?' When a call starts out that way, it is my experience that the partner is struggling with the question and what the client wants to do."[48] Stewart complained to a senior partner about Bass's removal. Duncan called Stewart and explained that two Enron executives, Richard Causey and John Echols, had pushed for Bass's removal.[49]

[48] Carl E. Bass, internal e-mail to John E. Stewart, "Subject: Enron," March 4, 2001.

[49] Anita Raghavan, "Accountable: How a Bright Star at Andersen Fell Along with Enron," *The Wall Street Journal,* May 15, 2002. Accessed from Factiva (February 25, 2005).

Case Questions

1. Consult PCAOB Ethics and Independence Rule 3520. What is *auditor independence,* and what is its significance to the audit profession? What is the difference between independence in appearance and independence in fact?

2. Refer to Section 201 of SARBOX. Identify the services provided by Arthur Andersen that are no longer allowed to be performed. Do you believe that Section 201 is needed? Why or why not?

3. Refer to Sections 203 and 206 of SARBOX. How would these sections of the law have impacted the Enron audit? Do you believe that these sections are needed? Why or why not?

4. Refer to Section 301 of SARBOX. Do you believe that Section 301 is important to maintaining independence between the auditor and the client? Why or why not?

5. Consider the principles, assumptions, and constraints of Generally Accepted Accounting Principles (GAAP). Define the *revenue recognition principle* and explain why it is important to users of financial statements.

6. Consider the Sithe Energies contract described in the case. Does the accounting for this contract provide an example of how Enron violated the revenue recognition principle? Why or why not? Please be specific.

7. Consult Paragraph 14 of PCAOB Auditing Standard No. 5 and Paragraph 68 of PCAOB Auditing Standard No. 12. Based on the case information, do you believe that Enron had established an effective system of internal control over financial reporting related to the contract revenue recorded in its financial statements? Why or why not?

8. Consult Paragraphs 4–8 of PCAOB Auditing Standard No. 15. As an auditor, what type of evidence would you want to examine to determine whether Enron was inappropriately recording revenue from the Sithe Energies contract?

9. Consult Paragraphs 3–6 of Quality Control Standard No. 20 (QC 20). Explain why an accounting and auditing research function (like Andersen's PSG) is important in the operations of a CPA firm. What role does the function play in completing the audit?

10. Consult Section 103 of SARBOX. Do you believe that the engagement leader of an audit (like David Duncan on the Enron audit) should have the authority to overrule the opinions and recommendations of the accounting and auditing research function (like the PSG)? Why or why not?

11. After Carl Bass was removed from the Enron account, he indicated to his boss that he did not believe Enron should have known about internal discussions regarding accounting and auditing issues. Do you agree with Bass's position? Why or why not?

12. Consult Section 203 of SARBOX. Do you believe that this provision of the law goes far enough? That is, do you believe the audit firm itself (and not just the partner) should have to rotate off an audit engagement every five years? Why or why not?

13. Consult Paragraphs 7–10 of PCAOB Auditing Standard No. 12. Based on your understanding of risk assessment and the case information, identify three specific factors about Enron's business model in the late 1990s that might cause you to elevate the risk of material misstatement at Enron.

14. Consult Paragraphs 5–7 of PCAOB Auditing Standard No. 13. Comment on how your understanding of the inherent risks identified at Enron (in Question 13) would influence the nature, timing, and extent of your audit work at Enron.

15. Consult Paragraphs 28–30 of PCAOB Auditing Standard No. 5. Next, consider how the change in industry regulation and Enron's resulting strategy shift would impact your risk assessment for the relevant assertions about revenue. Finally, identify the most relevant assertion for revenue before and after Enron's resulting strategy shift and briefly explain why.

16. Consult Paragraphs 52–53 of PCAOB Auditing Standard No. 12. How might a revenue recognition fraud occur under Enron's strategy in the late 1990s? Identify an internal control procedure that would prevent, detect, or deter such a fraudulent scheme.

17. Consult Paragraphs 65–69 of PCAOB Auditing Standard No. 12. Based on your understanding of fraud risk assessment, what three conditions are likely to be present when fraud occurs (the fraud triangle)? Based on the information provided in the case, which of these three conditions appears to have been the most prevalent at Enron, and why?

18. Consult Paragraph 25 of PCAOB Auditing Standard No. 5. Define what is meant by *control environment*. Why is the control environment so important to effective internal control over financial reporting at an audit client like Enron?

19. Consult Paragraphs 21–22 of PCAOB Auditing Standard No. 5. Comment on how your understanding of Enron's control environment and other entity-level controls would help you implement a top-down approach to an internal control audit at Enron.

20. Consult Sections 204 and 301 of SARBOX. What is the role of the audit committee in the financial reporting process? Do you believe that an audit committee can be effective in providing oversight of a management team like Enron's?

21. Consult Sections 302 and 305 and Title IX of SARBOX. Do you believe that these new provisions could help deter fraudulent financial reporting by an upper management group? Why or why not?

22. Based on your understanding of the information presented in the case, how did Enron's Chewco SPE fail to meet the outside equity requirement for nonconsolidation? Did Enron meet the control requirement for non-consolidation?

23. Consult Paragraphs 4–8 of PCAOB Auditing Standard No. 15. Based on your understanding of audit evidence, did Arthur Andersen rely on sufficient appropriate audit evidence in its audit of the Chewco transaction? Why or why not?

24. Consult Section 401 of SARBOX. How would Section 401 apply to the Enron audit? Do you think Section 401 would have improved the presentation of Enron's financial statements? Why or why not?

25. Consult Paragraphs 28–30 of PCAOB Auditing Standard No. 5. Identify at least one relevant financial statement assertion about the financial statement accounts related to the Chewco transaction. Provide adequate support for your answer.

26. Consider the role of the Enron employee who was responsible for applying MTM accounting rules to electric power contracts, like the Eli Lilly contract. Assuming the employee knew that the use of MTM accounting was beyond the scope of the SEC approval parameters, do you believe that the employee had a responsibility to report the behavior to the audit committee? Why or why not?

Case 6.2

Waste Management

Synopsis

In February 1998 Waste Management announced that it was restating its financial statements for 1993 through 1996. In its restatement, Waste Management said that it had materially overstated its reported pretax earnings by $1.43 billion. After the announcement, the company's stock dropped by more than 33 percent, and shareholders lost over $6 billion.

The SEC brought charges against the company's founder, Dean Buntrock, and five other former top officers. The charges alleged that management had made repeated changes to depreciation-related estimates to reduce expenses and had employed several improper accounting practices related to capitalization policies, also designed to reduce expenses.[1] In its final judgment, the SEC permanently barred Buntrock and three other executives from acting as officers or directors of public companies and required payment from them of $30.8 million in penalties.[2]

History

In 1956 Dean Buntrock took over Ace Scavenger, a garbage collector owned by his father-in-law, who had recently died. After merging Ace with a number of other waste companies, Buntrock founded Waste Management in 1968.[3] Under Buntrock's reign as its CEO, the company went public in 1971 and then expanded during the 1970s and 1980s through several acquisitions of local waste hauling companies and landfill operators. At one point the company was performing close to 200 acquisitions a year.[4]

From 1971 to 1991 the company enjoyed 36 percent average annual growth in revenue and 36 percent annual growth in net income. By 1991 Waste

[1] SEC, Accounting and Auditing Enforcement Release No. 1532, March 26, 2002.

[2] SEC, Accounting and Auditing Enforcement Release No. 2298, August 29, 2005.

[3] "Waste Management: Change with the Market or Die," *Fortune*, January 13, 1992.

[4] *SEC v. Dean L. Buntrock, Phillip B. Rooney, James E. Koenig, Thomas C. Hau, Herbert A. Getz, and Bruce D. Tobecksen,* Complaint No. 02C 2180 (Judge Manning).

Management had become the largest waste removal business in the world, with revenue of more than $7.5 billion.[5] Despite a recession, Buntrock and other executives at Waste Management continued to set aggressive goals for growth. For example, in 1992 the company forecast that revenue and net income would increase by 26.1 percent and 16.5 percent, respectively, over 1991's figures.[6]

Waste Management's Core Operations

Waste Management's core solid waste management business in North America consisted of the following major processes: collection, transfer, and disposal.

Collection

Solid waste management collection from commercial and industrial customers was generally performed under one- to three-year service agreements. Most residential solid waste collection services were performed under contracts with—or franchises granted by—municipalities giving the company exclusive rights to service all or a portion of the homes in their respective jurisdictions. These contracts or franchises usually ranged in duration from one to five years. Factors that determined the fees collected from industrial and commercial customers were market conditions, collection frequency, type of equipment furnished, length of service agreement, type and volume or weight of the waste collected, distance to the disposal facility, and cost of disposal. Similar factors determined the fees collected in the residential market.[7]

Transfer

As of 1995 Waste Management operated 151 solid waste transfer stations—facilities where solid waste was received from collection vehicles and then transferred to trailers for transportation to disposal facilities. In most instances, several collection companies used the services of these facilities, which were provided to municipalities or counties. Market factors, the type and volume or weight of the waste transferred, the extent of processing of recyclable materials, the transport distance involved, and the cost of disposal were the major factors that determined the fees collected.[8]

Disposal

As of 1995 Waste Management operated 133 solid waste sanitary landfill facilities, 103 of which were owned by the company. All of the sanitary landfill facilities were subject to governmental regulation aimed at limiting the possibility of water pollution. In addition to governmental regulation, land scarcity and

---

[5] Ibid.

[6] Ibid.

[7] 1995 10-K.

[8] Ibid.

local resident opposition also conspired to make it difficult to obtain permission to operate and expand landfill facilities in certain areas. The development of a new facility also required significant up-front capital investment and a lengthy amount of time, with the added risk that the necessary permits might not be ultimately issued. In 1993, 1994, and 1995 approximately 52 percent, 55 percent, and 57 percent, respectively, of the solid waste collected by Waste Management was disposed of in sanitary landfill facilities operated by it. These facilities were typically also used by other companies and government agencies on a noncontract basis for fees determined by market factors and by the type and volume or weight of the waste.[9]

Corporate Expansion

As the company grew, Waste Management expanded its international operations and into new industries, including hazardous waste management, waste to energy, and environmental engineering businesses. By the mid-1990s Waste Management had five major business groups that provided the following services: solid waste management; hazardous waste management; engineering and industrial services; trash to energy, water treatment, and air quality services; and international waste management. (See Table A.2.1 for a description of the primary services these groups provided and their revenues in 1993, 1994, and 1995.)

Challenges

By the mid-1990s the company's core North American solid waste business was suffering from intense competition and excess landfill capacity in some of its markets. New environmental regulations also added to the cost of operating a landfill, and they made it more difficult and expensive for Waste Management to obtain permits for constructing new landfills or expanding old ones.[10]

Several of Waste Management's other businesses (including its hazardous waste management business and several international operations) were also performing poorly. After a strategic review that began in 1994, the company was reorganized into four global lines of business: waste services, clean energy, clean water, and environmental and infrastructure engineering and consulting.[11]

In the summer of 1996 Dean Buntrock, who founded Waste Management in 1968, retired as CEO; but he continued to serve as chair of the board of directors. Buntrock was initially replaced by Phillip Rooney, who had started working at Waste Management in 1969. In early 1997 Rooney resigned as director and CEO because of mounting shareholder discontent.

---

[9] Ibid.

[10] *SEC v. Dean L. Buntrock, Phillip B. Rooney, James E. Koenig, Thomas C. Hau, Herbert A. Getz, and Bruce D. Tobecksen,* Complaint No. 02C 2180 (Judge Manning).

[11] 1995 10-K.

TABLE A.2.1 Waste Management's Major Business Groups

Business Group	Services	Revenues ($000)		
		1993	1994	1995
Solid waste management	Garbage collection, transfer, resource recovery, and disposal for commercial, industrial, municipal, and residential customers, as well as for other waste management companies. Included recycling of paper, glass, plastic, and metal; removal of methane gas from sanitary landfill facilities for use in electricity generation; and medical and infectious waste management services to hospitals and other health care and related facilities.	4,702,166	5,117,871	5,642,857
Hazardous waste management	Chemical waste treatment, storage, disposal, and related services provided to commercial and industrial customers, governmental entities, and other waste management companies by Waste Management and Chemical Waste Management (CWM), a wholly owned subsidiary; onsite integrated hazardous waste management services provided by Advanced Environmental Technical Services (AETS), a 60 percent owned subsidiary; and low-level radioactive waste disposal services provided by subsidiary Chem-Nuclear Systems.	661,860	649,581	613,883
Engineering and industrial	Through Rust International, a 60 percent owned subsidiary, provided environmental and infrastructure engineering and consulting services, primarily to clients in government and in the chemical, petrochemical, nuclear energy, utility, pulp and paper, manufacturing, environmental services, and other industries.	1,035,004	1,140,294	1,027,430
Trash to energy, water treatment, air quality	Through Wheelabrator Technologies Inc. (WTI), a 58 percent owned subsidiary, developed, arranged financing for, operated, and owned facilities that disposed of trash and other waste materials by recycling them into electrical or steam energy. Also designed, fabricated, and installed technologically advanced air	1,142,219	1,324,567	1,451,675

pollution control, and systems and equipment. WTI's clean water group was principally involved in design, manufacture, operation, and ownership of facilities and systems used to purify water, to treat municipal and industrial wastewater, and to recycle organic wastes into compost material usable for horticultural and agricultural purposes.

International waste management	Solid and hazardous waste management and related environmental services in 10 countries in Europe and in Argentina, Australia, Brazil, Brunei, Hong Kong, Indonesia, Israel, Malaysia, New Zealand, Taiwan, and Thailand. Also had a 20 percent interest in Wessex Water Plc, an English publicly traded company providing water treatment, water distribution, wastewater treatment, and sewerage services.	1,411,211	1,710,862	1,865,081
Intercompany revenue		(316,344)	(388,470)	(353,309)
Consolidated revenue		8,636,116	9,554,705	10,247,617

195

After a five-month search, Waste Management chose Ronald LeMay, the president and COO of Sprint, to assume its post of chair and CEO. Surprisingly, just three months into his new role, LeMay quit to return to his former job at Sprint.

In addition, several other key executives who, unlike LeMay, had worked for Waste Management for several years—including CFO James Koenig, Corporate Controller Thomas Hau, and Vice President of Finance Bruce Tobecksen—also resigned by the end of 1997.

Capitalization of Landfill Costs and Other Expenses[12]

Waste Management capitalized the costs related to obtaining the required permits to develop and expand its many landfills. It also capitalized interest on landfill construction costs, as well as costs related to systems development.

GAAP for Capitalizing Costs

Under GAAP, a cost can be capitalized if it provides economic benefits to be used or consumed in future operations. A company is required to write off, as a current period expense, any deferred costs at the time the company learns that the underlying assets have been either impaired or abandoned. Any costs to repair or return property to its original condition are required to be expensed when incurred. Finally, interest can be capitalized as part of the cost of acquiring assets for the period of time that it takes to put the asset in the condition required for its intended use. However, GAAP requires that the capitalization of interest must cease once the asset has become substantially ready for its intended use.

Capitalization of Landfill Permitting Costs

As part of its normal business operations, Waste Management allocated substantial resources toward development of new landfills and expansion of existing landfills. A significant part of the landfill development and expansion costs related to the process of obtaining required permits from the appropriate government authorities. Over the years, the company faced increased difficulty in obtaining the required landfill permits; it often invested significantly in projects that had to be abandoned or were materially impaired.

The company routinely capitalized the costs related to obtaining the required permits so that it could defer recording expenses related to the landfills until they were put in productive use. However, instead of writing off the costs related to impaired and abandoned landfill projects and disclosing the impact of such write-offs, management disclosed only the *risk* of future write-offs related to such projects.

---

[12] *SEC v. Dean L. Buntrock, Phillip B. Rooney, James E. Koenig, Thomas C. Hau, Herbert A. Getz, and Bruce D. Tobecksen,* Complaint No. 02C 2180 (Judge Manning), www.sec.gov/litigation/complaints/complr17435.htm.

The management team of Waste Management also allegedly transferred the costs of unsuccessful efforts to obtain permits for certain landfill sites to other sites that had received permits or other sites for which it was still seeking permits. In effect, the team was commingling impaired or abandoned landfill project costs with the costs of a permitted site (a practice known as *basketing*, which did not comply with GAAP). In addition to basketing, the company also allegedly transferred unamortized costs from landfill facilities that had closed earlier than expected to other facilities that were still in operation (a practice known as *bundling*, which also did not comply with GAAP). Management never disclosed the use of bundling or basketing in its form 10K.

In 1994, after its auditor Arthur Andersen discovered these practices, management allegedly agreed to write off $40 million related to dead projects over a span of 10 years; management also promised to write off future impairments and abandonments in a prompt manner. However, during 1994, 1995, 1996, and 1997, management effectively buried the write-offs related to abandoned and impaired projects by netting them against other gains, as opposed to identifying the costs separately.

Capitalization of Interest on Landfill Construction Costs

In accordance with GAAP, Waste Management was able to capitalize interest related to landfill development because of the relatively long time required to obtain permits, construct the landfill, and ultimately prepare it to receive waste. However, Waste Management utilized a method, referred to as the *net book value (NBV)* method, that essentially enabled it to avoid GAAP's requirement that interest capitalization cease once the asset became substantially ready for its intended use. Waste Management's auditor, Arthur Andersen, advised the company from its first use of the NBV method (in 1989) that this method did not conform to GAAP.

Corporate Controller Thomas Hau even admitted that the method was "technically inconsistent with FAS Statement No. 34 [the controlling GAAP pronouncement] because it included interest [capitalization] related to cells of landfills that were receiving waste." Yet the company wrote in the footnotes to its financial statements that "[i]nterest has been capitalized on significant landfills, trash-to-energy plants, and other projects under development in accordance with FAS No. 34."

Ultimately the company agreed to utilize a new method, one that conformed to GAAP, beginning January 1, 1994. Corporate Controller Thomas Hau and CFO James Koenig allegedly determined that the new GAAP method would result in an increased annual interest expense of about $25 million, and therefore they chose to phase in the new method over three years, beginning in 1995. However, the company appeared to still utilize the NBV method for interest capitalization as of 1997.

Capitalization of Other Costs

The company's management also chose to capitalize other costs, such as systems development costs, rather than record them as expenses in the period in which they were incurred. In fact, management allegedly used excessive amortization periods (10- and 20-year periods for the two largest systems) that did not recognize the impact of technological obsolescence on the useful lives of the underlying systems.

The SEC found evidence that the company's auditor Arthur Andersen proposed several adjusting journal entries to write off the improperly deferred systems development costs. Andersen also repeatedly advised management to shorten the amortization periods. In 1994 management finally agreed to shorten the amortization periods and to write off financial statement misstatements resulting from improperly capitalized systems costs over a period of five years. During 1995 management changed the amortization periods and wrote off improperly capitalized systems costs by netting them against other gains.

Waste Management's Major Fixed Assets

The major fixed assets of Waste Management's North American business consisted of garbage trucks, containers, and equipment, which amounted to approximately $6 billion in assets. The second largest asset of the company (after vehicles, containers, and equipment) was land, in the form of the more than 100 fully operational landfills that the company both owned and operated. Under GAAP, depreciation expense is determined by allocating the historical cost of tangible capital assets (less the salvage value) over the estimated useful life of the assets.

Unsupported Changes to the Estimated Useful Lives of Assets

From 1988 through 1996 management allegedly made numerous unsupported changes to the estimated useful lives and/or the salvage values of one or more categories of vehicles, containers, or equipment. Such changes reduced the amount of depreciation expense recorded in particular periods. In addition, such changes were recorded as top-side adjustments at the corporate level (detached from the operating unit level). Most often the entries were made during the fourth quarter and then improperly applied cumulatively from the beginning of the year. It appeared that management never disclosed the changes or their impact on profitability to investors.[13]

Carrying Impaired Land at Cost

Because of the nature of landfills, GAAP also requires that a company compare a landfill's cost to its anticipated salvage value, with any difference depreciated over its estimated useful life. Waste Management disclosed in the footnotes to the financial statements in its annual reports that "[d]isposal sites are carried

---

[13] *SEC v. Dean L. Buntrock, Phillip B. Rooney, James E. Koenig, Thomas C. Hau, Herbert A. Getz, and Bruce D. Tobecksen,* Complaint No. 02C 2180 (Judge Manning).

at cost and to the extent this exceeds end use realizable value, such excess is amortized over the estimated life of the disposal site." However, in reality, the SEC found evidence that Waste Management allegedly carried almost all of its landfills on the balance sheet at cost.[14]

Auditor Assessment[15]

In a letter to the management team dated May 29, 1992, Arthur Andersen's team wrote, "[i]n each of the past five years the Company added a new consolidating entry in the fourth quarter to increase salvage value and/or useful life of its trucks, machinery, equipment, or containers." Andersen recommended that the company conduct a "comprehensive, one-time study to evaluate the proper level of WMNA's salvage value and useful lives," and then send these adjustments to the respective WMNA groups. Top management continued to change depreciation estimates at headquarters, however.

In March 1994 Executive Vice President and CFO James Koenig, who had worked as an auditor at Arthur Andersen before joining Waste Management in 1977, allegedly instructed a purchasing agent to draft a memo concluding that the agent supported one of the company's salvage value estimates. In November 1995 a study was initiated to determine the appropriate lives and salvage values of the company's vehicles, equipments, and containers. Koenig allegedly ordered the study to be stopped after he was informed that the interim results of the study revealed that the company's salvage values should be reduced. Koenig also was said to have ordered the destruction of all copies of the memo that released the study's interim results and that the document be deleted from the author's computer. The memo was never provided to the company's auditors.

Regarding the issue of Waste Management's treatment of landfills on the balance sheet, Andersen issued a management letter to the board of directors recommending that the company conduct a "site by site analysis of its landfills to compare recorded land values with its anticipated net realizable value based on end use" after its 1988 audit. Andersen further instructed that any excess needed to be amortized over the "active site life" of the landfill. Andersen made similar demands after its audit in 1994. Despite this letter, management never conducted such a study and also failed to reduce the carrying values of overvalued land, despite its commitment to do so after Andersen's audit in 1994.

Top-Side Adjusting Journal Entries

Top-side adjusting journal entries are typically made by upper managers at the end of the reporting process, usually at corporate headquarters. Because these journal entries are typically not generated at the business process (such as

[14] Ibid.
[15] Ibid.

Internet sales) or the business unit level (such as the North American division), they can be used by upper managers to circumvent the internal control system and possibly perpetrate fraud.

Waste Management seemed to routinely use top-side adjusting entries when consolidating the results of several of its business units and entities in which the company had an interest, to prepare its annual and quarterly financial statements. Indeed, Waste Management's use of several unbudgeted and unsupported top-side adjustments in the early 1990s caused observers (including Arthur Andersen) to question whether management had employed these adjustments as tools to help manage reported earnings.

Waste Management set its earnings targets during an annual budget process. The company followed a top-down budgeting process whereby the CEO (Buntrock until 1996 and Rooney from Buntrock's retirement until early 1997) set goals for earnings growth, and the operating units would in turn determine their budgets based on the goals set at the top. The budgets were then consolidated to arrive at the budgeted consolidated earnings. At this time the upper managers also set budgets for the anticipated top-side adjustments, which were based on the existing accounting assumptions used.

As operating results were recorded by Waste Management's operating units at the end of each quarter, upper management allegedly monitored the gap between the results and the goals and made a number of different types of unbudgeted top-side adjusting entries to "close the gap." Management did not disclose to investors the impact of the top-side adjustments on the company's earnings. In fact, management did not inform its own internal operating units about the top-side adjusting entries that were made and their resulting expense reductions.

As early as 1992, the company's auditor Arthur Andersen advised management against its use of top-side adjusting entries as a tool to manage its earnings in a postaudit letter recommending accounting changes. Andersen auditors wrote that "individual decisions are not being evaluated on the true results of their operations" as a result of the extensive use of top-side adjustments. Andersen recommended that "all such corporate adjustments should be passed back to the respective" divisions. Yet top management allegedly increased the budget for the top-side adjustments from 1992 to 1997, and each year the actual adjustments made exceeded the budgeted adjustments. From the first quarter of 1992 through the first quarter of 1997, top management used unsupported top-side adjustments in 14 of 21 quarters to achieve reported results that ultimately fell within the range of the company's public earnings projections or its internal budgeted earnings.

In February 1998, Waste Management announced that it was restating the financial statements it had issued for the years 1993 through 1996. In its restatement, Waste Management said that it had materially overstated its reported pretax earnings by $1.43 billion and that it had understated elements of its tax expense by $178 million. When the company's improper accounting was revealed, the stock dropped by more than 33 percent and shareholders lost over $6 billion.

Waste Management's Relationship with Independent Auditor Arthur Andersen

Even before Waste Management became a public company in 1971, Arthur Andersen served as the company's auditor. In the early 1990s Waste Management capped Andersen's corporate audit fees at the prior year's level, although it did allow the firm to earn additional fees for "special work." Between 1991 and 1997 Andersen billed Waste Management approximately $7.5 million in audit fees.[16] During this seven-year period Andersen also billed Waste Management $11.8 million in fees related to the following services: $4.5 million for audit work under ERISA, special purpose letters (EPA), franchise audits and other reports, registration statements and comfort letters, international public offering, SFAS 106 and 109 adoption, accounting research/discussions and other (audit committee meetings); $4.5 million for various consulting services that included $450,000 for information systems consulting; and $1.1 million for miscellaneous other services.[17]

During the 1990s approximately 14 former Andersen employees worked for Waste Management.[18] While at Andersen, most of these individuals worked in the group responsible for auditing Waste Management's financial statements prior to 1991, and all but a few had left Andersen more than 10 years before the 1993 financial statement audit commenced.[19]

In fact, until 1997 every chief financial officer (CFO) and chief accounting officer (CAO) at Waste Management since it became public had previously worked as an auditor at Andersen. Waste Management's CAO and corporate controller from September 1990 to October 1997, Thomas Hau, was a former Andersen audit engagement partner for the Waste Management account. When Hau left Andersen, he was the head of the division within Andersen responsible for conducting Waste Management's annual audit, but he was not the engagement partner at that time.[20]

Andersen's Engagement Partners on the Waste Management Audit

In 1991 Andersen assigned Robert Allgyer, a partner at Andersen since 1976, to become the audit engagement partner for the Waste Management audit engagement. He held the title of partner-in-charge of client service and served as marketing director for Andersen's Chicago office. Among the reasons for Allgyer's selection as engagement partner were his "extensive experience in Europe,"

---

[16] SEC Auditing and Enforcement Release No. 1410, June 19, 2001.
[17] SEC Auditing and Enforcement Release No. 1405, June 19, 2001.
[18] SEC Auditing and Enforcement Release No. 1410, June 19, 2001.
[19] SEC Auditing and Enforcement Release No. 1405, June 19, 2001.
[20] Ibid.

his "devotion to client service," and his "personal style that ... fit well with the Waste Management officers."[21] In setting Allgyer's compensation, Andersen took into account fees for audit and nonaudit services.[22] Walter Cercavschi, who was a senior manager when he started working on the Waste Management engagement team in the late eighties, remained on the engagement after becoming partner in 1994.

In 1993 Edward Maier became the concurring partner on the engagement. As concurring partner, Maier's duties included reading the financial statements; discussing significant accounting, auditing, or reporting issues with the engagement partner; reviewing certain workpapers (such as the audit risk analysis, final engagement memoranda, summaries of proposed adjusting, and reclassifying entries); and inquiring about matters that could have a material effect on the financial statements or the auditor's report. Maier also served as the risk management partner for the Chicago office in charge of supervising such processes as client acceptance and retention decisions.[23]

Andersen's Proposed Adjusting Journal Entries

In early 1994 the Andersen engagement team quantified several current and prior period misstatements and prepared proposed adjusting journal entries (PAJEs) in the amount of $128 million for the company to record in 1993. If recorded, this amount would have reduced net income before special items by 12 percent. The engagement team also identified accounting practices that gave rise to other known and likely misstatements primarily resulting in the understatement of operating expenses.[24]

Allgyer and Maier consulted with Robert Kutsenda, the practice director responsible for Andersen's Chicago, Kansas City, Indianapolis, and Omaha offices. Kutsenda and the audit division head, who was also consulted, determined that the misstatements were not material and that Andersen could therefore issue an unqualified audit report on the 1993 financial statements. Nevertheless, they instructed Allgyer to inform management that Andersen expected the company to change its accounting practices and to reduce the cumulative amount of the PAJEs in the future.[25] After consulting with the managing partner of the firm, Allgyer proposed a "Summary of Action Steps" to reduce the cumulative amount of the PAJEs, going forward, and to change the accounting practices that gave rise to the PAJEs and to the other known and likely misstatements.[26]

[21] Ibid.

[22] Ibid.

[23] Ibid.

[24] Ibid.

[25] Ibid.

[26] Ibid.

Although the company's management agreed to the action steps, the company allegedly continued to engage in the accounting practices that gave rise to the PAJEs, and the other misstatements. Despite Waste Management's failure to make progress on the PAJEs, Andersen's engagement team continued to issue unqualified audit reports on Waste Management's financial statements. In fact, Waste Management's financial statements for the years 1993 through 1996 overstated the company's pretax income by more than $1 billion.[27]

The SEC brought charges against founder Buntrock and five other former top officers on charges of earnings management fraud. The SEC's charges alleged that top management had made several top-side adjustments in the process of consolidating the results reported by operating groups and intentionally hid these adjustments from the operating groups themselves. In addition, top management had allegedly employed several other improper accounting practices to reduce expenses and artificially inflate earnings.[28]

To help conceal the intentional understatement of expenses, top management allegedly used a practice known as *netting*, whereby one-time gains realized on the sale or exchange of assets were used to eliminate unrelated current period operating expenses, as well as accounting misstatements that had accumulated from prior periods. Top management also allegedly used *geography entries*, which involved moving millions of dollars to different line items on the income statement to make it harder to compare results across time. In addition, management allegedly made or authorized false and misleading disclosures in financial statements.[29]

Because the financial statements for the years 1993 through 1996 were not presented in conformity with GAAP, Waste Management's independent auditor, Arthur Andersen, came under fire for issuing unqualified opinions on these financial statements. The SEC filed suit against Andersen on charges that it knowingly or recklessly issued materially false and misleading audit reports for the period 1993 through 1996. Andersen settled with the SEC for $7 million, the largest ever civil penalty at the time, without admitting or denying any allegations or findings.[30]

Three Andersen partners who worked on the Waste Management audit during the period 1993 through 1996 were implicated in the SEC's charges: Robert Allgyer, the partner responsible for the Waste Management engagement; Edward Maier, the concurring partner on the engagement and the risk management partner for Andersen's Chicago office; and Walter Cercavschi, a partner

[27] SEC, "Arthur Andersen LLP Agrees to Settlement Resulting in First Antifraud Injunction in More Than 20 Years and Largest-Ever Civil Penalty ($7 million) in SEC Enforcement Action against a Big Five Accounting Firm," Press Release 2001–62.

[28] *SEC v. Dean L. Buntrock, Phillip B. Rooney, James E. Koenig, Thomas C. Hau, Herbert A. Getz, and Bruce D. Tobecksen,* Complaint No. 02C 2180 (Judge Manning).

[29] Ibid.

[30] SEC, "Arthur Andersen LLP Agrees to Settlement Resulting in First Antifraud Injunction in More Than 20 Years and Largest-Ever Civil Penalty ($7 million) in SEC Enforcement Action against a Big Five Accounting Firm," Press Release 2001–62.

on the engagement. Allgyer, Maier, and Cercavschi agreed to pay a civil penalty of $50,000, $40,000, and $30,000, respectively. Allgyer, Maier, and Cercavschi were also denied privileges of practicing before the SEC as accountants, with the right to request reinstatement after five years, three years, and three years, respectively. A fourth Andersen partner, Robert Kutsenda, the central region audit practice director responsible for Andersen's Chicago, Kansas City, Indianapolis, and Omaha offices, was also implicated in the SEC charges for improper conduct. Kutsenda was penalized by being denied the privilege of practicing before the SEC as an accountant. Kutsenda was given the right to request reinstatement after one year.[31]

[31] SEC Auditing and Enforcement Release No. 1410, June 19, 2001.

Case Questions

1. What is *auditor independence,* and what is its significance to the audit profession? In what ways was Arthur Andersen's independence potentially affected on the Waste Management audit, if any?

2. Consult Paragraphs 3–6 of Quality Control Standard No. 20 (QC 20). Considering the example in the Waste Management case, explain why a review by the practice director and the audit division head is important in the operations of a CPA firm. In your opinion, was this review effective at Waste Management? Why or why not?

3. Consult Paragraph 7 of PCAOB Auditing Standard No. 13. Do you believe that Andersen's final decision regarding the PAJEs was appropriate under the circumstances? Would your opinion change if you knew that all of the adjustments were based on subjective differences (such as a difference in the estimate of the allowance for doubtful accounts) as compared to objective differences (such as a difference in the account receivable balance of their biggest customer)?

4. Refer to Sections 203 and 206 of SARBOX. How would these sections of the law have impacted the Waste Management audit? Do you believe that these sections are needed? Why or why not?

5. Consider the principles, assumptions, and constraints of Generally Accepted Accounting Principles (GAAP). Define the *matching principle* and explain why it is important to users of financial statements.

6. Based on the case information provided, describe specifically how Waste Management violated the matching principle. In your description, please identify a journal entry that may have been used by Waste Management to commit the fraud.

7. Consult Paragraph 2 of PCAOB Auditing Standard No. 5. Do you believe that Waste Management had established an effective system of internal control over financial reporting related to the depreciation expense recorded in its financial statements? Why or why not?

8. Consult Paragraphs 5–6 of PCAOB Auditing Standard No. 15. As an auditor, what type of evidence would you want to examine to determine whether Waste Management's decision to change the useful life and salvage value of its assets was appropriate under GAAP?

9. Consider the principles, assumptions, and constraints of Generally Accepted Accounting Principles (GAAP). What is the specific definition of an *asset*?

10. Consider the practices of basketing and bundling. Briefly explain why each practice is not appropriate under GAAP.

11. Consult Paragraphs 6–7 of PCAOB Auditing Standard No. 13. Next, describe why netting would be effective for Waste Management's management team when trying to cover up their fraudulent behavior.

12. Consult Paragraph 10 of PCAOB Auditing Standard No. 15. As an auditor, what type of evidence would allow you to detect whether your client was engaging in behaviors designed to mask fraud (such as basketing, bundling, or netting)?

13. Consult Paragraphs 14–15 of PCAOB Auditing Standard No. 13. If you were auditing Waste Management, what type of documentary evidence would you require to evaluate the propriety of such a top-side adjusting journal entry?

14. Consult Paragraph 14 of PCAOB Auditing Standard No. 5. Based on the case information, do you think this paragraph relates to the use of top-side adjusting journal entries at an audit client like Waste Management? Why or why not?

15. Consult Paragraphs 26–27 of PCAOB Auditing Standard No. 5 and Paragraph 41 of PCAOB Auditing Standard No. 13. Do you believe that the period-end financial reporting process should always be evaluated by auditors as a significant and material process during an audit of internal control? Why or why not?

16. Consult Paragraphs 71–72 of PCAOB Auditing Standard No. 12. Identify one specific control procedure that could prevent or detect a misstatement related to a top-side adjusting journal entry.

17. Consult Paragraphs 65–69 of PCAOB Auditing Standard No. 12. Based on your understanding of fraud risk assessment, what three conditions are likely to be present when fraud occurs (the fraud triangle)? Based on the information provided in the case, which condition was most prevalent at Waste Management, and why?

18. Consult Sections 204 and 301 of SARBOX. What is the role of the audit committee in the financial reporting process? Do you believe that an audit committee can be effective in providing oversight of a management team such as that of Waste Management?

19. Consult Sections 302 and 305 and Title IX of SARBOX. Do you believe that these provisions will help to deter fraudulent financial reporting by a top management group such as that of Waste Management? Why or why not?

20. Consider the role of the Waste Management employee who was responsible for calculating depreciation expense and recording the proper amount in the financial statements. Assuming the employee knew that the consolidating entries in the fourth quarter recorded by upper management were fraudulent, do you believe that the employee had a responsibility to report the behavior to the audit committee? Why or why not?

21. Consider the decision by CFO James Koenig and Corporate Controller Thomas Hau to phase in the new GAAP method to capitalize interest expense over three years. Do you believe that this decision was in the best interests of the shareholders in the long run? Why or why not?

Case 6.3

WorldCom

Synopsis

On June 25, 2002, WorldCom announced that it would be restating its financial statements for 2001 and the first quarter of 2002. On July 21, 2002, WorldCom announced that it had filed for bankruptcy. It was later revealed that WorldCom had engaged in improper accounting that took two major forms: overstatement of revenue by at least $958 million and understatement of line costs, its largest category of expenses, by over $7 billion. Several executives pled guilty to charges of fraud and were sentenced to prison terms, including CFO Scott Sullivan (five years) and Controller David Myers (one year and one day). Convicted of fraud in 2005, CEO Bernie Ebbers was the first to receive his prison sentence: 25 years.

Growth through Acquisitions

WorldCom evolved from a long distance telephone provider named Long Distance Discount Services (LDDS), which had annual revenues of approximately $1.5 billion by the end of 1993. LDDS connected calls between the local telephone company of a caller and the local telephone company of the call's recipient by reselling long distance capacity it purchased from major long distance carriers (such as AT&T, MCI, and Sprint) on a wholesale basis.[1] LDDS was renamed WorldCom in 1995.

A change in industry regulation was the primary catalyst for WorldCom's growth. The Telecommunications Act of 1996 allowed long distance telephone service providers to enter the market for local telephone services and other telecommunications services, such as the Internet. Like many players in the industry, WorldCom turned to acquisitions to expand into these markets.

WorldCom's revenues grew rapidly as it embarked on these acquisitions. Between the first quarter of 1994 and the third quarter 1999, WorldCom's year-over-year revenue growth was over 50 percent in 16 of 23 quarters; the

[1] Board of Directors' Special Investigative Committee Report, June 9, 2003, pp. 44–45.

growth rate was less than 20 percent in only three quarters. WorldCom's stock price experienced rapid growth as well, from $8.17 at the beginning of January 1994 to $47.91 at the end of September 1999 (adjusted for stock splits). Its stock performance exceeded those of its largest industry competitors, AT&T and Sprint.[2]

MFS and Subsidiary UUNET

In late 1996 WorldCom acquired MFS, which provided local telephone services, for $12.4 billion. In that transaction WorldCom also gained an important part of the Internet backbone through MFS's recently acquired subsidiary, UUNET.[3]

Brooks Fiber Properties, CompuServe Corporation, and ANS Communications

In 1998 WorldCom purchased Brooks Fiber Properties for approximately $2.0 billion and CompuServe Corporation and ANS Communications (a three-way transaction valued at approximately $1.4 billion that included a five-year service commitment to America Online). Each of these companies expanded World-Com's presence in the Internet arena.

MCI

In September 1998 WorldCom acquired MCI, using approximately 1.13 billion of its common shares and $7.0 billion cash as consideration, for a total price approaching $40 billion. MCI's annual revenues of $19.7 billion in 1997 far exceeded WorldCom's 1997 annual revenues of $7.4 billion. As a result of this merger, WorldCom became the second largest telecommunications provider in the United States.

SkyTel Communications and Sprint

In October 1999 WorldCom purchased SkyTel Communications, adding wireless communications to its service offerings, for $1.8 billion. A few days after its Sky-Tel acquisition, WorldCom announced that it would merge with Sprint in a deal valued at $115 billion. In the proposed deal, WorldCom would gain Sprint's PCS wireless business, in addition to its long distance and local calling operations.[4]

Challenges

By 2000 WorldCom started to face some difficult challenges. It faced fierce competition in its industry. In addition, its proposed merger with Sprint failed to receive approval from the Antitrust Division of the U.S. Department of Justice. The companies officially terminated their discussions on July 13, 2000.[5]

[2] Ibid., p. 48.
[3] Ibid., p. 46.
[4] Ibid., pp. 47–48.
[5] Ibid., pp. 48–49.

Although WorldCom's revenue continued to grow, the rate of growth slowed. On November 1, 2000, it announced the formation of two tracking stocks: one—called WorldCom Group—to capture the growth of its data business, and the other—called MCI—to capture the cash generation of its voice business, which experienced low growth. WorldCom also announced reduced expectations for revenue growth of the consolidated company, from its previous guidance of 12 percent to between 7 percent and 9 percent in the fourth quarter of 2000 and all of 2001. By the close of market on the day of its announcement, WorldCom's stock price had fallen by 20.3 percent, from $23.75 on October 31, 2000, to $18.94.[6]

Industry conditions worsened in 2001. Both the local telephone services and Internet segments experienced downturns in demand. The impact of the downturn in the Internet segment was particularly severe because of the industry's increased investment in network capacity (supply). Many competitors found themselves mired in long-term contracts that they had entered into to obtain the capacity to meet anticipated customer demand. As the ratio of their expenses to revenues was increasing, industry revenues and stock prices plummeted. For example, the stock prices of WorldCom, AT&T, and Sprint lost at least 75 percent of their share price values between January 2000 and June 25, 2002.[7]

Independent Auditor's Risk Assessment

The special investigative committee of the board of directors did find evidence that Andersen understood the elevated risk associated with the WorldCom audit. Specifically, although Andersen's System for Managing Acceptance and Retention (SMART) Tool—which assessed the risks of business failure, fraud, and accounting and financial errors—rated WorldCom a "high risk" client, Andersen manually overrode this result and increased WorldCom to a "maximum risk" client. The committee reported that Andersen's workpapers revealed that the reasoning behind this elevation of risk was "the volatility in the telecommunications industry, the company's future merger and acquisition plans, and the company's reliance on a high stock price to fund those acquisitions."[8] Surprisingly, Andersen did not disclose that WorldCom was considered a "maximum risk" client to the audit committee.[9]

Because of the "maximum risk" classification, Andersen's internal policies required the engagement team to consult with Andersen's practice director, advisory partner, audit division head, and professional standards group (where appropriate) regarding all significant audit issues. In addition, the lead engagement partner was required to hold an annual expanded risk discussion with the

---

[6] Ibid., p. 50.

[7] Ibid., pp. 51–55.

[8] Ibid., pp. 232–233.

[9] Ibid., p. 27.

concurring partner, the practice director, and the audit division head to consider the areas that caused greater audit risk.

The outcome of this discussion after the 1999 and 2000 year-end audits was that Andersen did not find evidence of aggressive accounting or fraud at WorldCom.[10] However, during the expanded risk discussion held in December 2001, concerns were voiced over WorldCom's use of numerous top-side journal entries. Such entries were typically recorded at the corporate level, detached from the economic activity occurring at each of the business units or divisions within WorldCom. In fact, a handwritten note in Andersen's workpapers read, "Manual Journal Entries How deep are we going? Surprise w[ith] look [at] journal entries." Yet there was no indication of further testing of these entries.[11]

Line Cost Expenses

WorldCom generally maintained its own lines for local service in heavily populated urban areas. However, it relied on non-WorldCom networks to complete most residential and commercial calls outside these urban areas and paid the owners of the networks to use their services. For example, a call from a WorldCom customer in Boston to Rome might start on a local (Boston) phone company's line, flow to WorldCom's own network, and then get passed to an Italian phone company to be completed. In this example WorldCom would have to pay both the local Boston phone company and the Italian provider for the use of their services.[12] The costs associated with carrying a voice call or data transmission from its starting point to its ending point were called *line cost expenses.*

Line cost expenses were WorldCom's largest single expense. They accounted for approximately half of the company's total expenses from 1999 to 2001. WorldCom regularly discussed its line cost expenses in public disclosures, emphasizing, in particular, its "line cost E/R ratio"—the ratio of line cost expense to revenue.[13]

GAAP for Line Costs

Under Generally Accepted Accounting Principles (GAAP), WorldCom was required to estimate its line costs each month and to expense the estimated cost immediately, even though many of these costs would be paid later. To reflect an estimate of amounts that had not yet been paid, WorldCom would set up a liability account, known as an *accrual,* on its balance sheet. As the bills arrived from its outside parties, sometimes many months later, WorldCom would pay them and reduce the previously established accruals accordingly.[14]

Because accruals are estimates, a company was required under GAAP to reevaluate them periodically to see if they were stated at appropriate levels.

[10] Ibid., pp. 232–233.
[11] Ibid., p. 236.
[12] Ibid., p. 58.
[13] Ibid., pp. 58–59.
[14] Ibid., pp. 62–63.

If charges from service providers were lower than estimated, an accrual was "released." The amount of the release was set off against the reported line cost expenses in the period when the release occurred. For example, if an accrual of $500 million was established in the first quarter and $25 million of that amount was deemed excess or unnecessary in the second quarter, then $25 million should be released in that second quarter, thus reducing reported line cost expenses by $25 million.[15]

WorldCom's Line Cost Releases

Beginning in the second quarter of 1999, management allegedly started ordering several releases of line cost accruals, often without any underlying analysis to support the releases. When requests met resistance, management allegedly made the adjustments themselves. For example, in the second quarter of 2000 David Myers, a CPA who served as senior vice president and controller of WorldCom, requested that UUNET (a largely autonomous WorldCom subsidiary at the time) release $50 million in line cost accruals. UUNET's acting Chief Financial Officer David Schneeman asked that Myers explain the reasoning for the requested release, but Myers insisted that Schneeman book the entry without an explanation. When Schneeman refused, Myers wrote him in an e-mail, "I guess the only way I am going to get this booked is to fly to DC and book it myself. Book it right now, I can't wait another minute." After Schneeman refused again, Betty Vinson in general accounting allegedly completed Myers's request by making a top-side corporate-level adjusting journal entry releasing $50 million in UUNET accruals.[16]

In 2000 senior members of WorldCom's corporate finance organization reportedly directed a number of similar releases from accruals established for other reasons to offset domestic line cost expenses. For example, in the second quarter of 2000 Senior Vice President and Controller David Myers asked Charles Wasserott, director of domestic telco accounting, to release $255 million in domestic line cost accruals to reduce domestic line cost expenses. Wasserott refused to release such a large amount. It later emerged that the entire $255 million used to reduce line cost expenses came instead from a release of a mass markets accrual related to WorldCom's selling, general, and administrative expenses.[17]

The largest of the releases of accruals from other areas to reduce line cost expenses occurred after the close of the third quarter of 2000. During this time a number of entries were made to release various accruals that reduced domestic line cost expenses by $828 million.[18]

In addition to releasing line cost accruals without proper support for doing so and releasing accruals that had been established for other purposes, it was

[15] Ibid., pp. 63–64.
[16] Ibid., p. 83.
[17] Ibid., pp. 87–88.
[18] Ibid., pp. 88–89.

also alleged that WorldCom management had not released certain line costs in the periods in which they were identified. Rather, certain line cost accruals were kept as "rainy-day" funds that could be released when managers wanted to improve reported results.[19]

Andersen's Relationship with WorldCom

Andersen served as WorldCom's auditor from at least as far back as 1990 through April 2002. In a presentation to the audit committee on May 20, 1999, Andersen stated that it viewed its relationship with WorldCom as a "long-term partnership" in which Andersen would help WorldCom improve its business operations and growth in the future. In its Year 2000 audit proposal, Andersen told the audit committee that it considered itself "a committed member of [WorldCom's] team" and that WorldCom was "a flagship client and a 'crown jewel'" of its firm.[20]

In terms of the total amount of fees charged to clients, WorldCom was one of Andersen's top 20 engagements in 2000 and was the largest client of its Jackson, Mississippi, office. From 1999 through 2001 WorldCom paid Andersen $7.8 million in fees to audit the financial statements of WorldCom, Inc.; $6.6 million for other audits required by law in other countries; and about $50 million for consulting, litigation support, and tax services.[21]

Andersen's Restricted Access to Information

WorldCom allegedly severely restricted Andersen's access to information; several of Andersen's requests for detailed information and opportunities to speak with certain employees were denied. In fact, Andersen was denied access to WorldCom's computerized general ledger and had to rely on printed ledgers. According to the person in charge of security for WorldCom's computerized consolidation and financial reporting system, WorldCom's treasurer in 1998 allegedly instructed him not to give Andersen access to this reporting system.[22]

In addition, WorldCom's senior management allegedly berated employees who disclosed unauthorized information to Andersen. For example, in October 2000 Steven Brabbs, the director of international finance and control for EMEA (Europe, Middle East, and Africa), told Andersen's U.K. office that line cost expenses for EMEA were understated by $33.6 million because senior management had reduced its line cost accruals and that EMEA did not have any support for this entry. WorldCom's Senior Vice President and Controller David Myers reprimanded Brabbs and directed him never to do it again. In early 2002, after learning about another conversation between Brabbs and Andersen about a planned restructuring

---

[19] Ibid., p. 10.
[20] Ibid., p. 225.
[21] Ibid.
[22] Ibid., pp. 246–248.

charge, Myers specifically instructed U.K. employees that "NO communication with auditors is allowed without speaking with Stephanie Scott [Vice President of Financial Reporting] and myself. This goes for anything that might imply a change in accounting, charges or anything else that you would think is important." When Myers found out that the accountant had continued to speak with Andersen U.K. about the issue, he wrote the following to the accountant:[23]

> Do not have anymore meetings with Andersen for any reason. I spoke to Andersen this morning and hear that you are still talking about asset impairments and facilities. I do not want to hear an excuse just stop. Mark Wilson has already told you this once. Don't make me ask you again.

Although Andersen was aware that it was receiving less than full cooperation, it did not notify WorldCom's audit committee of this matter.[24]

Audit Approach

The special investigative committee of the board of the directors found that Andersen conducted only a limited amount of detailed substantive testing. Andersen's audit approach relied heavily on analytical procedures without taking into full account the possibility that management might be manipulating the results to eliminate significant financial statement variations. Further, Andersen gave WorldCom's senior management team a list of the auditing procedures that it anticipated performing in the areas of revenues, line costs, accounts receivable, capital expenditures, and data integrity. In addition, Andersen's testing of capital expenditures, line costs, and revenues did not change materially from 1999 through 2001.[25]

The special committee was surprised by Andersen's failure to detect significant deficiencies in WorldCom's procedures related to the proper documentary support of top-side accounting entries. For example, the committee found hundreds of large, round-dollar journal entries that were made by WorldCom's general accounting group staff without any support other than Post-it® Notes or written instructions directing the entry to be made. The documentary support was also found in a disorganized manner.[26]

Measurement and Monitoring of Revenue within WorldCom

Revenue growth was said to have been particularly emphasized within WorldCom. Sales groups' performances were regularly measured against the revenue plan. At meetings held every two to three months, each sales channel manager

---

[23] Ibid., pp. 250–251.
[24] Ibid., pp. 25–26.
[25] Ibid., p. 228.
[26] Ibid., p. 241.

was required to present and defend his or her sales channel's performance against the budgeted performance. Compensation and bonus packages for several members of senior management were also tied to double-digit revenue growth. In 2000 and 2001, for instance, three executives were eligible to receive executive bonuses only if the company achieved double-digit revenue growth over the first six months of each year.[27]

Monthly Revenue Report ("MonRev") and the Corporate Unallocated Schedule

The principal tool by which revenue performance was measured and monitored at WorldCom was the monthly revenue report ("MonRev"), which was prepared and distributed by the revenue reporting and accounting group (hereafter referred to as the revenue accounting group). The MonRev included dozens of spreadsheets detailing revenue data from all the company's channels and segments. The full MonRev contained the corporate unallocated schedule, an attachment detailing adjustments made at the corporate level and generally not derived from the operating activities of WorldCom's sales channels. WorldCom's Chief Financial Officer and Treasurer Scott Sullivan had ultimate responsibility for the items booked on the corporate unallocated schedule.[28]

In addition to CEO Ebbers and CFO Sullivan, only a handful of employees outside the revenue accounting group regularly received the full MonRev. Most managers at WorldCom received only those portions of the MonRev that were deemed relevant to their position; for example, most sales channel managers received only the MonRev components that reflected their own sales channel revenue information. It was alleged that Sullivan routinely reviewed the distribution list for the full MonRev to make sure he approved of everyone on the list.[29]

The total amounts reported in the corporate unallocated schedule usually spiked during quarter-ending months, with the largest spikes occurring in those quarters when operational revenue lagged furthest behind quarterly revenue targets—the second and third quarters of 2000 and second, third, and fourth quarters of 2001. Without the revenue booked in corporate unallocated, WorldCom would have failed to achieve the double-digit growth it reported in 6 out of 12 quarters between 1999 and 2001.[30]

In 1999 and 2000 the revenue accounting group attempted to track the impact of corporate unallocated and other accounting adjustments by generating two MonRevs—one that represented the company's operational revenues before any adjustments and a second representing the revenues as supplemented by any extraordinary accounting entries, such as those recorded in the corporate

---

[27] Ibid., pp. 133–134.
[28] Ibid., pp. 135–139.
[29] Ibid.
[30] Ibid.

unallocated revenue account. The extraordinary revenue items schedule captured the items that comprised the difference between the two documents. The group decided to stop preparing both reports—a decision they later said was principally based on the time required to produce the second version of the MonRev, given the limited resources in his group.[31]

Process of Closing and Consolidating Revenues

WorldCom maintained a fairly automated process for closing and consolidating operational revenue numbers. By the 10th day after the end of the month, the revenue accounting group prepared a draft preliminary MonRev that was followed by a final MonRev, which took into account any adjustments that needed to be made. In non-quarter-ending months, the final MonRev was usually similar, if not identical, to the preliminary MonRev.[32]

In quarter-ending months, however, revenue accounting entries, often large, were made during the quarterly close to hit revenue growth targets. Investigators later found notes made by senior executives in 1999 and 2000 that calculated the difference between "act[ual]" or "MonRev" results and "target" or "need[ed]" numbers and identified the entries that were necessary to make up that difference. It was alleged that CFO Scott Sullivan directed this process, which was implemented by Ron Lomenzo, the senior vice president of financial operations, and Lisa Taranto, an employee who reported to Lomenzo.[33]

Throughout much of 2001 WorldCom's revenue accounting group tracked the gulf between projected and targeted revenue—an exercise labeled "close the gap"—and kept a running tally of accounting "opportunities" that could be exploited to help make up that difference.[34]

Many questionable revenue entries were later found within the corporate unallocated revenue account. On June 19, 2001, as the quarter of 2001 was coming to a close, CFO Sullivan left a voicemail message for CEO Ebbers that indicated his concern over the company's growing use of nonrecurring items to increase revenues reported:

> Hey Bernie, it's Scott. This MonRev just keeps getting worse and worse. The copy, um the latest copy that you and I have already has accounting fluff in it . . . all one time stuff or junk that's already in the numbers. With the numbers being, you know, off as far as they are, I didn't think that this stuff was already in there. . . . We are going to dig ourselves into a huge hole because year to date it's disguising what is going on the recurring, uh, service side of the business.[35]

A few weeks later, Ebbers sent a memorandum to WorldCom's COO Ron Beaumont that directed him to "see where we stand on those one time events

---

[31] Ibid., pp. 140–141.
[32] Ibid.
[33] Ibid., p. 14.
[34] Ibid., p. 141.
[35] Ibid., p. 15.

that had to happen in order for us to have a chance to make our numbers." Yet Ebbers did not give any indication of the impact of nonrecurring items on revenues in his public comments to the market in that quarter or in other quarters. For that matter, the company did not address the impact of nonrecurring items on revenues in its earnings release or public filing either for that quarter or prior quarters.[36]

By the first quarter of 2002 management realized it was virtually impossible to deliver double-digit revenue growth. During a February 7, 2002, analyst call, CEO Ebbers announced guidance of "mid single-digits" revenue growth. Soon thereafter, both Ebbers and CFO Sullivan expressed confidence in achieving 5 percent revenue growth. Two weeks later, Ebbers was provided with an internal review of January 2002 revenue numbers, which showed that even those projections were ambitious; that is, January MonRev results showed a 6.9 percent year-over-year *decline* in revenue. In the first quarter of 2002 the WorldCom group ultimately reported revenues of $5.1 billion, a decline of approximately 2 percent from the first quarter of 2001. This publicly reported decline in revenue occurred despite the fact that approximately $132 million was booked in the WorldCom group corporate unallocated revenue account in the first quarter of 2002.[37]

Internal Audit Department Deficiencies

The audit committee of the board of directors at WorldCom had responsibility for ensuring that the company's systems of internal controls were effective. The internal audit department periodically gathered information related to aspects of the company's operational and financial controls, reporting its findings and recommendations directly to the audit committee. Dick Thornburgh, WorldCom's bankruptcy court examiner, wrote in his Second Interim Report, released on June 9, 2003, that "the members of the Audit Committee and the Internal Audit Department personnel appear to have taken their jobs seriously and worked to fulfill their responsibilities within certain limits."[38]

However, the bankruptcy court examiner also wrote that he found a number of deficiencies in both the internal audit department and the audit committee. Among the issues the bankruptcy court examiner noted in the internal audit department were as follows: its relationship with management, lack of budgetary resources, lack of substantive interaction with the external auditors, and its restricted access to relevant information.[39] The bankruptcy court examiner found that WorldCom's internal audit department focused its audits primarily on the areas that were expected to yield cost savings or result in additional

---

[36] Ibid.

[37] Ibid., p. 155.

[38] Second Interim Report of Dick Thornburgh, Bankruptcy Court Examiner, June 9, 2003, p. 12.

[39] Ibid., pp. 174–176.

revenues.[40] In planning its audits, the department did not seem to conduct any quantifiable risk assessment of the weaknesses or strengths of the company's internal control system. In addition, the examiner found that the department's lack of consultation with WorldCom's external auditor, Arthur Andersen, resulted in even further audit coverage gaps.[41]

Internal Audit Department's Relationship with Management

The SEC's investigation revealed that management's influence over the activities of the internal audit department appeared to supersede those of the audit committee. It appeared that management was able to direct the internal audit department to work on audits not previously approved by the audit committee and away from other audits that were originally scheduled. At most, the audit committee was advised of such changes after the fact.[42]

Although the audit committee annually approved the audit plans of the internal audit department, it had little input into the development of the scope of each audit or the disposition of any findings and/or recommendations. The audit committee also did not play any role in determining the day-to-day activities of the internal audit department. That responsibility appeared to belong to the CFO, who provided direction over the development of the scope of the department's audits and audit plans, the conduct of its audits, and the issuance of its conclusions and recommendations. The CFO also oversaw all personnel actions for the department, such as promotions and increases in salaries, bonuses, and stock options granted.[43]

The internal audit department distributed preliminary drafts of its internal audit reports to CFO Scott Sullivan and at times to CEO Bernie Ebbers. The internal audit also distributed preliminary drafts of its reports to the management that was affected by a particular report. All people on the distribution list provided their input on the conclusions and recommendations made in the reports. In contrast, the audit committee did not receive any preliminary drafts of the internal audit reports.[44]

At times, CFO Sullivan or CEO Ebbers would assign special projects to the internal audit department. Some of these projects were not audit-related, and the audit committee did not appear to have been consulted about such assignments.[45]

---

[40] Ibid., pp. 186–187.
[41] Ibid., pp. 194–195.
[42] Ibid.
[43] Ibid., pp. 190–191.
[44] Ibid., pp. 195–197.
[45] Ibid., pp. 190–191.

Impact of Lack of Budgetary Resources

According to the 2002 Global Auditing Information Network (GAIN) peer study conducted by the Institute of Internal Auditors, WorldCom's internal audit department (at a staff of 27 by 2002) was half the size of the internal audit departments of peer telecommunications companies. The head of the internal audit department, Cynthia Cooper (a vice president), presented the results of the GAIN study to the audit committee in May 2002. She advised the audit committee that her department was understaffed as well as underpaid. The minutes reflect that she advised the committee that the average cost of each of their internal auditors was $87,000 annually, well below the peer group average of $161,000.[46]

The budgetary resources allocated to the department seemed particularly inadequate given the international breadth and scope of the company's operations and the challenges posed by the company's various mergers and acquisitions over a relatively short time. For example, budget constraints restricted travel by internal audit staffers outside Mississippi, where most of the internal audit staff was located. Such a restriction made managing and conducting audits of company units located outside Mississippi, and particularly international audits, far more difficult.[47]

Lack of Substantive Interaction with External Auditors

Arthur Andersen's annual statement to the audit committee noted no material internal control weaknesses found as part of its annual audit of the company's financial statements. Yet in the same year the internal audit department had identified a number of seemingly important internal control weaknesses as part of its operational audits that impacted financial systems and the reporting of revenue. It appears that there was no communication between the internal and the external auditors to ensure awareness about all of the internal control weaknesses that were discovered. In fact, after 1997 internal audit had few substantive interactions with the company's external auditors other than at the quarterly audit committee meetings, where both groups made presentations.[48]

Restricted Access to Information

The internal audit department lacked consistent support throughout the company. In many instances management allegedly refused to answer or dodged

---

[46] Ibid., pp. 192–193.

[47] Ibid.

[48] Ibid., pp. 193–194.

certain questions asked by internal audit personnel. In several cases internal audit personnel would have to repeatedly request information, and their requests were not always answered in a timely manner.[49]

In addition, the internal audit department had limited access to the company's computerized accounting systems. Although the internal audit charter provided that internal audit had "full, free, and unrestricted access to all company functions, records, property, and personnel," few internal audit staff personnel had full systems access to the company's reporting system and the company's general ledgers.[50]

[49] Ibid., pp. 195–197.
[50] Ibid.

Case Questions

1. Consult PCAOB Ethics and Independence Rule 3520. What is *auditor independence,* and what is its significance to the audit profession? Based on the case information, do you believe that Andersen violated this rule? Why or why not?

2. Consult Paragraphs 5–7 of PCAOB Auditing Standard No. 13. Given the reluctance of WorldCom's management team to communicate with Andersen, do you believe that Andersen exercised due care and professional skepticism in completing its audit? Why or why not?

3. Consult Paragraphs 13–21 of PCAOB Auditing Standard No. 15. In terms of audit effectiveness and efficiency, briefly explain the difference between substantive analytical procedures and substantive tests of details. Do you believe it was appropriate for Andersen to rely primarily on substantive analytical procedures? Why or why not?

4. Consult Paragraph 14 and Paragraph A8 (in Appendix A) of PCAOB Auditing Standard No. 5. Provide examples of both a preventive control and a detective control that could address the risk that a fraudulent top-side adjusting journal entry could be made by a member of management.

5. Consider the principles, assumptions, and constraints of Generally Accepted Accounting Principles (GAAP). Define the *revenue recognition principle,* and explain why it is important to users of financial statements.

6. Provide one specific example of how WorldCom violated the revenue recognition principle in this situation. In your description, please identify a journal entry that may have been used by WorldCom to commit the fraud.

7. Consult Paragraph 2 of PCAOB Auditing Standard No. 5 and Paragraph 68 of PCAOB Auditing Standard No. 12. Do you believe that WorldCom had established an effective system of internal control over financial reporting related to the revenue recorded in its financial statements?

8. Consult Paragraph 25 of PCAOB Auditing Standard No. 5. Define what is meant by *control environment.* Explain why the control environment is so important to effective internal control over financial reporting at an audit client like WorldCom.

9. Consult Paragraphs 6–7 of PCAOB Auditing Standard No. 13. If you were auditing WorldCom, what type of documentary evidence would you require to evaluate the validity and propriety of a top-side adjusting journal entry made to a revenue account?

10. Consider the principles, assumptions, and constraints of Generally Accepted Accounting Principles (GAAP). Define the *matching principle,* and explain why it is important to users of financial statements.

11. Based on the case information provided, describe specifically how World-Com violated the matching principle. In your description, please identify a journal entry that may have been used by WorldCom to commit the fraud.

12. Consult Paragraph A5 (in Appendix A) of PCAOB Auditing Standard No. 5. Do you believe that WorldCom had established an effective system of internal control over financial reporting related to the line cost expense recorded in its financial statements? Why or why not?

13. Consult Paragraphs 13–21 of PCAOB Auditing Standard No. 15. As an auditor at WorldCom, what type of evidence would you want to examine to determine whether the company was inappropriately releasing line costs? Please be specific.

14. Consult Paragraphs 7–10 of PCAOB Auditing Standard No. 12. Based on your understanding of risk assessment and the case information, identify three specific factors about WorldCom's strategy that might cause you to elevate the risk of material misstatement.

15. Consult Paragraphs 5–7 of PCAOB Auditing Standard No. 13. Comment on how your understanding of the risks identified at WorldCom (in Question 14) would influence the nature, timing, and extent of your audit work at WorldCom.

16. Consult Paragraph 33 and Paragraph B10 (in Appendix B) of PCAOB Auditing Standard No. 5. If you were conducting an internal control audit of WorldCom, comment on how WorldCom's acquisition strategy would impact the nature, timing, and extent of your audit work at WorldCom.

17. Consult Paragraphs 65–66 of PCAOB Auditing Standard No. 12. Based on your understanding of fraud risk assessment, what three conditions are likely to be present when fraud occurs (the fraud triangle)? Based on the information provided in the case, which of these three conditions appears to have been the most prevalent at WorldCom, and why?

18. Consult Paragraph A5 (in Appendix A) of PCAOB Auditing Standard No. 5. Based on your understanding of WorldCom's internal audit department, do you believe that the department could have been helpful in the internal control process at WorldCom? Why or why not?

19. Consult Paragraph 56 of PCAOB Auditing Standard No. 12 and Sections 204 and 301 of SARBOX. Based on the case information, do you believe that WorldCom's audit committee was effective in its management of the internal audit department? Why or why not?

20. Consult Paragraphs .04–.08 of AU Section 322. Do you believe that auditors should be allowed to use the work of other professionals as evidence to support their own internal control audit opinions? Why or why not?

21. Consult Paragraphs 18–19 of PCAOB Auditing Standard No. 5. What specific factors must external auditors consider before using the work of other professionals as evidence to support their own internal control opinions?

22. Consult Paragraphs 1–2 of Ethics Rule 102 (ET 102). Next, consider the roles of Ron Lomenzo and Lisa Taranto. Assuming these employees were CPAs and knew that the entries being proposed by Scott Sullivan were fraudulent, do you believe that Lomenzo and Taranto should have recorded the journal entries as directed by Sullivan? Why or why not?

Case 6.4

Sunbeam

Synopsis

In April 1996 Sunbeam named Albert J. Dunlap as its CEO and chair. Formerly with Scott Paper Co., Dunlap was known as a turnaround specialist and was nicknamed "Chainsaw Al" because of the cost-cutting measures he typically employed. Almost immediately Dunlap began replacing nearly all of the upper management team and led the company into an aggressive corporate restructuring that included the elimination of half of its 12,000 employees and the elimination of 87 percent of Sunbeam's products.

Unfortunately, in May 1998 Sunbeam disappointed investors with its announcement that it had earned a worse-than-expected loss of $44.6 million in the first quarter of 1998.[1] CEO and Chair Dunlap was fired in June 1998. In October 1998 Sunbeam announced that it would need to restate its financial statements for 1996, 1997, and 1998.[2]

Sunbeam's History[3]

The early beginnings of Sunbeam Corporation can be traced back to the Chicago Flexible Shaft Company, founded by John Stewart and Thomas Clark in 1897. Although it was not until 1946 that the company changed its name to Sunbeam, it adopted the name Sunbeam in its advertising shortly after it expanded into manufacturing electrical appliances in 1910.

Successful products in the 1930s included the Sunbeam Mixmaster, a stationary food mixer; the Sunbeam Shavemaster Shaver; the first automatic coffeemaker; and the first pop-up electric toaster. Later appliances included the hair dryer (1949), humidifier (1950), ice crusher (1950), knife sharpener (1950), the Sunbeam Egg Cooker (1950), the Sunbeam Controlled Heat fry pan (1953), and an electric blanket (1955). The company acquired rival household appliance maker Oster in 1960.

---

[1] Robert Frank and Joann S. Lublin. "Dunlap's Ax Falls—6,000 Times—at Sunbeam," *The Wall Street Journal*, November 13, 1996, p. B1.

[2] GAO-03-138, Appendix XVII "Sunbeam Corporation," 201.

[3] Hoovers Online.

In 1981 Sunbeam was acquired by industrial conglomerate Allegheny International, which fell into bankruptcy in 1988 because of economic difficulties in its other divisions. Michael Price, Michael Steinhardt, and Paul Kazarian bought Allegheny from its creditors in 1990 and named the company Sunbeam-Oster. Kazarian assumed the positions of CEO and chair. Under Kazarian's leadership, the company paid off its debt, reorganized operations, and cut its workforce dramatically.[4]

The company went public in 1992. Kazarian was forced out in 1993 and replaced by Roger Schipke, a former manager of General Electric's appliance division. Kazarian was subsequently awarded $160 million in a lawsuit he filed for being forced out. The company was renamed Sunbeam in 1995. That year the company faced stagnant product prices and other difficult industry conditions, such as the growth of discount chains. In the face of these conditions, Sunbeam introduced new product lines, made acquisitions, and invested in greater production capacity.[5] After several quarters of disappointing sales and earnings results, Schipke tendered his resignation in April 1996. The company named as Schipke's successor Albert J. Dunlap, chief of Scott Paper Co.

Sunbeam in 1996

Sunbeam Corporation had five major product lines in its domestic operations: household appliances, health care products, personal care and comfort products, outdoor cooking products, and "away from home" business. It also had international sales that accounted for approximately 19 percent of its total net sales.[6]

Household appliances (29 percent of 1996 domestic net sales) included blenders, food steamers, bread makers, rice cookers, coffeemakers, toasters, and irons. Examples of health care products (11 percent) were vaporizers, humidifiers, air cleaners, massagers, and blood pressure monitors. Sunbeam's line of personal care and comfort products (21 percent) included shower massagers, hair clippers and trimmers, and electric warming blankets. Some of its major outdoor cooking products (29 percent) were electric, gas, and charcoal grills, as well as grill accessories. Its "away from home" business (5 percent) marketed clippers and related products for the professional and veterinarian trade, as well as products to commercial and institutional channels.

Executive Leadership

Chair and CEO Albert J. Dunlap assumed leadership in 1996. Dunlap invested $3 million of his own money in Sunbeam shares. "If I make a lot of money here

---

[4] Robert Frank and Joann S. Lublin, "Dunlap's Ax Falls—6,000 Times—at Sunbeam," *The Wall Street Journal,* November 13, 1996.

[5] Ibid.

[6] 1996 10K filing to SEC, Item 1 ("Business").

[at Sunbeam]—which I certainly intend to do—then the shareholders will make a lot. . . . I'm in lockstep with the shareholders."[7]

Dunlap immediately hired Russell Kersh as Sunbeam's chief financial officer. Dunlap and Kersh both entered lucrative three-year employment agreements that gave them strong financial incentives to raise the share price of the company. Dunlap then replaced almost all of top management, and their replacements were each provided with strong financial incentives to improve the company's share price.[8]

Corporate Restructuring and Plans for Growth

Under Dunlap's reign Sunbeam embarked on an aggressive restructuring that would involve the elimination of half of the company's 12,000 employees; the sale or consolidation of 39 of its 53 facilities; the divestiture of several lines of businesses, such as its furniture business; the elimination of 87 percent of Sunbeam's product list; and the replacement of six regional headquarters in favor of a single office in Delray Beach, Florida. "We planned this like the invasion of Normandy. . . . We attacked every aspect of the business," said Dunlap.[9]

Dunlap publicly predicted that as a result of the restructuring, the company would attain operating margins of 20 percent of sales in 1997 and increase its sales by 20 percent, 30 percent, and 35 percent, respectively, in 1997, 1998, and 1999. This meant that the company would have to double its sales to $2 billion by 1999.[10] Other goals were to introduce 30 new products each year domestically and to triple international sales to $600 million by 1999.[11]

Sunbeam's Reported Restructuring Charges in 1996

Associated with its operational restructuring, Sunbeam's 1996 results included a pretax charge to earnings of $337.6 million, which was allocated as follows:[12]

Restructuring, impairment, and other costs	$154.9 million
Cost of goods sold	$ 92.3 million
Selling, general, and administrative (SG&A)	$ 42.5 million
Estimated loss from discontinued operations	$ 47.9 million
Total	$337.6 million

[7] Joann S. Lublin and Martha Brannigan. "Sunbeam Names Albert Dunlap as Chief, Betting He Can Pull Off a Turnaround," *The Wall Street Journal,* July 19, 1996, p. B2.

[8] SEC Accounting and Auditing Enforcement Release No. 1706, January 27, 2003.

[9] Robert Frank and Joann S. Lublin. "Dunlap's Ax Falls—6,000 Times—at Sunbeam," *The Wall Street Journal,* November 13, 1996, p. B1.

[10] SEC Accounting and Auditing Enforcement Release No. 1706, January 27, 2003.

[11] 1996 10K filing to SEC, Item 1 ("Business").

[12] 1996 10K filing to SEC. Also see 1997 10K SEC filing, Note 8 ("Restructuring, Impairment, and Other Costs").

Restructuring, Impairment, and Other Costs

The "restructuring, impairment, and other costs" category included the following cash items: severance and other employee costs ($43.0 million); lease obligations and other exit costs associated with facility closures ($12.6 million); and back-office outsourcing start-up costs and other costs related to the implementation of the restructuring and growth plan ($7.5 million). Noncash items in this category ($91.8 million) were related to asset write-downs for disposals of excess facilities and equipment and noncore product lines; write-offs of redundant computer systems from the administrative back-office consolidations and outsourcing initiatives; and intangible, packaging, and other asset write-downs related to exited product lines and SKU reductions.

Importantly, this amount also included approximately $18.7 million of items that benefited future activities, such as costs of redesigning product packaging, costs of relocating employees and equipment, and certain consulting fees.[13] Inclusion of these items was not allowed under GAAP.

Cost of Goods Sold, SG&A, and Estimated Loss from Discontinued Operations

As part of its operational restructuring, Sunbeam sold the inventory of its eliminated products to liquidators at a substantial discount. As such, the cost of goods sold portion of the restructuring charge related principally to inventory write-downs and costs of inventory liquidation programs.

The SG&A portion of the restructuring charge related principally to increases in environmental, litigation, and other reserves. The litigation reserve was created for a lawsuit alleging Sunbeam's potential obligation to cover a portion of the cleanup costs for a hazardous waste site. To establish a litigation reserve under GAAP, management must determine that the reserved amount reflects a loss that is probable and able to be reasonably estimated. However, the SEC found that the amount of Sunbeam's reserve was improbable to be incurred.[14] Finally, the estimated loss from the discontinued operations portion of the restructuring reserve was related to the divestiture of the company's furniture business.[15]

Using Excess Reserves to Offset Current Expenses

In the first quarter of 1997 Sunbeam used $4.3 million of these restructuring reserves to offset against costs incurred in that period. This improved Sunbeam's 1997 income by approximately 13 percent. Sunbeam failed to disclose this "infrequent item" in its quarterly filing. In the second quarter of 1997 Sunbeam offset $8.2 million in second-quarter costs against the restructuring and other reserves created at year-end 1996 without making the appropriate disclosures.

---

[13] SEC Accounting and Auditing Enforcement Release No. 1706, January 27, 2003.

[14] Ibid.

[15] 1996 10K filed with the SEC.

It made a similar offset of current period expenses in the third and fourth quarters of 1997: $2.9 million and $1.5 million, respectively.[16]

Restatement of Restructuring Charge

In November 1998 Sunbeam ultimately restated the pretax restructuring charge from $337.6 million to $239.2 million, which was allocated as follows:[17]

Restructuring, impairment, and other costs	$110.1 million
Cost of goods sold	$ 60.8 million
Selling, general, and administrative (SG&A)	$ 10.1 million
Estimated loss from discontinued operations	$ 58.2 million
Total	$239.2 million

Restructuring, Impairment, and Other Costs

Restructuring, impairment, and other costs were restated as follows: severance and other employee costs of $24.7 million; lease obligations and other exit costs associated with facility closures of $16.7 million. Noncash items totaled $68.7 million—related to asset write-downs for disposals of excess facilities, and equipment and noncore product lines; write-offs of redundant computer systems from the administrative back-office consolidations and outsourcing initiatives; and intangible, packaging, and other asset write-downs related to exited product lines and SKU reductions.[18]

Cost of Goods Sold, SG&A, and Estimated Loss from Discontinued Operations

Contributing to the company's need to restate its cost of goods sold expense related to restructuring was the fact that in calculating their estimate for year-end inventory of household products, management failed to distinguish excess and obsolete inventory from inventory that was part of continuing product lines. Thus the value of Sunbeam's inventory from its continuing household product lines had been understated by $2.1 million on its balance sheet. Its restatement to its SG&A included a revision of a $12 million litigation reserve that initially was improperly overstated by at least $6 million.[19]

Sunbeam's Customer Discounts and Other Incentives

Under GAAP sales revenue can be recognized only if the buyer assumes the risks and rewards of ownership of merchandise—for example, the risk of damage or physical loss. A sale with a right of return can be recognized as revenue

---

[16] SEC Accounting and Auditing Enforcement Release No. 1393, May 15, 2001.

[17] Amended 1997 10K filed with the SEC.

[18] Ibid.

[19] SEC Accounting and Auditing Enforcement Release No. 1393, May 15, 2001.

only if the seller takes a reserve against possible future returns. The size of this reserve must be based on history with returns; the sales revenue may not be recorded if no such history exists.

Beginning with the first quarter of 1997, Sunbeam began offering its customers discounts and other incentives if they placed their orders in the current period rather than holding off until the next period. Sunbeam did not disclose this practice of accelerating expected sales from later periods, however. In the other quarters of 1997, Sunbeam also relied on additional price discounting and other incentives in an attempt to accelerate the recognition of revenue from future periods.[20]

One example of a special arrangement with a customer took place at the end of March 1997, just before the first quarter closed. Sunbeam recognized $1.5 million in revenue and contributed $400,000 toward net income from the sale of barbecue grills to a wholesaler. The contract with the wholesaler provided that the wholesaler could return all of the merchandise, with Sunbeam paying all costs of shipment and storage, if it was unable to sell it. In fact, the wholesaler wound up returning all of the grills to Sunbeam during the third quarter of 1997, and the wholesaler incurred no expenses in the transaction.[21]

Bill and Hold Sales

In the second quarter of 1997 Sunbeam recognized $14 million in sales revenue and contributed over $6 million toward net income from bill and hold sales. By the fourth quarter, Sunbeam was able to recognize $29 million in revenues and contributed $4.5 million toward net income in bill and hold sales after it began promoting its bill and hold program. Bill and hold sales contributed to 10 percent of the fourth quarter's revenue.[22]

At year-end 1997 Sunbeam disclosed in its annual filing to the SEC that "the amount of [the] bill and hold sales at December 29, 1997, was approximately 3 percent of consolidated revenues." It did not disclose that bill and hold sales had been booked primarily in the final quarter to pull revenue from 1998 to 1997.[23]

Revenue Recognition Criteria for Bill and Hold Sales

The SEC had stipulated that the following criteria must be met for revenue to be recognized in bill and hold transactions:[24]

- The risks of ownership must have passed to the buyer.
- The buyer must have made a fixed commitment to purchase the goods.
- The buyer must request that the transaction be on a bill and hold basis and must have a substantial business purpose for this request.
- There must be a fixed schedule for delivery of the goods.

[20] Ibid.
[21] Ibid.
[22] SEC Accounting and Auditing Enforcement Release No. 1394, May 15, 2001.
[23] Ibid.
[24] Staff Accounting Bulletin No. 101.

- The seller must not have retained any specific performance obligations such that the earning process is not complete.
- The ordered goods must be segregated from the seller's inventory.
- The goods must be complete and ready for shipment.

Characteristics of Sunbeam's Bill and Hold Sales

The SEC found that Sunbeam's bill and hold sales were not requested by Sunbeam's customers and served no business purpose other than to accelerate revenue recognition by Sunbeam. Sunbeam's bill and hold sales were typically accompanied by financial incentives offered to customers, such as discounted pricing, to encourage the "sale" to occur long before the customer actually needed the goods. Sunbeam would then hold the product until delivery was requested by the customer. Sunbeam also paid the costs of storage, shipment, and insurance related to the products. In addition, Sunbeam's customers had the right to return the unsold products.[25]

Sales to Distributors

In December 1997 Sunbeam devised a distributor program that would help improve the company's sales in 1997. Sunbeam accelerated recognition of sales revenue for merchandise it placed with distributors in advance of actual retail demand. Sunbeam used favorable payment terms, discounts, guaranteed markups, and, consistently, the right to return unsold products as incentives for distributors to participate in the program.

The sales under the distributor program represented a new distribution channel for the company. Therefore, Sunbeam was unable to set an appropriate level of reserves for returns.[26]

Restatement of Revenues and Other Significant Developments

In 1998 Sunbeam restated its revenues for 1997 from $1,168,182 to $1,073,090. In an amended filing of its 10K to the SEC, management wrote, "Upon examination, it was determined certain revenue was improperly recognized (principally 'bill and hold' and guaranteed sales transactions)."[27] The company had reversed all bill and hold sales, which amounted to $29 million in 1997, and about $36 million in guaranteed or consignment sales, whose liberal return policies made the recognition of their revenue improper.[28]

[25] SEC Accounting and Auditing Enforcement Release No. 1393, May 15, 2001.
[26] SEC Accounting and Auditing Enforcement Release No. 1706, January 27, 2003.
[27] Amended 1997 10K filing to SEC.
[28] Martha Brannigan, "Sunbeam Slashes Its 1997 Earnings in Restatement," *The Wall Street Journal,* October 21, 1998, p. 1.

Following several quarters of disappointing sales and earnings results, Sunbeam's CEO Roger Schipke tendered his resignation in April 1996. The company named as Schipke's successor Albert J. Dunlap, chief of Scott Paper Co. and a turnaround specialist who was nicknamed "Chainsaw Al" because of his typical cost-cutting measures. Despite Dunlap's efforts to achieve a successful turnaround, Sunbeam disappointed investors with lower-than-expected results in the fourth quarter of 1997 and the first quarter of 1998. CEO and Chair Dunlap was fired in June 1998.

It was later uncovered that Sunbeam's results in 1996, 1997, and 1998 were fraudulent in several aspects. In October 1998 Sunbeam announced that the audit committee of its board of directors had determined that the company would need to restate its prior financial statements, as follows: to reduce the 1996 net loss by $20 million (9 percent of reported losses); to reduce 1997 net income by $71 million (65 percent of reported earnings); and to increase 1998 earnings by $10 million (21 percent of reported losses).[29]

Sunbeam's auditor, Arthur Andersen, came under fire for having issued unqualified opinions on the company's financial statements for 1996 and 1997. In January 1999 a class action lawsuit alleging violation of federal securities laws was filed in the U.S. District Court for the Southern District of Florida against Sunbeam, Arthur Andersen, and Sunbeam executives. The suit reached a settlement in August 2002. As part of the settlement, Andersen agreed to pay $110 million.[30]

Phillip Harlow, the engagement partner in charge of the Sunbeam audit from 1993 to the summer of 1998, also found himself under fire for his work on the audits. The SEC barred Harlow from serving as a public accountant for three years after it found that Harlow failed to exercise professional care in performing the audits of Sunbeam's financial statements.[31]

1996 and 1997 Audits

Through the 1996 audit Andersen partner Phillip Harlow allegedly became aware of several accounting practices that failed to comply with GAAP. In particular, he allegedly knew about Sunbeam's improper restructuring costs, excessive litigation reserves, and an excessive cooperative advertising figure.

Harlow also allegedly discovered several items that were not compliant with GAAP during the 1997 audit. These items related to revenue, restructuring reserves, and inventory in particular. In several cases Harlow made proposed adjustments that management refused to make. In response to management's refusal, Harlow acquiesced, however. By the end of 1997 it appears that Harlow knew that approximately 16 percent of Sunbeam's reported 1997 income came

[29] GAO-03-138, Appendix XVII "Sunbeam Corporation," p. 201.

[30] Nicole Harris, "Andersen to Pay $110 Million to Settle Sunbeam Accounting-Fraud Lawsuit," *The Wall Street Journal,* May 2, 2001, p. B11.

[31] Cassell Bryan-Low, "Deals & Deal Makers," *The Wall Street Journal,* January 28, 2003, p. C5.

from items that he found to be noncompliant with GAAP.[32] In fact, at least $62 million of Sunbeam's reported $189 million of income before tax failed to comply with GAAP.[33]

Improper Restructuring Costs

During the 1996 audit Harlow allegedly identified $18.7 million in items within Sunbeam's restructuring reserve that were improperly classified as restructuring costs because they benefited Sunbeam's future operations. Harlow proposed that the company reverse the improper accounting entries, but management rejected his proposed adjustments for these entries. Harlow relented after deciding that the items were immaterial for the 1996 financials.[34]

Excessive Litigation Reserves

Sunbeam also failed to comply with GAAP on a $12 million reserve that was recorded for a lawsuit that alleged Sunbeam's potential obligation to cover a portion of the cleanup costs for a hazardous waste site. Management did not take appropriate steps to determine whether the amount reflected a probable and reasonable estimate of the loss. Had it done so, the reserve would not have passed either of the criteria. The SEC determined that Harlow relied on statements from Sunbeam's general counsel and did not take additional steps to determine whether the litigation reserve level was in accordance with GAAP.[35]

Bill and Hold Sales

The SEC also wrote in its findings that Harlow "knew or recklessly disregarded facts indicating that the fourth quarter bill and hold transactions did not satisfy required revenue recognition criteria."[36] Among other things, Sunbeam's revenues earned through bill and hold sales should not have been recognized because these sales were not requested by Sunbeam's customers and served no business purpose other than to accelerate revenue recognition by Sunbeam. Sunbeam offered its customers in the sales the right to return unsold products. Further, several of Sunbeam's bill and hold sales were also characterized by Sunbeam offering its customers financial incentives, such as discounted pricing, to write purchase orders before they actually needed the goods.[37]

---

[32] SEC Accounting and Auditing Enforcement Release No. 1706, January 27, 2003.

[33] SEC Accounting and Auditing Enforcement Release No. 1393, May 15, 2001.

[34] Ibid.

[35] SEC Accounting and Auditing Enforcement Release No. 1706, January 27, 2003.

[36] Ibid.

[37] SEC Accounting and Auditing Enforcement Release No. 1393, May 15, 2001.

Sale of Inventory

Sunbeam's fourth-quarter revenue included $11 million from a sale of its spare parts inventory to EPI Printers, which, prior to this transaction, had satisfied spare parts and warranty requests for Sunbeam's customers on an as-needed basis. As part of the transaction, Sunbeam agreed to pay certain fees and guaranteed a 5 percent profit for EPI Printers on the resale of the inventory. The contract with EPI Printers also stipulated that it would terminate in January 1998 if the parties did not agree on the value of the inventory underlying the contract.

Harlow allegedly knew that revenue recognition on this transaction did not comply with GAAP because of the profit guarantee and the indeterminate value of the contract. Thus he proposed an adjustment to reverse the accounting entries that reflected the revenue and income recognition for this transaction. Yet Harlow acquiesced to management's refusal to reverse the sale.[38]

Improper Use of Reserves

In the fourth quarter of 1997 Sunbeam improperly used excessive restructuring reserves to reduce current expenses. In fact, this use of reserves increased fourth-quarter income by almost 8 percent. Harlow proposed an adjustment to reverse this improper reduction. However, when management refused to make the adjustment, Harlow complied.[39]

Times of Trouble

After the first quarter of 1997, Dunlap heralded the success of the company's turnaround efforts:

> The impressive growth in both revenues and earnings is proof that the revitalization of Sunbeam is working. In fact, the sales growth in the first quarter is the highest level achieved without acquisitions since Sunbeam became public in 1992. ... The substantially higher earnings in the quarter from ongoing operations were due to increased sales coupled with the successful implementation of our restructuring efforts.[40]

---

[38] SEC Accounting and Auditing Enforcement Release No. 1706, January 27, 2003.

[39] Ibid.

[40] Ibid.

Yet by the fourth quarter of 1997, Sunbeam's results had fallen below expectations. Its first-quarter results in 1998 earned a worse-than-expected loss of $44.6 million.[41] CEO and Chair Dunlap was fired in June 1998. In October 1998 Sunbeam announced that the audit committee of its board of directors had determined that the company would need to restate its prior financial statements, as follows: to reduce the 1996 net loss by $20 million (9 percent of reported losses); to reduce 1997 net income by $71 million (65 percent of reported earnings); and to increase 1998 earnings by $10 million (21 percent of reported losses).[42]

Sunbeam filed for Chapter 11 bankruptcy protection in February 2001. In May 2001 the SEC brought charges of fraud against several former Sunbeam officials. At the end of 2002, the company emerged from Chapter 11 and changed its name to American Household. In early 2005 it was acquired by Jarden to be part of its consumer solutions division.

---

[41] Robert Frank and Joann S. Lublin, "Dunlap's Ax Falls—6,000 Times—at Sunbeam," *The Wall Street Journal,* November 13, 1996, p. B1.

[42] GAO-03-138, Appendix XVII "Sunbeam Corporation," p. 201.

Case Questions

1. Consider the principles, assumptions, and constraints of Generally Accepted Accounting Principles (GAAP). Define the *revenue recognition principle* and explain why it is important to users of financial statements.

2. Provide one specific example of how Sunbeam violated the revenue recognition principle in this case. In your description, please identify a journal entry that may have been used by Sunbeam to commit the fraudulent act.

3. Consult Paragraph 2 of PCAOB Auditing Standard No. 5. Do you believe that Sunbeam had established an effective system of internal control over financial reporting related to revenue recorded in its financial statements? Why or why not? Consult Paragraphs 7–9 of PCAOB Auditing Standard No. 15. As an auditor, what type of evidence would you want to examine to determine whether Sunbeam was inappropriately recording revenue from special discount sales?

4. Consult Paragraphs 4–8 of PCAOB Auditing Standard No. 15. Next, consider the alleged accounting improprieties related to increased expenses from the 1996 audit. If you were auditing Sunbeam, what type of evidence would you like to review to determine whether Sunbeam had recorded the litigation reserve amount and the cooperative advertising amount in accordance with GAAP?

5. For the excessive litigation reserves and excessive cooperative advertising amount, identify the journal entry that is likely to have been proposed by Andersen to correct each of these accounting improprieties. Why would Sunbeam be interested in recording journal entries that essentially reduced its income before tax in 1996?

6. Consult Paragraphs 17–23 of PCAOB Auditing Standard No. 14. As discussed in the case, during both the 1996 and 1997 audits, Phillip Harlow allegedly discovered a number of different accounting entries made by Sunbeam that were not compliant with Generally Accepted Accounting Principles (GAAP). Speculate about how Harlow might have explained his decision not to require Sunbeam to correct these alleged misstatements in the audit working papers.

7. Consult Sections 204 and 301 of SARBOX. In the post-Sarbanes audit environment, which of the issues that arose in 1996 and 1997 would have to be reported to the audit committee at Sunbeam? Do you believe that communication to the audit committee would have made a difference in Harlow's decision not to record the adjusting journal entries? Why or why not?

8. Consult Paragraphs 5–8 of PCAOB Auditing Standard No.8 and Paragraphs 7–10 of PCAOB Auditing Standard No. 12. Based on your understanding of inherent risk assessment and the case information, identify three specific factors about Sunbeam that might cause you to elevate inherent risk.

9. Consult Paragraphs 8–10 of PCAOB Auditing Standard No. 13. Comment on how your understanding of the inherent risks identified at Sunbeam (in Question 8) would influence the nature, timing, and extent of your audit work at Sunbeam.

10. Consult Paragraphs 29 and 32 of PCAOB Auditing Standard No. 5. Briefly identify the types of revenue earned by Sunbeam. Do you believe that any of the different types of revenue earned by Sunbeam might be subject to significantly differing levels of inherent risk? Why or why not?

11. Consult Paragraphs 52–53 of PCAOB Auditing Standard No. 12. For one of Sunbeam's revenue types (please choose one), brainstorm about how a fraud might occur. Next identify an internal control procedure that would prevent, detect, or deter such a fraudulent scheme.

12. Consult Paragraphs 13–21 of PCAOB Auditing Standard No. 15. What is meant by a *restructuring reserve*? As an auditor, what type of evidence would you want to examine to determine whether a company was inappropriately accounting for its restructuring reserve?

13. Consult Paragraphs 29 and 32 of PCAOB Auditing Standard No. 5. As an auditor, do you believe that the different components of a restructuring reserve might be subject to significantly differing levels of inherent risk? Why or why not?

14. Consult Paragraphs 28–30 of PCAOB Auditing Standard No. 5. Identify at least one relevant financial statement assertion related to the restructuring reserve account. Why is it relevant?

15. This case describes a situation in which a company overstated its recorded expenses in 1996 (as compared to understating recorded expenses). Why would a company choose to overstate its expenses and understate its net income?

16. Consider a customer who receives extraordinary discounts and terms to purchase merchandise at the end of the year (e.g., the wholesaler that purchased grills from Sunbeam). Do you believe that the customer has a moral obligation to report these actions to a company's audit committee? Why or why not?

Case 6.5

Qwest

Synopsis

When Joseph Nacchio became Qwest's CEO in January 1997, the company's existing strategy began to shift from building only a nationwide fiber-optic network to include increasing communications services. By the time it released earnings in 1998, Nacchio proclaimed Qwest's successful transition from a network construction company to a communications services provider. "We successfully transitioned Qwest . . . into a leading Internet protocol-based multimedia company focused on the convergence of data, video, and voice services."[1]

During 1999 and 2000, Qwest consistently met its aggressive revenue targets and became a darling to its investors. Yet, when the company announced its intention to restate revenues in August 2002, its stock price plunged to a low of $1.11 per share in August 2002, from a high of $55 per share in July 2000.[2] Civil and criminal charges related to fraudulent activitity were brought against several Qwest executives, including CEO Joseph Nacchio. Nacchio was convicted on 19 counts of illegal insider trading, and was sentenced to six years in prison in July 2007. He was also ordered to pay a $19 million fine and forfeit $52 million that he gained in illegal stock sales.[3]

Strategic Direction Qwest Communications International

In the mid-1990s Qwest Communications International embarked on building a fiber-optic network across major cities within the United States. The network would consist of a series of cables that contained strands of pure glass that

---

[1] *SEC v. Joseph P. Nacchio, Robert S. Woodruff, Robin R. Szeliga, Afshin Mohebbi, Gregory M. Casey, James J. Kozlowski, Frank T. Noyes, Defendants,* Civil Action No. 05-MK-480 (OES), pp. 11–14.

[2] *SEC v. Qwest,* pp. 1–2.

[3] Dionne Searcey, "Qwest Ex-Chief Gets 6 Years in Prison for Insider Trading," *The Wall Street Journal,* July 28, 2007, p. A3.

could transmit data by using light and the appropriate equipment. Qwest's initial strategy was to build the network of fiber cable and sell it in the form of an indefeasible right of use (IRU)—an irrevocable right to use a specific amount of fiber for a specified period.

However, when Joseph Nacchio became Qwest's CEO in January 1997, the strategy of the company shifted toward communications services. Nacchio envisioned that Qwest had the potential of becoming a major telecommunications company that offered Internet and multimedia services over its fiber-optic network, in addition to offering traditional voice communications services.[4]

Qwest's Construction Services Business

A fiber-optic network consists of a series of cables that contain strands of pure glass and allow data transmission between any two connected points by using beams of light. While each cable of the fiber-optic network typically contains at least 96 strands of fiber, Qwest intended to hold 48 of the fiber strands for its own use and to sell the remaining strands to help finance the cost of network construction.[5] Total revenues from its construction services business were approximately $224.5 million, $688.4 million, and $581.4 million in 1999, 1998, and 1997, respectively.[6]

As of 1999 Qwest faced competition from three other principal facilities-based long distance fiber-optic networks: AT&T, Sprint, and MCI WorldCom. In its 1999 annual filing with the SEC, Qwest warned investors that others—including Global Crossing, GTE, Broadwing, and Williams Communications—were building or planning networks that could employ advanced technology similar to Qwest's network. Yet Qwest assured investors that it was at a significant advantage because its network would be completed in mid-1999—at least a year ahead of the planned completion of other networks—and that it could extend and expand the capacity on its network using the additional fibers that it had retained.[7]

Qwest's Communications Services Business

As part of its communications services business, Qwest provided traditional voice communications services, as well as Internet and multimedia services, to business customers, governmental agencies, and consumers in domestic and

---

[4] *SEC v. Joseph P. Nacchio, Robert S. Woodruff, Robin R. Szeliga, Afshin Mohebbi, Gregory M. Casey, James J. Kozlowski, Frank T. Noyes, Defendants,* Civil Action No. 05-MK-480 (OES), pp. 11–14.

[5] 1997 10-K, p. 10.

[6] 1999 10-K, p. 12.

[7] 1999 10-K, p. 13.

international markets. Qwest also provided wholesale services to other communications providers, including Internet service providers (ISPs) and other data service companies. Total revenues from its communications services business were approximately $3,703.1 million, $1,554.3 million, and $115.3 million in 1999, 1998, and 1997, respectively.[8]

The impact of regulatory change was significant in the highly regulated telecommunications industry. The Telecommunications Act of 1996 increased competition in the long distance market by allowing the entry of local exchange carriers and others. Indeed, Qwest warned investors in its 1999 annual filing with the SEC that its costs of providing long distance services could be affected by changes in the rules controlling the form and amount of access charges long distance carriers had to pay local exchange carriers to use the local networks they needed to provide the local portion of long distance calls.[9]

Qwest's primary competitors in its communications services business included AT&T, Sprint, and MCI WorldCom, all of which had extensive experience in the traditional long distance market. In addition, the industry faced continuing consolidation, such as the merger of MCI and WorldCom.

In the markets for Internet and multimedia services, Qwest competed with a wide range of companies that provided Web hosting, Internet access, and other Internet protocol (IP) products and services. Significant competitors included GTE, UUNET (a subsidiary of MCI WorldCom), Digex, AboveNet, Intel, and Exodus.[10]

Qwest's Mergers and Acquisitions

To facilitate its growth in its communications services revenue, Quest unveiled an aggressive acquisition strategy in the late 1990s. From October 1997 to December 1998 it acquired SuperNet, Inc., a regional ISP in the Rocky Mountain region; in March 1998 it acquired Phoenix Network, Inc., a reseller of long distance services; in April 1998 it acquired EUnet International Limited, a leading European ISP; in June 1998 it purchased LCI International, Inc., a provider of long distance telephone services; and in December 1998 it acquired Icon CMT Corp., a leading Internet solutions provider.[11] In many of these acquisitions Qwest used its own company stock as the tender (instead of cash) that was needed to acquire the companies.

---

[8] 1999 10-K, p. 10.
[9] 1999 10-K, pp. 14–17.
[10] 1999 10-K, p. 13.
[11] 1998 10-K, p. 5.

Qwest's string of acquisitions culminated during 1999 when it entered a merger agreement with telecommunications company US West on July 18, 1999. The merger agreement required Qwest to issue $69 worth of its common stock for each share of US West stock, and it gave US West the option to terminate the agreement if the average price of Qwest stock was below $22 per share or the closing price was below $22 per share for 20 consecutive trading days. Less than a month after the merger announcement, Qwest's stock price had dropped from $34 to $26 per share. So to prevent any further drops in its stock price, executives and managers were pressured by CEO Nacchio to meet earnings targets to ensure that price per share did not fall below the level specified in the agreement. Although Qwest's stock price had dropped from $34 to $26 per share less than a month after the merger announcement, Qwest stock was trading above $50 per share by June 2000; Qwest was therefore able to acquire US West by using Qwest's common stock.

Following the merger, Qwest's senior management set ambitious targets for revenue and earnings of the merged company.[12] These targets were especially ambitious in the face of difficult industry conditions. For example, in Qwest's earnings release for the second quarter 2000, on July 19, 2000, Nacchio said that Qwest would "generate compound annual growth rates of 15–17 percent revenue . . . through 2005." At a January 2001 all-employee meeting, Nacchio stated his philosophy on the importance of meeting targeted revenues:

> [T]he most important thing we do is meet our numbers. It's more important than
> any individual product, it's more important than any individual philosophy,
> it's more important than any individual cultural change we're making. We stop
> everything else when we don't make the numbers.

Challenges

By 1999 Qwest encountered several obstacles that challenged its ability to meet its aggressive revenue and earnings targets. It faced increased competition from long distance providers, steep declines in the demand for Internet services, an overcapacity in the market resulting from the formation of other major fiber-optic networks, and a decline in the price at which Qwest could sell its excess fiber-optic capacity due to the increase in capacity.[13]

Despite these significant industry challenges, Qwest's senior management publicly claimed that the company would continue its pattern of dramatic revenue increases because of a "flight to quality" that customers would enjoy when they left competitors to use Qwest's services. Within the company, Qwest senior management exerted extraordinary pressure on its subordinate managers and employees to meet or exceed the publicly announced revenue targets. In addition, it paid bonuses to management and employees only for periods when they achieved targeted revenue.[14]

[14] *SEC v. Qwest,* p. 8.

[12] *SEC v. Qwest,* pp. 6–7.

[13] *SEC v. Qwest,* pp. 7–8.

Sale of Network Assets Initially Held for Use and Capital Equipment

To help meet revenue targets, senior management also began to sell portions of its own domestic fiber-optic network. Originally this network was to be held for Qwest's own use and had previously been identified as the principal asset of Qwest. Qwest sold indefeasible rights of use (IRUs) for specific fiber capacity that it had constructed and used in its own communications services business. In addition, Qwest sold pieces of the network it had acquired from other third parties. Finally, Qwest also sold used capital equipment to generate additional revenue.

Unlike recurring service revenue from its communication services business that produced a predictable amount of revenue in future quarters, revenue from IRUs and other equipment sales had no guarantee of recurrence in future quarters. In fact, both IRUs and equipment sales were referred to internally as "one hit wonders."[15]

In its earnings releases during 1999 through 2001, Qwest executives would often fail to disclose the impact of nonrecurring revenues. In its earnings releases and in the management's discussion and analysis portion of its SEC filings, Qwest improperly characterized nonrecurring revenue as service revenue, often within the "data and Internet service revenues" line item on the financial statements. Qwest's nonrecurring revenue was included primarily in the wholesale services segment and, to a lesser extent, the retail services segment.[16]

IRU Swap Transactions

An IRU is an irrevocable right to use specific fiber-optic cable or fiber capacity for a specified period. In IRU swap transactions, Qwest would sell IRUs to customers in exchange for purchasing fiber or capacity in similar dollar amounts from those same customers. Under GAAP, no revenue should be recognized in this type of swap transaction unless Qwest had a legitimate business need to purchase the IRU capacity simultaneously from the other telecommunications company. Unfortunately, based on the available evidence, it appears that many of Qwest's IRU swap transactions failed to meet this requirement to recognize revenue. In addition, in some cases Qwest's executives backdated documents for IRU swap transactions to enable earlier revenue recognition.

---

[15] *SEC v. Qwest*, pp. 9–10.
[16] *SEC v. Qwest*, pp. 12–13.

Business Need for Assets Purchased in IRU Swap Transactions

Beginning in 1999 Qwest found it increasingly difficult to sell IRUs to customers unless it purchased fiber or capacity in similar dollar amounts from those same customers in swap transactions. As an example, in the third quarter 2001, Qwest agreed to purchase $67.2 million of capacity in Pan America from Global Crossing in a swap transaction because Global Crossing could deliver the capacity by the close of the third quarter, a necessary element for booking revenue on Qwest's simultaneous sale to Global Crossing.[17] In fact, many of the assets Qwest purchased in swap transactions seemingly did not have a legitimate business purpose besides their role in the completion of a swap transaction.

Qwest's Failure to Use Assets Purchased in Swap Transactions

In most cases Qwest did not use the assets it purchased. For example, on September 29, 2000, Qwest purchased from Global Crossing $20.8 million in capacity across the Pacific Ocean as part of a swap transaction. Qwest never activated the capacity and, six months later, returned the $20.8 million in capacity as a credit toward the purchase of different capacity from Global Crossing.[18] In fact, members of Qwest's senior management directed and established quotas for the IRU sales teams to resell capacity that Qwest "[took] on as a result of trades with other carriers that we do not intend to use."[19]

Qwest's Purchase of Assets That Duplicated Other Assets It Owned

Many of the routes Qwest purchased in IRU swaps duplicated network assets that Qwest already possessed. For example, Qwest purchased similar East Asia capacity during 2001 in four swap transactions with Cable & Wireless, Global Crossing, Flag Telecom, and TyCom Networks. Because the routes were redundant, Qwest did not have a business use for at least three of the four routes. In another example, Qwest engaged in a swap with Enron on December 21, 1999, whereby it bought fiber between Denver and Dallas for $39.2 million. However, Qwest had already built and completed a route between those cities that had excess capacity and the ability to be expanded.[20]

Interaction of IRU Sales Staff with Network Planning Department

Although Qwest's network planning department was responsible for determining what capacity was needed to expand or develop Qwest's fiber-optic network, Qwest's IRU salespeople did not generally consult with the network

[17] *SEC v. Qwest,* p. 31.
[18] *SEC v. Qwest,* p. 32.
[19] *SEC v. Qwest,* p. 30.
[20] *SEC v. Qwest,* pp. 32–33.

planning department before purchasing assets in a swap.[21] In those few instances when Qwest's network planning department was consulted, it recommended against the purchase of capacity because Qwest had little or no need for the IRU.[22] For example, prior to the purchase of a large amount of fiber from Enron in a third-quarter 2001 swap, in which Qwest recognized $85.5 million in revenue on the sale, Qwest's network planning group allegedly made it clear that the Qwest network had no need for the majority of Enron's fiber route and other assets.[23]

Study of Use of International Capacity Purchased in IRU Swaps

In late 2001 through early 2002 Qwest conducted a study to determine how to use the international capacity it had purchased in IRU swaps. The study concluded that Qwest could possibly use or resell only one-third of the capacity it had purchased in the swaps. The remaining two-thirds of the capacity purchased was not needed by Qwest, could not be resold, and was therefore worthless.[24]

Accounting for Swap Transactions

In accounting for swaps, Qwest recognized large amounts of revenue immediately, which was an aggressive method relative to the rest of the telecommunications industry. Yet Qwest capitalized its costs related to purchasing capacity from others as long-term assets that were amortized over the 20–25 year terms of the IRUs.[25]

During 2000 and 2001 the frequency, dollar amount, and number of swap transactions grew as Qwest tried to meet its aggressive revenue targets in the face of declining demand for fiber optic assets. Internally some Qwest managers and employees referred to these transactions using the acronym of "SLUTS," which stood for simultaneous, legally unrelated transactions. In fact most of Qwest's swaps were completed as directed by members of senior management in the waning days and hours of each quarter in desperate attempts to achieve previously stated revenue targets.[26]

Pressure from senior management allegedly even motivated employees to backdate contracts to falsely demonstrate that a contract was "completed" by the end of the quarter. For example, the company recorded revenue of $69.8 million in the first quarter of 2001 on a swap transaction with Cable & Wireless that had not closed until after the quarter (on April 12, 2001) by backdating the contract to March 30, 2001. In another example of backdating, in the third quarter

[21] *SEC v. Qwest,* p. 31.
[22] Ibid.
[23] Ibid.
[24] *SEC v. Qwest,* p. 30.
[25] *SEC v. Qwest,* p. 24.
[26] Ibid.

of 2001 Qwest recognized $85.5 million of revenue on the sale of IRU capacity in a swap with Enron. The parties' agreements, which were dated September 30, 2001, were not executed until October 1, 2001—after the close of the quarter.[27]

Premature Revenue Recognition

Included within the $3.8 billion of revenues that were fraudulently recognized by Qwest were prematurely recognized revenues from sales of IRUs for its network. Qwest treated IRU sales as sales-type leases, which allow a seller to treat a lease transaction as a sale of an asset with complete, up-front revenue recognition. According to GAAP, this type of up-front revenue recognition required (1) completion of the earnings process; (2) that the assets sold remain fixed and unchanged; (3) full transfer of ownership, with no continuing involvement by the seller; and (4) an assessment of the fair market value of the revenue components. In addition, as part of the completion of the earnings process, the assets being sold had to be explicitly and specifically identified.

Portability

Qwest generally allowed customers of IRUs the ability to *port*, or exchange, IRUs purchased for other IRUs. By mid-2001 Qwest had ported at least 10 percent of its assets sold as IRUs. Portability was not uncommon in the telecommunications industry because companies needed the flexibility to change their networks as demand changed.[28]

However, Qwest salespeople often granted customers the right to port through secret side agreements or verbal assurances—allegedly due to the fact that the practice of porting jeopardized Qwest's ability to recognize revenue on IRUs up front. For example, in the fourth quarter of 2000 Qwest sold to Cable & Wireless $109 million of capacity in the United States (and recognized $108 million in up-front revenue) by providing a secret side agreement guaranteeing that Cable & Wireless could exchange the specific capacity it purchased at a later date.[29]

As another example, in the first quarter of 2001 Qwest sold IRU capacity to Global Crossing and recognized $102 million of up-front revenue after it gave secret verbal assurances to Global Crossing that Qwest would agree to exchange the capacity when the IRU capacity that Global Crossing actually wanted became available.[30]

Ownership Transfer

Qwest also allegedly had a significant continuing involvement with all IRUs sold in the form of ongoing administrative, operating, and maintenance activities.

[27] *SEC v. Qwest*, pp. 28–29.
[28] *SEC v. Qwest*, p. 20.
[29] *SEC v. Qwest*, pp. 26–27.
[30] Ibid.

While Qwest's IRU sales agreements generally provided for title transfer at the end of the lease terms, conditions also allegedly existed that would require that the titles remain with Qwest in reality.[31]

Interestingly, there was no statutory title transfer system for IRUs that is comparable to what exists for real property. In addition, some of Qwest's right of way agreements on the underlying IRUs actually expired prior to the end of the IRU terms. Further, some of the underlying IRU agreements (concerning IRUs that Qwest purchased from a third party and then resold) did not allow Qwest to sublease its rights of way or did not provide title to Qwest. Therefore Qwest could not legally provide those rights to a third party.[32]

The SEC found evidence that in some IRU contracts Qwest specifically stated that the purchasers did not receive any ownership interest in the fiber. Similarly, there was also evidence that in many contracts Qwest prohibited the purchasers from assigning, selling, or transferring the fiber-optic capacity without Qwest's prior written consent. For example, on March 31, 2000, Qwest entered a $9.6 million IRU transaction with Cable & Wireless in which Qwest included a clause preventing assignment, sale, or transfer without Qwest's consent.[33]

Other Characteristics That Failed to Comply with GAAP

Qwest's up-front revenue recognition of IRUs was also premature because Qwest routinely neglected to specify the assets it was selling. For example, in the first quarter ended March 31, 2001, Qwest sold $105 million of fiber-optic capacity to Global Crossing and recognized approximately $102 million in revenue on the sale. This was done despite the fact that the majority of the capacity was not specified in the contract by the end of the quarter. Rather, the contract exhibit intended to list the assets sold simply stated "to be identified." Further, Global Crossing and Qwest did not identify the geographic termination points of some of the capacity purchased by Qwest until June 2001, three months after Qwest recognized the revenue on the sale transaction.[34]

In addition, to circumvent problems on its network or to optimize the network's efficiency, Qwest often moved IRUs previously sold, without customer consent, to different wavelengths and different routes as required. This process was known as *grooming*. During the third and fourth quarters of 2001, Qwest senior management allegedly knew of numerous IRUs that had been rerouted on different fibers. Qwest personnel allegedly informed senior management that the IRUs could not be restored to their original routes and advised senior management to reverse the revenue recognized from the IRU sales. Qwest senior

---

[31] *SEC v. Qwest*, pp. 22–23.
[32] *SEC v. Qwest*, p. 22.
[33] Ibid.
[34] *SEC v. Qwest*, p. 28.

management, however, allegedly rejected the employees' recommendations. From the fourth quarter of 2001 through early 2002, Qwest continued to reroute IRU fibers as necessary.[35]

Dex's Changes to Publication Dates and Lives of Directories

Qwest executives allegedly often made false and misleading disclosures concerning revenues from its directory services unit, Qwest Dex Inc. (Dex). In addition, executives were charged with having manipulated revenue from Dex for 2000 and 2001 by secretly altering directory publication dates and the lives of directories.

Dex published telephone directories year-round in approximately 300 markets in 14 states. It earned revenue by selling advertising space in its directories. Each of its directories typically had a life of 12 months, and Qwest traditionally recognized directory revenue over the life of the directory. However, in late 1999 Dex adopted a "point of publication" method of accounting and began to recognize all advertising revenue for a directory as soon as Dex began deliveries of that directory to the public.

In August 2000 Dex executives allegedly informed Qwest senior management that Dex would be unable to achieve the aggressive 2000 earnings' targets that management had set for it. As one option for making up for the shortfall, Dex suggested that it could publish Dex's Colorado Springs directory in December 2000 rather than January 2001 as scheduled, thereby allowing Qwest to recognize revenue from the directory in 2000 rather than 2001. One Dex executive expressed opposition, citing his concern that such a schedule change would severely reduce 2001 revenue and earnings. He also expressed his view that Qwest probably would be required to disclose the change in the regulatory filings with the SEC. Despite this executive's opposition, Qwest senior management allegedly instructed Dex to move forward with the proposed change.

By recognizing revenue from the Colorado Springs directory in 2000, Qwest generated $28 million in additional revenue and $18 million in additional earnings before interest and tax, depreciation, and amortization (EBITDA) for the year. The additional revenue generated in 2000 accounted for about 30 percent of Dex's 2000 year-over-year revenue increase. It further allowed Dex to show 6.6 percent year-over-year revenue growth versus 4.6 percent if the schedule change had not been made.

In Qwest's 2000 Form 10-K, Qwest informed investors that Dex's revenue for 2000 increased by almost $100 million. It wrote that the increase was due in part to "an increase in the number of directories published." At the same time, it failed to inform investors that Dex generated nearly one-third of that amount by publishing the Colorado Springs directory twice in 2000. It also did not inform investors that the schedule change would produce a corresponding decline in Dex revenue for the first quarter of 2001.

[35] *SEC v. Qwest,* p. 21.

ablished revenue and EBITDA targets
management believed was possible
is allegedly $80–$100 million greater
ved was achievable. The SEC found
vest's senior management about the
nagement not only allegedly refused
ow Dex a reduction in the targets to
rado Springs directory that was rec-

rith some of Qwest's senior manage-
the first two quarters of 2001 in an
s. One idea was to advance the pub-
llowing Dex to recognize revenue in
ien the lives of other directories from
ill each advertiser for one additional
inagers at Qwest allegedly instructed
nges, as well as others to allow it to
targets.

ion dates or extended the lives of 34
ed $42 million in additional revenue
vest's Forms 10-Ks for the first three
iod improvements in Dex's revenue
and/or the "lengths" of directories
eports did not include any informa-
r the reasons for those changes.

ndersen and the SEC

an, the global managing partner at
Qwest from 1999 to 2002—alleging
ient's false representations that cer-
liate revenue recognition on IRUs
others, the SEC ordered that Iwan
ticing before the SEC as an accoun-

Specifically, the SEC found that Iwan learned that Qwest's porting of
capacity had risen to approximately 10 percent of the capacity sold by mid-2001.
Although Iwan required Qwest to stop the practice of porting, he allegedly did
not go back and ensure that the prior revenue recognition was in conformity
with GAAP. Rather, Iwan relied exclusively on management's representations
that "Qwest had made no commitments to allow its customers to port capacity,
that it was never Qwest's intention to allow customers to port capacity, and that
Qwest would not honor any future request to port capacity."[36]

[36] A.A.E.R. No. 2220, pp. 3–4.

The SEC also found that Iwan relied on representations from Qwest's management and legal counsel that title did actually transfer on IRUs. In fact, Iwan allegedly knew by early 2000 that Qwest senior tax personnel believed there were "significant uncertainties as to whether title transfer would occur," and thus Qwest would treat IRUs as operating leases for tax purposes. Surprisingly, Iwan failed to reconcile Qwest's position on title transfer for IRUs for income tax reporting purposes with its position for financial reporting purposes under GAAP (which was different).[37]

In 2001 Iwan required Qwest to obtain an outside legal opinion that Qwest had the ability to transfer title to the IRUs it had sold over the past three years. Qwest provided to Iwan an abridged summary of the legal opinion that contained significant assumptions, qualifications, ambiguities, and limitations that were critical to evaluating whether Qwest met the ownership transfer requirements. Yet Iwan continued to rely on the representations of management and legal counsel in this regard.[38]

---

[37] Ibid.
[38] Ibid.

Case Questions

1. Consider the principles, assumptions, and constraints of Generally Accepted Accounting Principles (GAAP). Define the *full disclosure principle* and explain why it is important to users of financial statements.

2. Explain specifically why Qwest's failure to disclose the extent of nonrecurring revenue violated the full disclosure principle.

3. Consult Paragraph 67 of PCAOB Auditing Standard No. 12. Do you believe that Qwest had established an effective system of internal control over financial reporting related to the presentation and disclosure of its nonrecurring revenue? Why or why not?

4. Consult Paragraph 25 of PCAOB Auditing Standard No. 5. Define what is meant by *control environment*. Why does the "tone at the top" have such an important effect on internal control over financial reporting? Based on the case information, do you believe that the proper "tone at the top" was established at Qwest? Why or why not?

5. Consult Paragraph A4 (in Appendix A) of PCAOB Auditing Standard No. 5. What is the auditor's responsibility related to information disclosed by management at the time of an earnings release, if any? What is the auditor's responsibility related to the information disclosed by management in the management's discussion and analysis section, if any? Do you agree with these responsibilities? Why or why not?

6. Consider the principles, assumptions, and constraints of Generally Accepted Accounting Principles (GAAP). Define the *revenue recognition principle* and explain why it is important to users of financial statements.

7. Describe specifically why the revenue recognition practices of Dex were not appropriate under GAAP.

8. Consult Paragraph A5 (in Appendix A) of PCAOB Auditing Standard No. 5 and Paragraph 68 of PCAOB Auditing Standard No. 12. Do you believe that Qwest had established an effective system of internal control over financial reporting related to the revenue recorded by Dex in its financial statements? Why or why not?

9. Consult Paragraphs 65–66 of PCOAB Auditing Standard No. 12. Based on your understanding of fraud risk assessment, what three conditions are likely to be present when fraud occurs (the fraud triangle)? Based on the information provided in the case, which of these three conditions appears to have been the most prevalent at Qwest, and why?

10. Consult Paragraphs 5–8 of PCAOB Auditing Standard No.8 and Paragraphs 7–10 of PCAOB Auditing Standard No. 12. Based on your understanding of inherent risk assessment and the case information, identify three specific factors about Qwest's business model that might cause you to elevate inherent risk if you were conducting an audit of internal control over financial reporting at Qwest.

11. Consult Paragraphs 8–10 of PCAOB Auditing Standard No. 13. Comment on how your understanding of the inherent risks identified at Qwest (in Question 10) would influence the nature, timing, and extent of your audit work at Qwest.

12. Consult Paragraphs 29 and 32 of PCAOB Auditing Standard No. 5. Next consider revenue earned in the construction services and the communication services businesses. Do you believe that any of the different types of revenue earned by Qwest might be subject to significantly differing levels of inherent risk? Why or why not?

13. Describe specifically why the up-front revenue recognition practice for sales of IRUs by Qwest was not appropriate under Generally Accepted Accounting Principles (GAAP).

14. Consult Paragraphs 4–6 of PCAOB Auditing Standard No. 15. Based on your understanding of audit evidence, did Arthur Andersen rely on sufficient and competent audit evidence in its audit of Qwest's up-front revenue recognition processes? Why or why not?

15. Consult Paragraphs 28–30 of PCAOB Auditing Standard No. 5. Identify one relevant financial statement assertion related to revenue recognized for IRU sales by Qwest. Why is it relevant?

16. Consult Paragraphs 39–41 and Paragraph A5 (in Appendix A) of PCAOB Auditing Standard No. 5. For the assertion identified in Question 15, identify a specific internal control activity that would help *prevent* or *detect* a misstatement related to the practice of up-front revenue recognition of IRUs by Qwest.

17. Describe why the recognition of revenue for IRU swaps for fiber optic assets that were not actually needed by Qwest was inappropriate under GAAP. Next, consult Paragraphs 7–8 of PCAOB Auditing Standard No. 15. As an auditor, what type of evidence would allow you to determine whether such recognition of revenue would be appropriate under GAAP?

18. Consult Paragraphs 11–12 of PCAOB Auditing Standard No. 15. Identify one relevant financial statement assertion related to the revenue account that is impacted by an IRU swap. Why is it relevant?

19. Consult Paragraphs 39–41 and Paragraph A5 (in Appendix A) of PCAOB Auditing Standard No. 5. For the assertion identified in Question 18, identify a specific internal control activity that would help *prevent* a misstatement related to the recognition of revenue for IRU swaps.

20. Next, for the assertion identified in Question 18, identify a specific internal control activity that would help *detect* a misstatement related to the recognition of revenue for IRU swaps.

21. Do you believe it is ethical for a CEO to establish a company's earnings expectation at an unreasonably high number and then require the company's employees to meet or exceed that expectation to keep their jobs? Why or why not?

22. Consider the role of an upper manager at Dex. Do you believe that a "point of publication" method of accounting is allowable under Generally Accepted Accounting Principles? If so, please make an argument that supports the recognition of revenue related to the Colorado Springs directory in December 2000, as opposed to 2001. Do you believe that the actions of the upper managers at Dex were ethical? Why or why not?

Case

6.6

The Baptist Foundation of Arizona

Synopsis

The Baptist Foundation of Arizona (BFA) was organized as an Arizona nonprofit organization primarily to help provide financial support for various Southern Baptist causes. Under William Crotts's leadership, the foundation engaged in a major strategic shift in its operations. BFA began to invest heavily in the Arizona real estate market and also accelerated its efforts to sell investment agreements and mortgage-backed securities to church members.

Two of BFA's most significant affiliates were ALO and New Church Ventures. It was later revealed that BFA had set up these affiliates to facilitate the sale of its real estate investments at prices significantly above fair market value. In so doing, BFA's management perpetrated a fraudulent scheme that cost at least 13,000 investors more than $590 million. In fact, Arizona Attorney General Janet Napolitano called the BFA collapse the largest bankruptcy of a religious nonprofit in the history of the United States.[1]

Background

The Baptist Foundation of Arizona (BFA) was an Arizona religious nonprofit 501(c)(3) organization that was incorporated in 1948 to provide financial support for Southern Baptist causes. It was formed under the direction of the Arizona Southern Baptist Convention, which required BFA to be a profitable, self-sustaining independent entity (that is, it could not accept money from any other source). In BFA's early days, it focused its attention on funding church start-ups and providing aid for children and elderly people. In 1962 Pastor Glen Crotts became its first president and was succeeded in 1984 by his son, William P. Crotts.

[1] Terry Greene Sterling, "Arthur Andersen and the Baptists," *Salon.com,* February 7, 2002.

Under William Crotts's leadership, the foundation engaged in a major strategic shift in its operations. BFA began to invest heavily in the Arizona real estate market and also accelerated its efforts to sell investment agreements and mortgage-backed securities to church members. Soon after the decline in the Arizona real estate market in 1989, management decided to establish a number of related affiliates. These affiliates were controlled by individuals with close ties to BFA, such as former board members. In addition, BFA gained approval to operate a trust department that would serve as a nonbank passive trustee for individual retirement accounts (IRAs). To do so, BFA had to meet certain regulatory requirements, which included minimum net worth guidelines.

Related Parties

Two of BFA's most significant affiliates were ALO and New Church Ventures. A former BFA director incorporated both of these nonprofit entities. The entities had no employees of their own, and both organizations paid BFA substantial management fees to provide accounting, marketing, and administrative services. As a result, both ALO and New Church Ventures owed BFA significant amounts by the end of 1995. Overall BFA, New Church Ventures, and ALO had a combined negative net worth of $83.2 million at year-end 1995, $102.3 million at year-end 1996, and $124.0 million at year-end 1997.[2]

New Church Ventures

Although the stated purpose of New Church Ventures was to finance new Southern Baptist churches in Arizona, its major investment activities were similar to those of BFA. That is, New Church Ventures raised most of its funds through the sale of investment agreements and mortgage-backed securities, and then invested most of those funds in real estate loans to ALO. Thus the majority of New Church Ventures' assets were receivables from ALO. New Church Ventures' two main sources of funding were BFA's marketing of its investment products to IRA investors and loans it received from BFA.[3]

ALO

Contrary to its purported purpose to invest and develop real estate, one of ALO's primary activities in the 1990s was buying and holding BFA's nonproducing and overvalued investments in real estate so that BFA could avoid recording losses (write-downs) on its real estate. In fact, ALO owned many of the real estate investments that were utilized as collateral for IRA investor loans.

---

[2] Notice of Public Hearing and Complaint No. 98.230-ACY, Before the Arizona State Board of Accountancy, pp. 3–4.

[3] Ibid., pp. 8–9.

However, BFA's 1991 through 1997 financial statements did not include a set of summarized financial statements for ALO. ALO incurred operating losses each year since its inception in 1988. By the end of 1997, ALO's total liabilities of $275.6 million were over two times its assets, leaving a negative net worth of $138.9 million. In total, ALO owed New Church Ventures $173.6 million and BFA $70.3 million, respectively.[4]

BFA's Religious Exemptions

BFA operated in a manner similar to a bank in many respects. Its investment products were similar to those sold by financial institutions. Its trust department, which was fully authorized by the federal government to serve as a passive trustee of IRAs, was similar to a trust department at a bank. BFA also made real estate loans in a manner similar to a bank. Because of its banklike operations and products, BFA faced several risk factors that affect banks and other savings institutions, such as interest rate risk and liquidity risk.[5]

Yet because of its status as a religious organization, BFA's product offerings were not subject to the same regulatory scrutiny as a bank's products.[6] That is, although BFA underwrote its own securities offerings and used its staff to sell the investment instruments (like a bank), it was able to claim a religious exemption from Arizona statutes that regulate such activities. BFA also claimed exemption from Arizona banking regulations on the basis that its investment products did not constitute deposits as defined by Arizona banking laws.[7]

Passive Trustee Operation

BFA gained approval to operate a trust department that would serve as a nonbank passive trustee for IRAs. To operate a trust department, BFA had to comply with certain regulatory requirements, such as maintaining an appropriate minimum net worth. In addition to the minimum net worth requirement, treasury regulations also required BFA to conduct its affairs as a fiduciary; that is, it could not manage or direct the investment of IRA funds. In addition, BFA had to subject itself to an audit that would detect any failures to meet these regulatory requirements. In cases where the minimum net worth was not achieved, treasury regulations prohibited a trustee from accepting new IRA accounts and required the relinquishment of existing accounts.[8]

---

[4] Ibid.
[5] Ibid., pp. 4–5.
[6] Ibid., p. 5.
[7] Ibid., pp. 4–5.
[8] Ibid., pp. 15–20.

BFA's Independent Auditors

From 1984 to 1998 BFA engaged Arthur Andersen as its independent auditor. Arthur Andersen was also hired by BFA or BFA's attorneys to perform other accounting and auditing, management consulting, and tax services. From 1984 to 1997 Arthur Andersen issued unqualified audit opinions on BFA's combined financial statements.

From 1992 to 1998 Jay Steven Ozer was the Arthur Andersen engagement partner with the ultimate responsibility for the conduct of the BFA audits, including the review of all audit work performed, resolution of all accounting issues, evaluating the results of all audit procedures, and signing the final audit opinions. Ann McGrath was an auditor on the BFA engagement from 1988 to 1998. In 1991 she began her role as manager of the audit engagements. For audit years 1991 to 1998 McGrath had primary responsibility for all audit planning and field work, which included assessing areas of inherent and control risk, supervising the audit team, and reviewing all audit workpapers.[9]

Employees' Concerns over ALO's Deficit

In April 1996 several BFA accountants and one attorney were sufficiently concerned about ALO's deficit situation and related financial viability issues to confront BFA's senior management team. The response by management was perceived as inadequate by the employees. Due to their concerns about this lack of response by the BFA senior management team, most of these employees resigned during 1996, citing their concerns in their letters of resignation. One BFA accountant who showed concern was Karen Paetz.

Karen Paetz's Concerns

Karen Paetz was familiar with the financial condition of ALO and the interrelationships among ALO, New Church Ventures, and BFA because one of her responsibilities had been to supervise the preparation of the financial statements of New Church Ventures and ALO. In 1994, at the request of BFA President Crotts, Paetz produced a detailed analysis of the fair market value of ALO's assets compared to the cost basis of its assets. Her analysis revealed a $70.1 million negative net worth.[10] Paetz's misgivings about ALO, New Church Ventures, and BFA prompted her to resign as a BFA accountant in July 1996.

During the seven years Paetz was employed by BFA, she interacted frequently with the Arthur Andersen auditors during each year's audit. In February 1997, during the field work for Arthur Andersen's 1996 audit of BFA, Paetz decided to contact Arthur Andersen auditor Ann McGrath and set up a lunch meeting with McGrath to voice her concerns. At the meeting, Paetz expressed her

---

[9] Ibid., pp. 3–4.

[10] Ibid., pp. 29–30.

concern about ALO's deficit, which was in excess of $100 million and ALO's monthly losses, which were approximately $2.5 million. In addition, Paetz noted that the money from BFA and New Church Ventures was being used to service ALO's substantial debt to BFA. Paetz specifically advised McGrath to ask BFA, during the 1996 audit, for detailed financial statements for both ALO and New Church Ventures.

Arthur Andersen's Response to Concerns

McGrath reported her meeting with Paetz to the engagement partner, Ozer. However, Arthur Andersen's audit workpapers, and its analysis of fraud risk, did not refer to the Paetz meeting in February 1997 because McGrath and Ozer considered the meeting to be a "nonevent."[11] Arthur Andersen did, however, expand its audit procedures for the 1996 audit and requested from BFA the detailed financial statements of ALO and New Church Ventures. However, BFA refused to make the detailed financial statements for both ALO and New Church Ventures available to McGrath and Ozer.

McGrath and Ozer decided not to insist that ALO's financial statements be provided, although the financial statements were necessary to properly assess ALO's ability to repay its loans to BFA and affiliate New Church Ventures. Fortunately, the financial statements of ALO were a matter of public record and part of a four-page annual disclosure statement that ALO had filed with the Arizona Corporation Commission on March 19, 1997, during Arthur Andersen's field work for the 1996 audit. This four-page annual report showed a $116.5 million negative net worth as of year-end 1996 and a $22 million net loss for the year.[12] New Church Ventures' unaudited detailed financial statements were available for years 1995, 1996, and 1997. These financial statements revealed that substantially all of New Church Ventures' notes receivable were from ALO.[13]

Disclosure of ALO and New Church Ventures in 1996 Financial Statements

Footnote 3 to BFA's combined financial statements as of December 31, 1996, included an unaudited condensed balance sheet for New Church Ventures (identified only as "a company associated with Southern Baptist causes") as of year-end 1996, which reported net assets of $2.5 million and total assets of $192.5 million. The footnote did not disclose ALO's financial position or that approximately 81 percent of New Church Ventures' assets were notes receivable from ALO.

[11] Ibid., pp. 50–51.
[12] Ibid., pp. 30–31.
[13] Ibid., pp. 30–32.

To the extent that New Church Ventures' receivables from ALO were uncollectible due to ALO's negative net worth, New Church Ventures would not be able to meet its liabilities, which included liabilities to IRA holders by year-end 1996 that totaled $74.7 million.[14]

Year-End Transactions

In December of each year, BFA engaged in significant year-end transactions with its related parties, ALO and New Church Ventures. These related party transactions primarily included real estate sales, gifts, pledges, and charitable contributions. Without these year-end transactions, BFA, on a stand-alone basis, would have been forced to report a significant decrease in net assets in each year from 1991 to 1994. Yet BFA did not disclose any information about these material related party transactions in its financial statements for the years 1991 to 1994.[15]

As an example, the significant real estate transactions that occurred in December 1995 with Harold Friend, Dwain Hoover, and subsidiaries of ALO enabled BFA to report an increase in net assets of $1.6 million for the year ended December 31, 1995, as opposed to the decrease in net assets that would have been reported. Importantly, for BFA to recognize a gain on these transactions in accordance with GAAP, the down payment for a buyer's initial investment could not be "funds that have been or will be loaned, refunded, or directly or indirectly provided to the buyer by the seller, or loans guaranteed or collateralized by the seller for the buyer."[16] However, in reality, the cash for the initial down payments on many of these real estate sales can be traced back to BFA via transactions with affiliates of ALO and New Church Ventures.

Foundation Investments, Inc.'s Sale of Santa Fe Trails Ranch II, Inc., Stock

Santa Fe Trails Ranch II, Inc., was a subsidiary of Select Trading Group, Inc., which was a subsidiary of ALO. The only significant asset owned by Santa Fe Trails Ranch II was 1,357 acres of undeveloped land in San Miguel County, New Mexico.

On December 26, 1995, 100 percent of the issued and outstanding common stock of Santa Fe Trails Ranch II was transferred from Select Trading Group to ALO. ALO then sold the stock to New Church Ventures in exchange for a $1.6 million reduction in ALO's credit line that was already owed to New Church Ventures. On the same day, New Church Ventures sold the Santa Fe Trails

[14] Ibid., pp. 31–32.
[15] Ibid., pp. 19–20.
[16] Ibid., p. 25.

Ranch II stock to Foundation Investments, Inc., a BFA subsidiary, in exchange for a $1.6 million reduction in the New Church Ventures' credit line that was already owed to Foundation Investments. Also on the same day, Foundation Investments sold the Santa Fe Trails Ranch II stock to Harold Friend for $3.2 million, resulting in Foundation Investments recognizing a gain of $1.6 million in its financial statements.

The terms of the sale of the Santa Fe Trails Ranch II stock by Foundation Investments to Friend for $3.2 million was a 25 percent cash down payment ($800,000) with the balance of $2.4 million in a carryback note receivable to Foundation Investments. To audit the transaction, Arthur Andersen's senior auditor John Bauerle vouched the payment received from Friend via wire transfer back to the December 31, 1995, bank statement. However, he did not complete any additional work to determine the source of the cash down payment.

To assess the true nature and purpose of this series of transactions, Arthur Andersen reviewed a feasibility study and 1993 cash flow analysis for the proposed development of Cedar Hills. An independent appraisal was not obtained. Arthur Andersen prepared a net present value calculation using the 1993 cash flow analysis to support the $3.2 million value that Friend paid to Foundation Investments on December 26, 1995. Arthur Andersen accepted the $3.2 million value without questioning why that same property was valued at only $1.6 million when New Church Ventures sold it to Foundation Investments on the same day.

TFCI's Sale to Hoover[17]

In December 1995 The Foundation Companies, Inc., a for-profit BFA subsidiary, sold certain joint venture interests in real estate developments to Dwain Hoover and recognized a gain on the transaction of approximately $4.4 million. In this particular transaction, the cash down payment from Hoover to The Foundation Companies of approximately $2.9 million was funded by a loan to Hoover from FMC Holdings, Inc., a subsidiary of ALO. Importantly, FMC received its own funding from BFA and New Church Ventures.

The details of this transaction were documented in Arthur Andersen's workpapers primarily through a memorandum prepared by Arthur Andersen senior auditor John Bauerle on April 13, 1996. According to his memo, Bauerle concluded that the transaction did meet the criteria for gain recognition pursuant to SFAS No. 66. However, Bauerle's memorandum did not include any documentation to support how Arthur Andersen tested the source of the cash down payment to help ensure that the down payment was not directly or indirectly provided by BFA.

In early 1996 Arthur Andersen was auditing The Foundation Companies and prepared its annual management representation letter to be signed by The Foundation Companies' Chief Financial Officer Ron Estes. However, because of

[17] Ibid., pp. 27–28.

the previously described Hoover transaction, Estes refused to sign the management representation letter. CFO Estes had protested against the Hoover transaction and ultimately resigned in June 1996. Arthur Andersen's audit workpapers related to The Foundation Companies' 1995 audit did not address the absence of Estes's signature on the final management representation letter or indicate if it asked Estes why he refused to sign the letter.

Related Parties Disclosure, 1991–1994

In addition to its affiliates, BFA's related parties included its subsidiaries, BFA senior management, and their immediate families, as well as any former or current members of the board of directors. Yet except for information provided about New Church Ventures in its 1994 financial statements, the transactions and balances due from the following individuals and companies were *not* disclosed as related parties in the financial statements for the years 1991 through 1994:

- Dwain Hoover, BFA board member.
- Harold Friend, former BFA board member.
- Jalma Hunsinger, owner of ALO, former BFA board member, and New Church Ventures board member.
- ALO and its subsidiaries and affiliates.
- New Church Ventures and its subsidiaries and affiliates.[18]

1995

In the footnotes to BFA's 1995 financial statements, rather than using their names, BFA described its related parties according to their titles or roles in the business. This practice made it far more difficult and time-consuming for users to identify the true related parties. For example, BFA disclosed its related parties as follows: "Director A [Dwain Hoover] and his companies"; "Benefactor A [Harold Friend] and his companies"; and "Benefactor B [Jalma Hunsinger] and his companies." ALO was a Benefactor B company, and New Church Ventures was "a company associated with Southern Baptist causes."[19]

Related Party Pseudonyms

- Director A = Dwain Hoover.
- Benefactor A = Harold Friend.
- Benefactor B = Jalma Hunsinger.

[18] Ibid., pp. 16–17.
[19] Ibid., p. 21.

- ALO = a Benefactor B company.
- New Church Ventures = a company associated with Southern Baptist causes.

BFA disclosed in Footnote 13 of its 1995 financial statements, titled "Related Parties," that "a substantial portion of BFA's transactions involve individuals or companies associated with Southern Baptist causes."[20] In Footnote 13 it described "some of the more significant transactions involving related parties," including notes receivable from "Director A, Benefactor A, and Benefactor B or their companies" totaling $8,825,063, $2,400,000, and $53,797,827 (notes owed from ALO). Footnote 13 did not include an additional $37,400,000 in notes receivable owed to BFA from New Church Ventures, which was discussed in Footnote 3, titled "Notes Receivable."[21]

The footnotes to the 1995 financial statements did not disclose the material nature of the total notes receivable owed to BFA from related parties ALO and New Church Ventures, which accounted for 63 percent of BFA's total notes receivable—or 30 percent of BFA's total assets and more than 10 times as much as BFA's total net assets. This substantial concentration of credit given to ALO and New Church Ventures was also not disclosed in Footnote 2 in a subsection titled "Concentration of Credit Risk," which stated, "Concentration of credit risk with respect to notes receivable is limited due to the fact that BFA requires notes receivable to be adequately collateralized."[22]

1996–1997[23]

In connection with its 1996 audit of BFA, Arthur Andersen commented in a "Memorandum on Internal Control Structure" on BFA's lack of review, analysis, and proper documentation of related party transactions.

Andersen also criticized the fact that the collateral on related party notes receivable was not adequately monitored. It noted that "certain of the notes receivable from individuals and companies affiliated with Southern Baptist causes had outstanding balances in excess of the current value of the underlying collateral." Yet Arthur Andersen did not require BFA to take a reserve or write-down on its notes receivable. Rather, in BFA's 1996 financial statements a footnote merely stated that "certain of the notes have outstanding balances that may be in excess of underlying collateral."

Again for year-end 1997, Arthur Andersen assessed BFA's internal controls and criticized BFA for lack of review, analysis, and proper documentation of related party transactions and for failing to adequately monitor collateral on related party notes receivable. The criticisms stated in the 1997 internal control memorandum were practically identical to those made by Arthur Andersen

---

[20] Ibid.

[21] Ibid., pp. 20–22.

[22] Ibid., pp. 22–23.

[23] Ibid., pp. 40–41.

in 1996. In fact, in the 1997 memorandum Arthur Andersen noted that its 1996 audit recommendations regarding related parties had not been fully implemented and encouraged management to do so.

The 1997 memorandum repeated, almost verbatim, Arthur Andersen's observation "that certain of the notes receivable from individuals and companies affiliated with Southern Baptist causes had outstanding balances, which appeared to be in excess of the current value of the underlying collateral."

As in 1996, Arthur Andersen issued an unqualified opinion on BFA's 1997 financial statements without requiring adequate disclosures regarding the concentration of credit risk with related parties and the nature of the relationships with ALO and New Church Ventures. The footnote disclosures regarding the amounts due from related parties also appeared to be inadequate and misleading to financial statement users.

Case Questions

1. Consider the principles, assumptions, and constraints of Generally Accepted Accounting Principles (GAAP). Define the *conservatism constraint* and explain why it is important to users of financial statements.

2. Consider the significant year-end transactions consummated by BFA. Do you believe that the accounting for these transactions violated the conservatism constraint? Why or why not? Please be specific.

3. Consult Paragraph 14 of PCAOB Auditing Standard No. 5. Do you believe that BFA had established an effective system of internal control over financial reporting related to its significant year-end transactions? Why or why not?

4. Consult Paragraphs 12–15 of PCAOB Auditing Standard No. 13. Consider the sale of the Santa Fe Trails Ranch II stock by Foundation Investments to Friend. Do you believe that the auditor should have completed any additional testing beyond vouching the payment received from Friend? Provide the rationale for your decision.

5. Consult Paragraphs 5–8 of PCAOB Auditing Standard No. 8 and Paragraphs 7–10 of PCAOB Auditing Standard No. 12. Based on your understanding of inherent risk assessment, identify three specific factors about BFA that might cause you to elevate inherent risk. Briefly provide your rationale for each factor that you identify.

6. Consult Paragraphs .04–.06 of AU Section 334. Comment on why the existence of related parties (such as ALO and New Church Ventures) presents additional risks to an auditor. Do you believe that related party transactions deserve special attention from auditors? Why or why not?

7. Assume you are an investor in BFA. As an investor, what type of information would you be interested in reviewing before making an investment in BFA? Do you believe that BFA should have been exempt from Arizona banking laws? Why or why not?

8. Consult Paragraph 7 of PCAOB Auditing Standard No. 9. Consider the planning phase for the audit of BFA's trust department operations. As an auditor, what type of evidence would you want to collect and examine to determine whether BFA was meeting the U.S. Treasury regulations for non-bank passive trustees of IRA accounts?

9. Consult Paragraphs 23–25 of PCAOB Auditing Standard No. 12. Define what is meant by *control environment*. Based on the information provided in the case, explain why the control environment is so important to effective internal control over financial reporting at an audit client like BFA.

10. Consult Sections 204 and 301 of SARBOX. What is the role of the audit committee in the financial reporting process? Can you provide an example of how the audit committee might have been helpful in the BFA situation?

11. Consult Paragraph 56 of PCAOB Auditing Standard No. 12. What is meant by the term *whistleblower* within the context of the financial reporting process? Do you think that all whistleblower complaints should go directly to the audit committee? Why or why not? Do you think that a whistleblower program would have been helpful at BFA? Why or why not?

12. Consult Paragraph 5 of PCAOB Auditing Standard No. 10. Do you believe the Arthur Andersen auditors responded appropriately to the information received from BFA's former accountant, Karen Paetz? Why or why not?

13. Consult Section 401 of SARBOX. How would Section 401 apply to the BFA audit? Do you believe that Section 401 would have improved the presentation of BFA's financial statements?

14. Define what is meant by *a transaction being executed on an arm's-length basis*. Next, consult paragraphs 52–53 of PCAOB Auditing Standard No. 12. Explain why gains recorded on transactions with related parties would have greater inherent risk of being overstated.

15. Consult Paragraphs 28–30 of PCAOB Auditing Standard No. 5. What is the most relevant financial statement assertion about the related party transaction activity at BFA? Why?

16. Consult Paragraphs 39–41 and Paragraph A5 (in Appendix A) of PCAOB Auditing Standard No. 5. For the assertion identified in Question 15, identify a specific internal control activity that would help to prevent or detect a misstatement related to the related party transaction activity at BFA.

17. Consider the role of president at BFA. Next assume that as president you are representing the upper management team at the Foundation's annual meeting. During the question-and-answer session, an investor asks you to justify the creation of ALO and whether the real estate transactions between BFA and ALO were legitimate. Develop a response that could potentially satisfy the investor's curiosity. Next state the type of documentary evidence you would request if you were the investor.

Case

6.7

The Fund of Funds

Synopsis

As total assets reached $617 million in 1967, the Fund of Funds (FOF) was the most successful of the mutual funds offered by Investor Overseas Services, Limited. In the late 1960s FOF diversified into natural resource asset investments. To do so, it formed a relationship with John King, a Denver oil, gas, and mineral investor and developer, whereby FOF would purchase oil and gas properties directly from his company, King Resources. By the 1970s FOF was forced into bankruptcy.

It was later uncovered that King Resources had dramatically overcharged FOF for the properties that it sold to FOF. FOF's bankruptcy trustee sued FOF's independent auditor Arthur Andersen for failing to inform FOF that it was being defrauded by King Resources. As a result, Arthur Andersen was ultimately found liable and forced to pay around $70 million in civil damages, while John King was charged and convicted for masterminding the fraud against FOF.

Background

The Investors Overseas Services, Limited (IOS) was a Canadian company headquartered in Switzerland that offered diversified financial services that included the management of mutual funds. IOS was founded in 1956 by Bernie Cornfield, a former Philadelphia social worker. One of IOS's most successful mutual funds was its Fund of Funds (FOF). The FOF was also a Canadian company that had operations directed from Switzerland; however, its corporate records were maintained in Ferney-Voltaire, France. FOF's total assets reached $617 million by the end of 1967.[1]

FOF incorporated FOF Proprietary Funds, Ltd. (FOF Prop) as an umbrella for specialized investment accounts that were managed by investment advisers. FOF Prop's investments were heavily concentrated in American securities. Each investment adviser had a duty to act in FOF's best interests and to avoid conflicts

---

[1] "I.O.S. Lists Records Sales of Investments Programs," Special to *The New York Times*, *The New York Times*, February 23, 1968. Accessed from ProQuest Historical Newspapers, *The New York Times*, p. 52.

of interest. In addition, they were compensated based on the realized and unrealized (paper) appreciation of their portfolios.[2]

Challenges Faced by IOS and Its Affiliates

During the middle to late 1960s, IOS and its affiliates began to face several difficult conditions. The industry had become increasingly competitive as new competitors entered the field. In addition, the entire industry was negatively impacted by a decline in stock market prices. The industry was also impacted by significant regulatory changes: A number of national authorities had put more regulatory controls on fund selling.[3]

In 1966 the SEC brought charges that IOS had violated U.S. law by selling unregistered securities. As part of its settlement with the SEC, IOS and its affiliates agreed to the following restrictions:[4]

- Will not engage in any activities subject to SEC jurisdiction.
- Will cease substantially all sales of securities to U.S. citizens or nationals, wherever located.
- Will not buy more than 3 percent of the stock of any registered investment company.
- Will dispose of its interests in Investors Planning Corp. of America, a registered broker-dealer, and Investors Continental Services, Ltd., a wholly owned Investors Overseas subsidiary and also a registered broker-dealer.
- Will withdraw the SEC broker-dealer registration of five investment companies owned by FOF.
- Will not acquire a controlling interest in any financial organization doing business in the United States.

FOF Expands into Natural Resource Assets[5]

FOF's strategy for dealing with the SEC's sanctions and the prospect of a potential stock market downturn in the late 1960s was to diversify its holdings

---

[2] *The Fund of Funds, Limited, F.O.F. Proprietary Funds, Ltd., and IOS Growth Fund, Limited, A/K/A Transglobal Growth Fund, Limited, Plaintiffs, v. Arthur Andersen & Co., Arthur Andersen & Co. (Switzerland), and Arthur Andersen & Co., S.A., Defendants*, No. 75 Civ. 540 (CES), United States District Court for the Southern District of New York, 545 F. Supp. 1314; 1982 U.S. Dist. Lexis 9570; Fed. Sec. L. Rep. (Cch) P98,751, July 16, 1982. Available from LexisNexis Academic.

[3] Clyde H. Farnsworth, "Beleaguered Empire," *The New York Times*, April 27, 1970. Accessed from ProQuest Historical Newspapers, *The New York Times*, p. 53.

[4] "Investors Overseas Ltd. Agrees with SEC to Leave U.S. Securities Field," *The Wall Street Journal*, May 25, 1967. Accessed from ProQuest Historical Newspapers, *The Wall Street Journal*, p. 8.

[5] *The Fund of Funds, Limited, F.O.F. Proprietary Funds, Ltd., and IOS Growth Fund, Limited, A/K/A Transglobal Growth Fund, Limited, Plaintiffs, v. Arthur Andersen & Co., Arthur Andersen & Co. (Switzerland), and Arthur Andersen & Co., S.A., Defendants*, No. 75 Civ. 540 (CES), United States District Court for the Southern District of New York, 545 F. Supp. 1314; 1982 U.S. Dist. Lexis 9570; Fed. Sec. L. Rep. (Cch) P98,751, July 16, 1982.

into assets less affected by the stock market, such as natural resource assets. To set up an investment account that specialized in natural resource assets, the officers of FOF contacted John King, a Denver oil, gas, and mineral investor and developer. In February 1968 a formal contract designating a subsidiary of King's company, King Resources Corporation (KRC), as an investment adviser to FOF Prop was circulated between Edward Cowett, the chief operating officer (COO) of FOF, and Timothy Lowry, counsel for KRC. The agreement was not finalized, and ultimately no written investment advisory agreement was ever entered into by the parties.

However, in a presentation at a meeting of the FOF board of directors in Acapulco, Mexico, on April 5, 1968, King suggested to the board of FOF that it establish a proprietary account with an initial allocation of $10 million that should be invested in a minimum of 40 natural resource properties. In the presentation, King described the role of KRC as follows: "that of a vendor of properties to the proprietary account, with such properties to be sold on an arms-length basis at prices no less favorable to the proprietary account than the prices charged by KRC to its 200-odd industrial and other purchasers." The board approved the idea, and the National Resources Fund Account (NRFA) was established.

The clear intent of FOF was to use King's expertise, as it did that of other account advisers, to locate and purchase speculative investments in oil, gas, and mineral assets. FOF had no means of valuing the assets proposed for investment and no means of participating in any work requirements. FOF's dependence was encouraged by King in two ways: King's own corporate documents represented that KRC was an investment adviser to FOF, and its prospect summaries barely outlined the geologic and financial information that would be necessary for an informed, independent investment decision.

Yet investments in natural resource interests were different from other FOF Prop investments in one important aspect: The interest purchased in every natural resource transaction was a portion of an interest that was owned or had previously been owned by a member of the King group.

KRC's Pricing Policy

As FOF's COO, Cowett's general understanding of the pricing policy was stated in a memorandum written on April 19, 1968: KRC would offer properties to FOF "from time to time and on a more or less continuous basis," the terms of sale are to be "no less favorable than those offered by [KRC] to other nonaffiliated purchasers [and] all transactions will be arms-length in nature." Cowett also stated his understanding of the relationship and pricing policy in a letter dated November 11, 1970.[6]

---

[6] *The Fund of Funds, Limited, et al. v. Arthur Andersen & Co., et al.* United States District Court for the Southern District of New York, 545 F. Supp. 1314; 1982 U.S. Dist. Lexis 9570; Fed. Sec. L. Rep. (Cch) P98,751, July 16, 1982. Available from LexisNexis Academic.

Revaluations

FOF was required to value its investment portfolio daily because the company redeemed shares on the basis of its daily share value. The daily share value was determined by dividing the net asset value of FOF's entire portfolio by the number of outstanding shares. FOF relied on the advice of KRC for the revaluations of its natural resource assets contained in the NRFA. Because of their speculative nature and the lack of an active trading market, determining the value of natural resource interests was very difficult.[7]

Fox–Raff

In late 1968 KRC's founder and owner John King arranged a deal with Robert Raff, president of a Seattle brokerage firm, whereby Raff would purchase 10 percent of a specific natural resource interest that was owned by FOF. The sale was designed to provide a basis for the revaluation of FOF's remaining 90 percent interest in the natural resource interest. The purchase price for Raff's 10 percent interest totaled $440,000, with an $88,000 down payment required. The transaction provided a basis for FOF to write up the valuation of its 90 percent interest in the specific natural resource interest by $820,000.

To execute the deal, King actually advanced Raff all of the money that was needed to make the down payment, assuring Raff that no further financial commitment was necessary. Raff intended to sell the investment within six months so that he would never have to meet the remaining financial obligations to FOF. When FOF pressed for payment, KRC provided Raff with the means to pay.

Independent auditor Arthur Andersen questioned whether the 10 percent sale was sufficient enough to establish the value of the whole parcel. It also questioned the basis for the write-up due to the short holding period for the interest, as well as the lack of any oil strikes or any new geological information that would justify the revaluation of the parcel. Arthur Andersen resolved to express these concerns in a letter to the board of directors of FOF but ultimately never sent such a letter. The Arthur Andersen partner working on the year-end 1968 FOF audit, John Robinson, told Edward Cowett, the COO of FOF, that Andersen could accept the Fox–Raff transaction as a basis for revaluation only because it was immaterial to the financial statements as a whole.

Development of Guidelines for Revaluation[8]

In the fall of 1969 independent auditor Andersen sought to help FOF establish guidelines for unrealized appreciation or revaluations to allow for "substantive independent evidence for reviewing the reasonableness of

---

[7] Ibid.

[8] Ibid.

the client's valuations." A November 7, 1969, memorandum set out Arthur Andersen's proposal:

> Any *significant increase* in the value of natural resource properties over original cost to FOF must, for audit purposes, be supported by either
>
> 1. An appraisal report rendered by a competent, independent expert, or
> 2. An arms-length [*sic*] sale of a sufficiently large enough portion of a property to establish a proportionate value for the portion retained. . . .
>
> On the question of what constitutes adequate sales data for valuation purposes (i.e., the 10% question), we have proposed the following to King Resources Company:
>
> 1. *No* unrealized appreciation would be allowed on sales of relatively small percentages of properties to *private investors or others who do not have the necessary expertise* to determine a realistic fair market value. By "relatively small," we envision approximately 50% as being a minimum level in this type of sale to establish proportionate values for the remaining interests. This would preclude any unrealized appreciation on sales such as the December, 1968, sales to Fox–Roff, [*sic*] Inc. since it could not be reasonably sustained that a brokerage firm has the expertise necessary to evaluate primarily undeveloped resource interests.
> 2. Appreciation *would be allowed* if supported by arms-length [*sic*] sales to *knowledgeable outside parties.* For example, if King Resources Company sold a 25% interest in the Arctic permits to Texaco or another major oil company, we believe it would be appropriate to ascribe proportionate value to the 75% retained. Just where to draw the line on the percentage has not been clearly established. We feel 10% would be a bare minimum and would like to see a higher number.

The senior Andersen partner responsible for audit practices, John March, suggested a sale of a "25–30 percent minimum," as a more conservative figure, and stated that it "must be a cash deal with no take-out option." Yet the guideline finally adopted by FOF for inclusion in the 1969 annual report did not specify a fixed percentage that must be sold and also did not refer to the identity or attributes of a buyer.

Arctic Revaluation[9]

In late 1969 King arranged for a sale of 9.375 percent of his group's Arctic interest to John Mecom and Consolidated Oil & Gas (COG) to justify a revaluation for FOF. Essentially this sale was the basis for a $119 million increase in the valuation of FOF's interest in the Arctic interest. Details of the transaction were provided in the 1970 FOF annual report.

John Mecom, who also owned U.S. Oil of Louisiana, Inc., which had lost $11,458,000 for the year ending September 30, 1969, faced debts of over $132,000,000 at this time. As a result of Mecom's overall cash problems at that time, King agreed to provide the entire $266,000 down payment for the Arctic transaction, with the subsequent $10 million in payments being provided by

---

[9] Ibid.

KRC's projected usage of Mecom's oil and drilling equipment. Interestingly, Arthur Andersen also audited Mecom from its Houston office and therefore knew of his financial difficulties.[10]

In addition, COG was a Denver-based oil and gas concern headed by John King's personal friend. King Resources had joined together with COG in several previous business transactions, a fact that Arthur Andersen was well aware of. To facilitate the Arctic transaction, King arranged for COG to get a $600,000 loan from a Tulsa, Oklahoma, bank, without which COG would not have entered into the Arctic transaction.

Andersen obtained representation letters from KRC that the Arctic sale was bona fide. Although Andersen obtained representation letters from Mecom and COG confirming the terms of the Arctic purchase agreement, no inquiry was made of Mecom or COG about the existence of possible side agreements. Andersen also obtained a Dun & Bradstreet report on Mecom, which likely would have showed his cash flow problems. In May 1970, prior to issuing FOF's report, Andersen learned of a *Wall Street Journal* article that cast doubt on COG's obligation related to the sale. Andersen obtained a reconfirmation from KRC, discussed the matter with COG's principal, and obtained a reconfirmation specifically excluding side deals; but no further inquiry about side deals was made to Mecom. In late May 1970 Andersen decided that a "subject to" qualification was necessary in issuing its report concerning FOF as of year-end 1969.

Andersen's Relationships with FOF and KRC[11]

Both KRC and FOF, including its NRFA, were audited by Arthur Andersen. Andersen also audited John King's personal accounts. The partner in charge and the manager of the KRC audit held the same respective positions on the NRFA audit, and other Andersen staffers sometimes worked contemporaneously on the KRC and NRFA audits. Andersen used records from KRC to perform many aspects of its audit of NRFA. Andersen's auditors possessed minutes of an FOF board of directors' meeting describing the NRFA as "essentially a discretionary account managed by King Resources Corporation." Andersen's auditors themselves noted KRC's "carte blanche authority to buy oil and gas properties for [NRC]" and its "quasi-fiduciary" duty to FOF.

Prior to the year-end 1968 KRC audit, and as early as 1966, Andersen viewed John King and his companies as a difficult client, one that posed risks to Andersen itself. In fact, Andersen personnel had repeated, serious difficulties

---

[10] In February 1968 Leonard Spacek, Andersen's managing partner, met with King and Mecom to discuss integration of the King and Mecom organizations. Spacek also discussed a role for KRC in refinancing Mecom's debts in May 1968 and, in December 1968, Spacek discussed the possibility of a King–Mecom joint venture with the Houston office of AA.

[11] *The Fund of Funds, Limited, et al. v. Arthur Andersen & Co., et al.* No. 75 Civ. 540 (CES), United States District Court for the Southern District of New York, 545 F. Supp. 1314; 1982 U.S. Dist. Lexis 9570; Fed. Sec. L. Rep. (Cch) P98,751, July 16, 1982. Available from LexisNexis Academic.

with John King as a client at least since 1961. For example, King often spoke directly with the highest echelon of the Andersen partnership in Chicago when he was displeased with the Denver office's resolution of certain issues. Andersen also viewed FOF as presenting its own set of problems and risks.

In addition to performing substantial work on the audit of NRFA for FOF, Andersen's Denver office had primary responsibility for the KRC audits. Therefore, Andersen's Denver office was aware of the advisory relationship between KRC and FOF because the relationship was described in KRC filings with the SEC. The Denver office was also aware of the lack of a written contract evidencing the terms of the relationship between KRC and FOF. In addition, it sought confirmation of the nature of any KRC–FOF agreement from KRC for a KRC audit, although it surprisingly did not seek any such information from FOF with respect to the NRFA audit.

As part of its primary responsibility for audits of the NRFA occurring after year-end 1968, the Denver office of Andersen determined the cost value of NRFA purchases by using the books of KRC. Andersen reviewed the valuations set by KRC only to assess whether they were presented in accordance with FOF's guidelines. Surprisingly, it did not determine the market value of the NRFA interests as part of the FOF audit scope.

FOF's Natural Interest Purchases[12]

Beginning immediately after the board of directors' meeting where NRFA was established, on April 5, 1968, it began to purchase oil, gas, and mineral interests from KRC. King reported to the FOF board of directors on August 2, 1968, that $3 million of the initial authorization of $10 million was committed. For the year-end 1968 audit of FOF, the Denver office of Andersen prepared a series of comparisons of prices charged by the King group to FOF, other King affiliates, and other knowledgeable industry purchasers. The "Summary of 1968 Sales" showed the following with respect to sales to the King affiliates:

	Current Sales	Current Cost [to KRC]	Current Profit	Profit as a Percentage of Sales
Sales to IAMC	$ 9,876,271	$8,220,324	$1,655,947	16.8%
Sales to Royal	6,566,491	4,085,544	2,480,947	37.8%
Sales to IOS	11,325,386	4,307,583	7,017,803	62.0%

[12] *The Fund of Funds, Limited, F.O.F. Proprietary Funds, Ltd., and IOS Growth Fund, Limited, A/K/A Transglobal Growth Fund, Limited, Plaintiffs, v. Arthur Andersen & Co., Arthur Andersen & Co. (Switzerland), and Arthur Andersen & Co., S.A., Defendants,* No. 75 Civ. 540 (CES), United States District Court for the Southern District of New York, 545 F. Supp. 1314; 1982 U.S. Dist. Lexis 9570; Fed. Sec. L. Rep. (Cch) P98,751, July 16, 1982. Available from LexisNexis Academic.

In the same document, Andersen's auditors also computed the comparative profits for KRC, excluding interests sold to Royal and to IOS (which was essentially FOF). After subtracting those sales with higher markups, KRC's profits as percentages of sales on its sales to its affiliates, Royal and IAMC, were substantially smaller than the profits on its sales to FOF.

In fact, KRC's "Consolidated Sales to Industry," dated September 30, 1969, illustrated that KRC's profits on sales to FOF were 68.2 percent, as compared with average profits on all sales of nearly 36 percent. In comparing only the seven industry customers that purchased over $1 million of interests from KRC, FOF had the highest profit/sales ratio, at 68.2 percent. After FOF, the next highest profit/sales ratio, earned by KRC on sales to such customers, was 24.4 percent; the lowest profit/sales ratio was 5 percent.

Andersen's Knowledge of the Purchases[13]

By Andersen's account, "the earliest date when anyone employed by Andersen would have become aware of KRC's 1968 sales to FOF was in early 1969." At the same time, evidence exists that some FOF–KRC transactions were reviewed for the 1968 year-end audit in Andersen's Denver office before January 28, 1969. Andersen auditors from its Denver office also testified that they did some "information gathering" on the NRFA for the FOF Prop audit as of December 31, 1968. They also testified that they obtained documents related to the FOF audit from KRC. Andersen's auditors contended that their duty of confidentiality to KRC would prohibit them from having disclosed to FOF any relevant knowledge they may have had related to KRC's costs.

[13] Ibid.

Case Questions

1. Consider the principles, assumptions, and constraints of Generally Accepted Accounting Principles (GAAP). Define the *conservatism constraint* and explain why it is important to users of financial statements.

2. Explain why FOF's decision to record substantial increases in its natural resource assets violated the conservatism constraint. Please be specific.

3. Consult Paragraph 2 and Paragraph A5 (in Appendix A) of PCAOB Auditing Standard No. 5. Do you believe that FOF established an effective system of internal control over financial reporting related to the valuation of its natural resource assets? Why or why not?

4. Consider the valuation assertion related to natural resources assets. Do you think it is reasonable for an auditor to rely on a recent sale of a 10 percent interest as evidence to justify a revaluation of FOF's remaining 90 percent interest in natural resource assets? Why or why not?

5. Consult Paragraphs 7–8 of PCAOB Auditing Standard No. 15. What other evidence could an auditor seek to justify the valuation of an asset where there is no active trading market? Comment on whether Arthur Andersen's guidelines for the appreciation of national resource properties were appropriate under the circumstances. Why or why not?

6. Consult PCAOB Ethics and Independence Rule 3520. What is *auditor independence*, and what is its significance to the audit profession? What is the difference between independence in appearance and independence in fact? Based on the case information, do you believe that Arthur Andersen violated any principles of auditor independence? Why or why not?

7. Consider that both KRC and FOF, including its NRFA, were audited by Arthur Andersen. In addition, Arthur Andersen audited King's personal accounts. Do you believe these relationships impaired the independence of Arthur Andersen? Why or why not?

8. Would your answer differ if the fact pattern changed so that different partners were assigned to both the KRC audit and the NRFA audit? Assume that both audit teams were completely different. Why or why not would your answer change?

9. Refer to Sections 201, 203, and 206 of SARBOX. Based on your understanding of the FOF audit, do you believe these sections are needed? Why or why not? Be specific.

10. Consult Paragraphs 7–10 of PCAOB Auditing Standard No. 12. Based on your understanding of inherent risk assessment, identify three specific factors about IOS and/or FOF that would be likely to impact your audit procedures if you were conducting an audit of IOS and/or FOF.

11. Consult Paragraphs .04–.06 of AU Section 334. Given that all of FOF Prop's investments in natural resources had also been owned (or were currently owned) by a member of the King group, comment on why the existence of related parties (such as King Resources and FOF) presents additional risks to an auditor.

12. If you were auditing one of the transactions between King Resources and FOF, what type of evidence would you seek to examine to determine whether the transaction was consummated on an arm's-length basis?

13. Consult Paragraphs 4–6 of PCAOB Auditing Standard No. 15. Based on your understanding of audit evidence, did Arthur Andersen rely on competent and sufficient audit evidence in auditing the valuation assertion related to FOF's natural resources assets? Why or why not?

14. Consider the series of comparisons prepared by the Denver office of Arthur Andersen of prices charged by the King group to FOF, King affiliates, and other knowledgeable industry purchasers. Can you think of any additional evidence that would have strengthened the "Summary of 1968 Sales"?

15. Consult Paragraphs .09–.10 of AU Section 329. Explain the primary purpose of substantive analytical procedures. If you completed such procedures on FOF, do you think you could use KRC's "Consolidated Sales to Industry,"

which illustrated that KRC's profits on sales to FOF were 68.2 percent, as compared to 36 percent on all other sales, to help execute the procedures? How?

16. Do you believe Andersen's contention that they had a duty of client confidentiality to KRC that would prohibit the firm from disclosing to FOF any relevant knowledge it may have had related to KRC's costs? Why or why not?